FANTASTIC FOUR VOL. 1: THE FALL OF THE FANTASTIC FOUR. Contains material originally published in magazine form as FANTASTIC FOUR #1-5. First printing 2014. ISBN# 978-0-7851-5474-7. Published by MARVEL WORLDWIDE, INC., a subsidiary of MARVEL ENTERTAINMENT, LLC. OFFICE OF PUBLICATION: 135 West 50th Street, New York, NY 10020. Copyright © 2014 Marvel Characters, Inc. All rights reserved. All characters featured in this issue and the distinctive names and likenesses thereof, and all related indicia are trademarks of Marvel Characters, Inc. No similarity between any of the names, characters, persons, and/or institutions in this magazine with those of any living or dead person or institution is intended, and any such similarity which may exist is purely coincidental. **Printed in Canada.** ALAN FINE, EVP - Office of the President, Marvel Worldwide, Inc. and EVP & CMO Marvel Characters B.V.; DAN BUCKLEY, Publisher & President - Print, Animation & Digital Divisions; JOE QUESADA, Chief Creative Officer; TOM BREVOORT, SVP of Publishing; DAVID BOGART, SVP of Operations & Procurement, Publishing; C.B. CEBULSKI, SVP of Creator & Content Development; DAVID GABRIEL, SVP Print, Sales & Marketing; JIM O'KEEFE, VP of Operations & Logistics; DAN CARR, Executive Director of Publishing Technology; SUSAN CRESPI, Editorial Operations Manager; ALEX MORALES, Publishing Operations Manager; STAN LEE, Chairman Emeritus. For information regarding advertising in Marvel Comics or on Marvel.com, please contact Niza Disla, Director of Marvel Partnerships, at ndisla@marvel.com. For Marvel subscription inquiries, please call 800-217-9158. **Manufactured between 7/4/2014 and 8/11/2014 by SOLISCO PRINTERS, SCOTT, QC, CANADA.**

10 9 8 7 6 5 4 3 2 1

THE FALL OF THE FANTASTIC FOUR

Writer: James Robinson
Penciler: Leonard Kirk
Inkers: Karl Kesel [#1-4], Jay Leisten [#4-5] and Rick Magyar [#5]
Colorists: Jesus Aburtov [#1-5] with Rachelle Rosenberg [#2]
Letterer: VC's Clayton Cowles
Cover Art: Leonard Kirk with Laura Martin [#1-2]; John Romita Jr., Tom Palmer & Dean White [#3]; and Leonard Kirk with Jesus Aburtov [#4-5]

Guest Artists [#5]:
Fantastic Four #1 flashback & Doom vs. Fantastic Four flashback:
Chris Samnee & Matthew Wilson
Thing vs. Hulk flashback: Dean Haspiel & Jim Charalampidis
Sub-Mariner Invasion flashback: Paul Rivoche & Felix Serrano
Inhuman flashback: Phil Jiminez & Rachelle Rosenberg
Galactus flashback: Mike Allred & Laura Allred
Annihilus and Blaastar flashback: Jim Starlin,
Andy Smith & Nolan Woodard
Malice flashback: Jerry Ordway & Jim Charalampidis
Doom and Val: Derlis Santacruz & Israel Silva
Future Foundation: June Brigman, Roy Richardson & Vero Gandini

Assistant Editor: Emily Shaw
Editor: Mark Paniccia

Collection Editor: Sarah Brunstad
Associate Managing Editor: Alex Starbuck
Editors, Special Projects: Jennifer Grünwald & Mark D. Beazley
Senior Editor, Special Projects: Jeff Youngquist
Book Designer: Nelson Ribeiro
SVP Print, Sales & Marketing: David Gabriel

Editor in Chief: Axel Alonso
Chief Creative Officer: Joe Quesada
Publisher: Dan Buckley
Executive Producer: Alan Fine

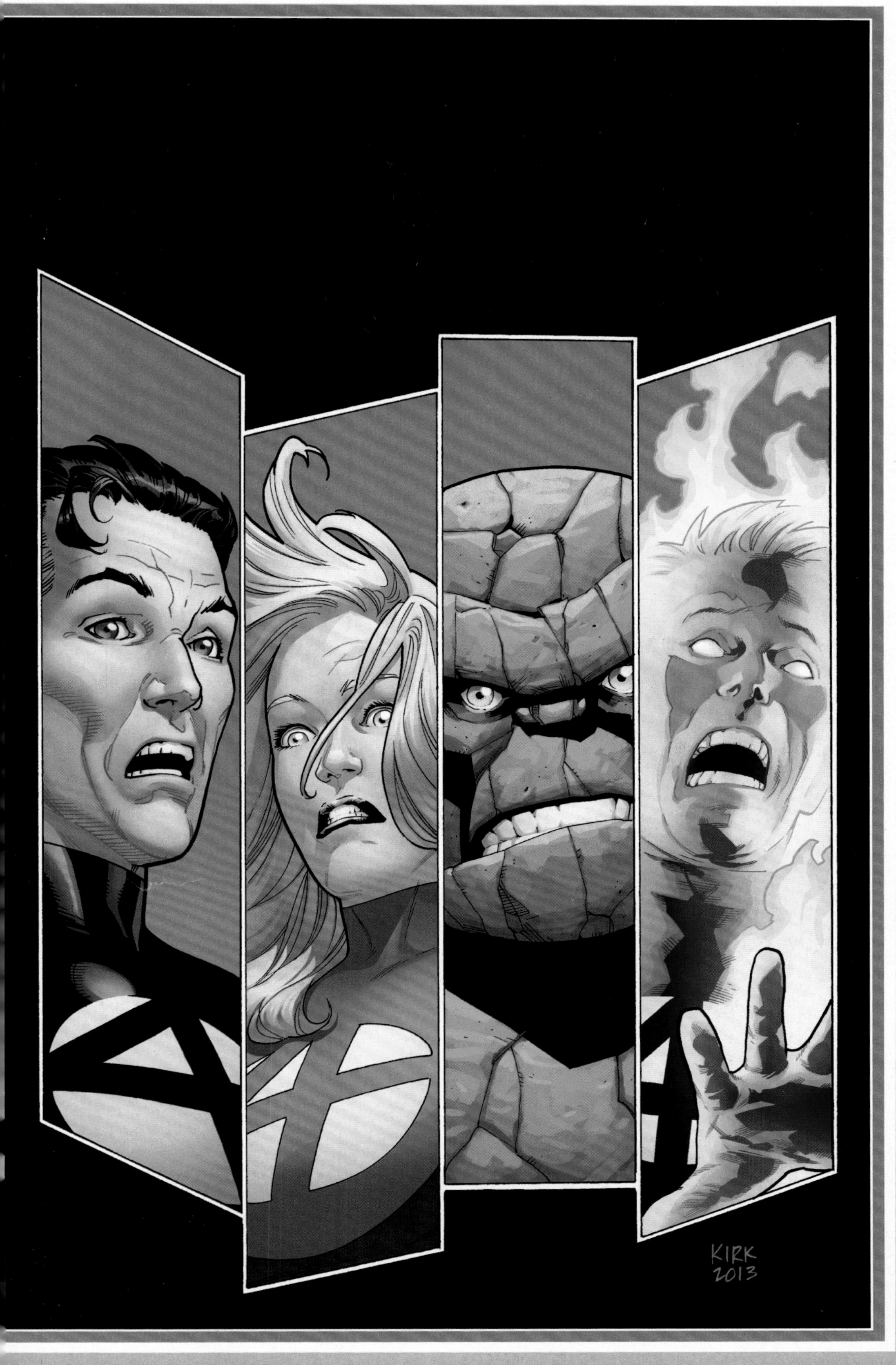
KIRK
2013

ONE

A brilliant scientist—his best friend—the woman he loves—and her fiery-tempered kid brother! Together, they braved the unknown terrors of outer space and were changed by cosmic rays into something more than merely human! MR. FANTASTIC! THE THING! THE INVISIBLE WOMAN! THE HUMAN TORCH! Now they are the FANTASTIC FOUR, and the world will never be the same again!

SUSAN STORM

REED RICHARDS

BEN GRIMM

JOHNNY STOR

THE INVISIBLE WOMAN

MR. FANTASTIC

THE THING

THE HUMAN TOR

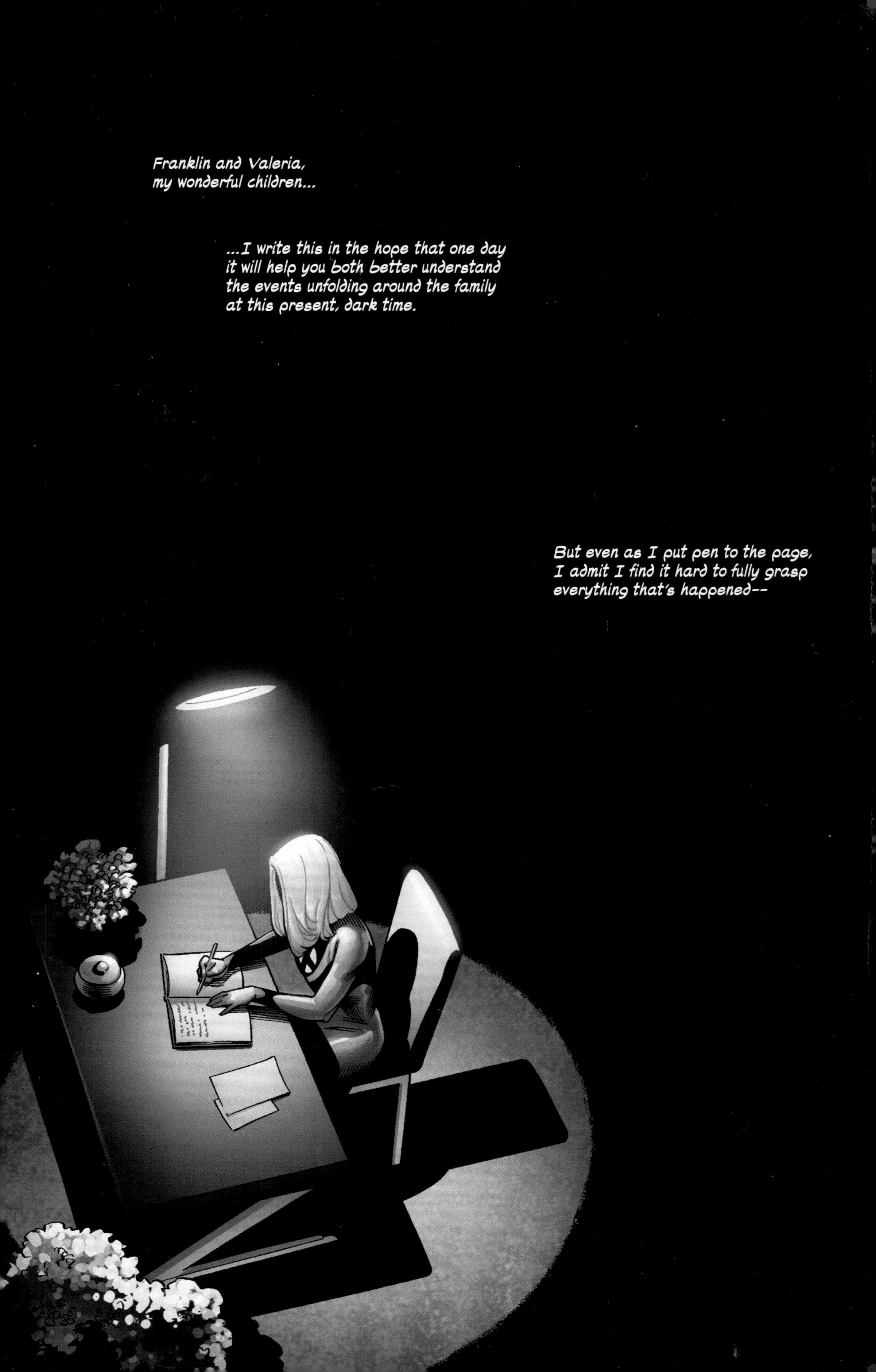
Franklin and Valeria, my wonderful children...
...I write this in the hope that one day it will help you both better understand the events unfolding around the family at this present, dark time.
But even as I put pen to the page, I admit I find it hard to fully grasp everything that's happened--

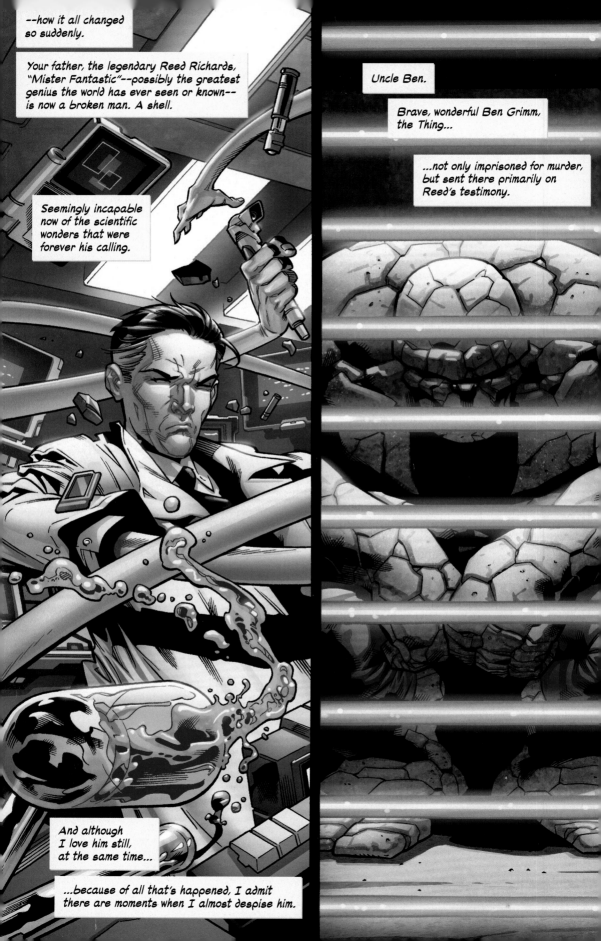

--how it all changed so suddenly.

Your father, the legendary Reed Richards, "Mister Fantastic"--possibly the greatest genius the world has ever seen or known-- is now a broken man. A shell.

Seemingly incapable now of the scientific wonders that were forever his calling.

Uncle Ben.

Brave, wonderful Ben Grimm, the Thing...

...not only imprisoned for murder, but sent there primarily on Reed's testimony.

And although I love him still, at the same time...

...because of all that's happened, I admit there are moments when I almost despise him.

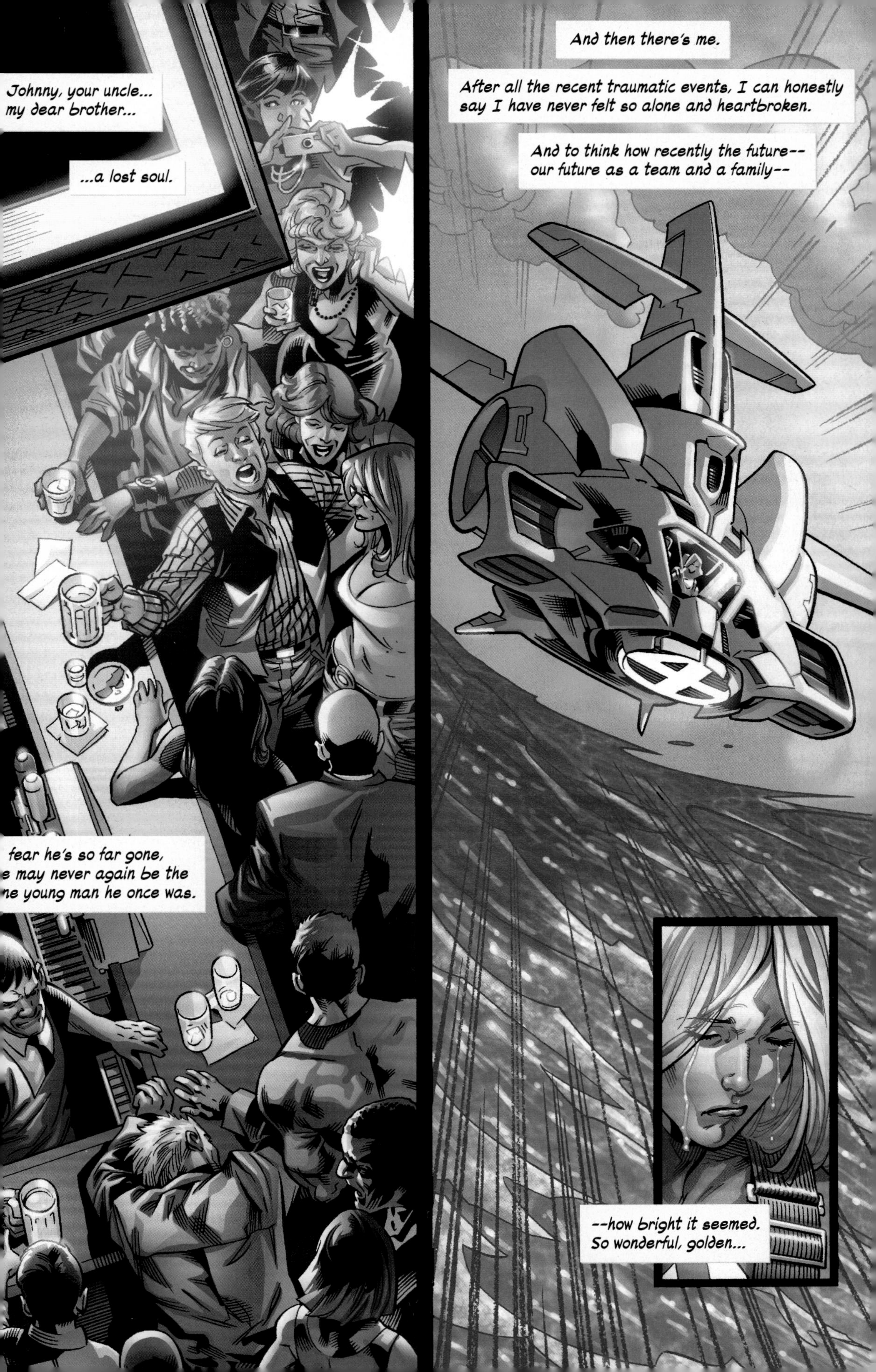
Johnny, your uncle... my dear brother...
...a lost soul.
fear he's so far gone,
e may never again be the
ne young man he once was.
And then there's me.
After all the recent traumatic events, I can honestly say I have never felt so alone and heartbroken.
And to think how recently the future-- our future as a team and a family--
--how bright it seemed. So wonderful, golden...

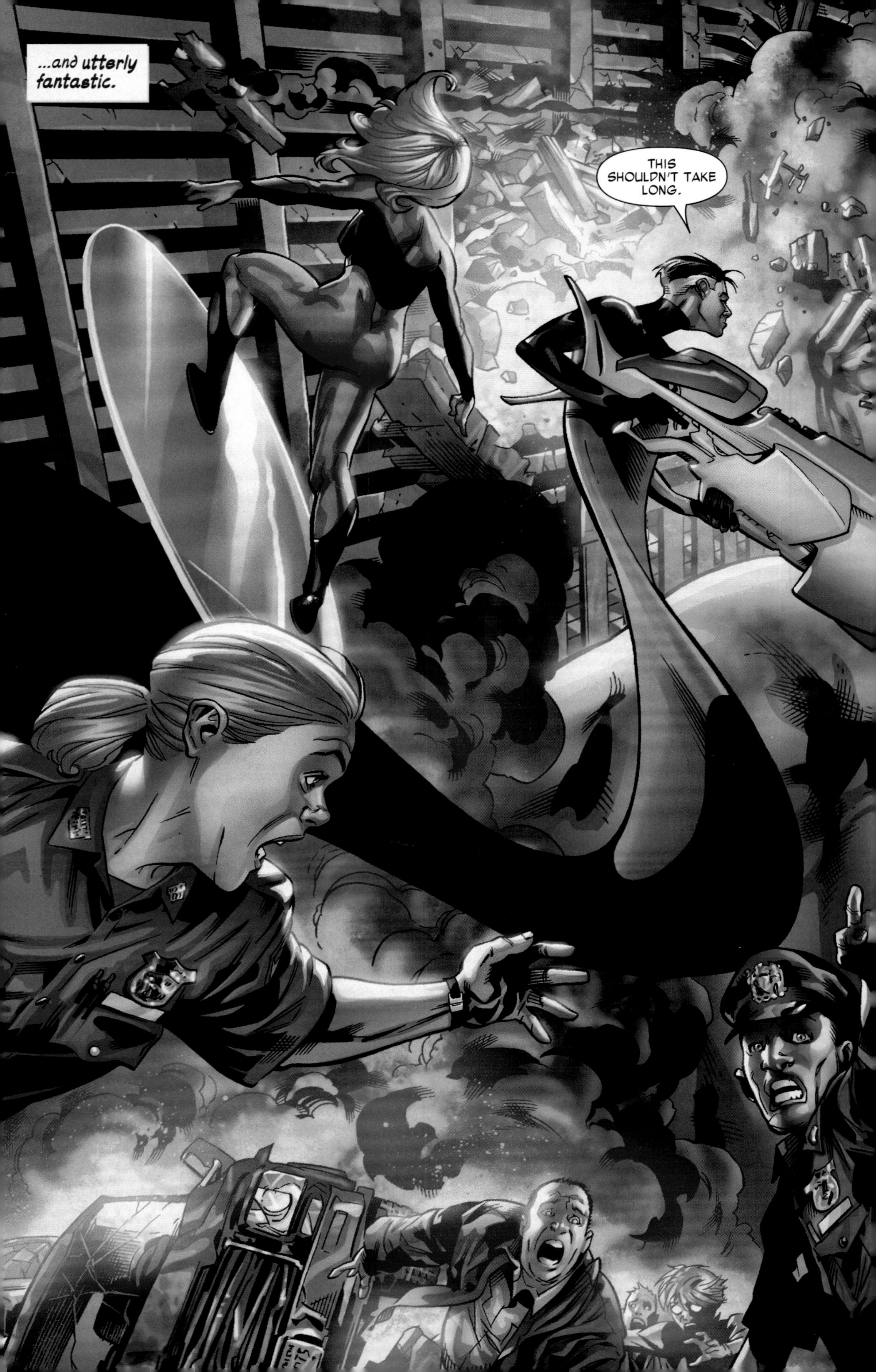
...and utterly fantastic.
THIS SHOULDN'T TAKE LONG.

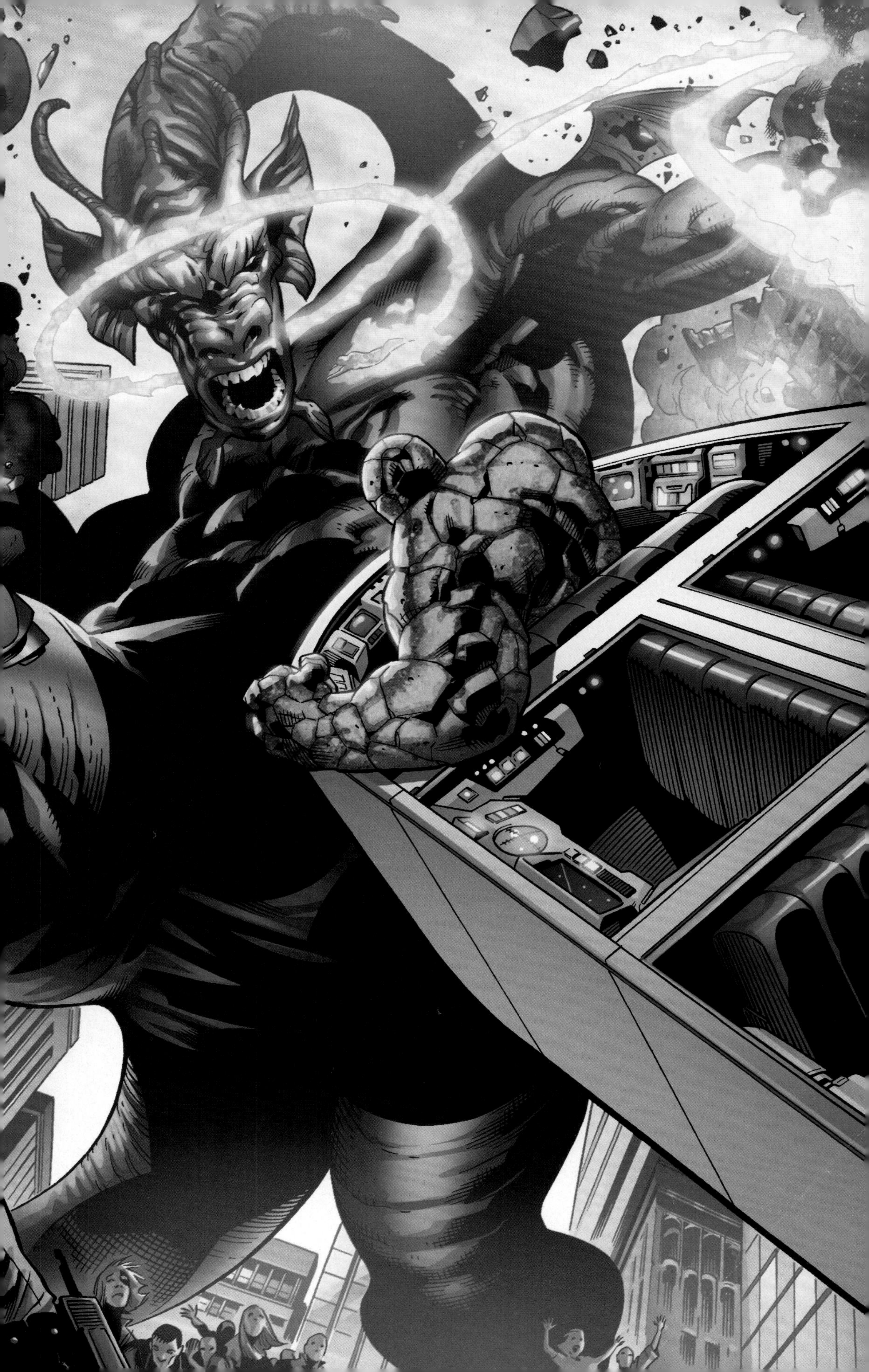

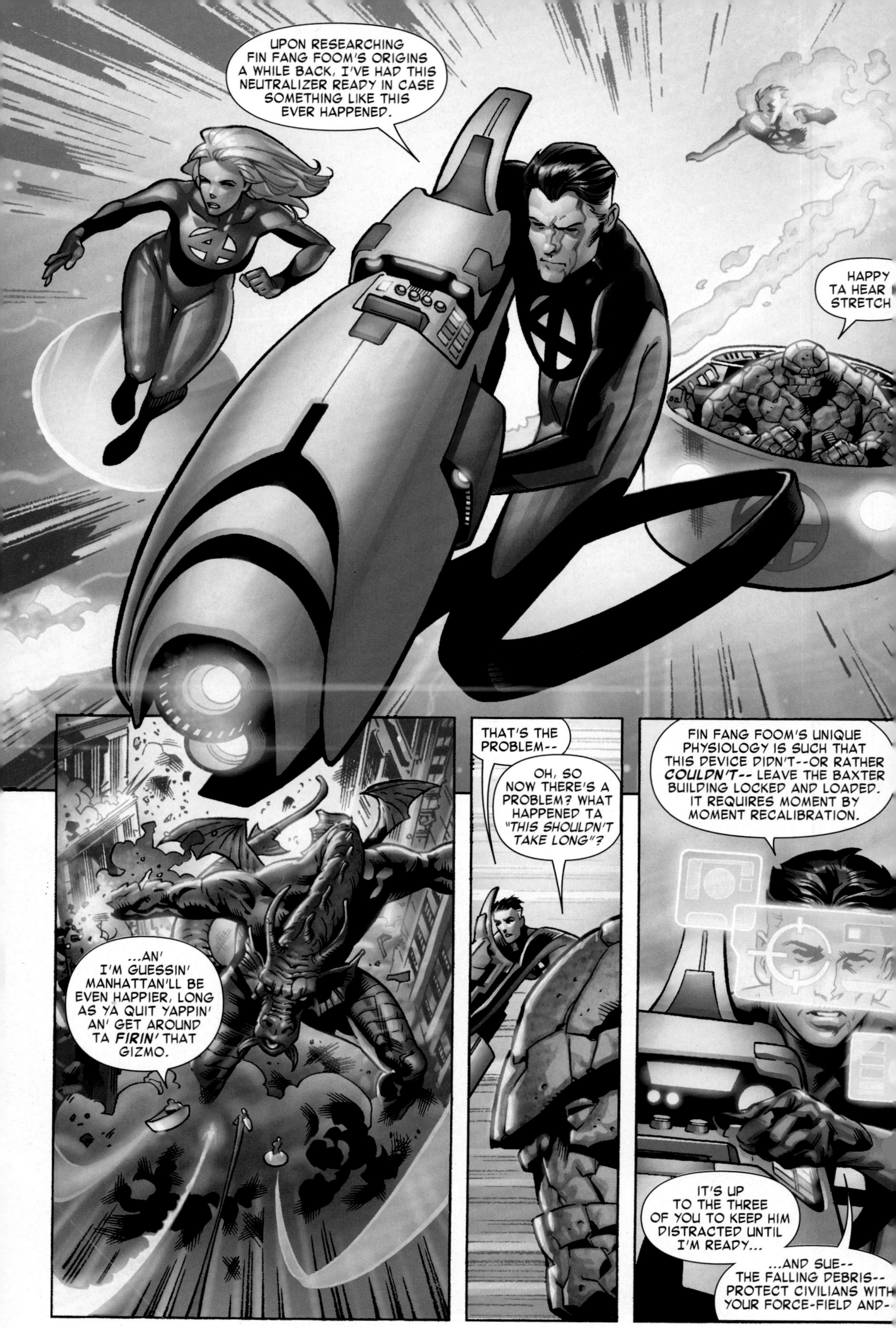
UPON RESEARCHING FIN FANG FOOM'S ORIGINS A WHILE BACK, I'VE HAD THIS NEUTRALIZER READY IN CASE SOMETHING LIKE THIS EVER HAPPENED.
HAPPY TA HEAR STRETCH
...AN' I'M GUESSIN' MANHATTAN'LL BE EVEN HAPPIER, LONG AS YA QUIT YAPPIN' AN' GET AROUND TA FIRIN' THAT GIZMO.
THAT'S THE PROBLEM--
OH, SO NOW THERE'S A PROBLEM? WHAT HAPPENED TA "THIS SHOULDN'T TAKE LONG"?
FIN FANG FOOM'S UNIQUE PHYSIOLOGY IS SUCH THAT THIS DEVICE DIDN'T--OR RATHER COULDN'T-- LEAVE THE BAXTER BUILDING LOCKED AND LOADED. IT REQUIRES MOMENT BY MOMENT RECALIBRATION.
IT'S UP TO THE THREE OF YOU TO KEEP HIM DISTRACTED UNTIL I'M READY...
...AND SUE-- THE FALLING DEBRIS-- PROTECT CIVILIANS WITH YOUR FORCE-FIELD AND-

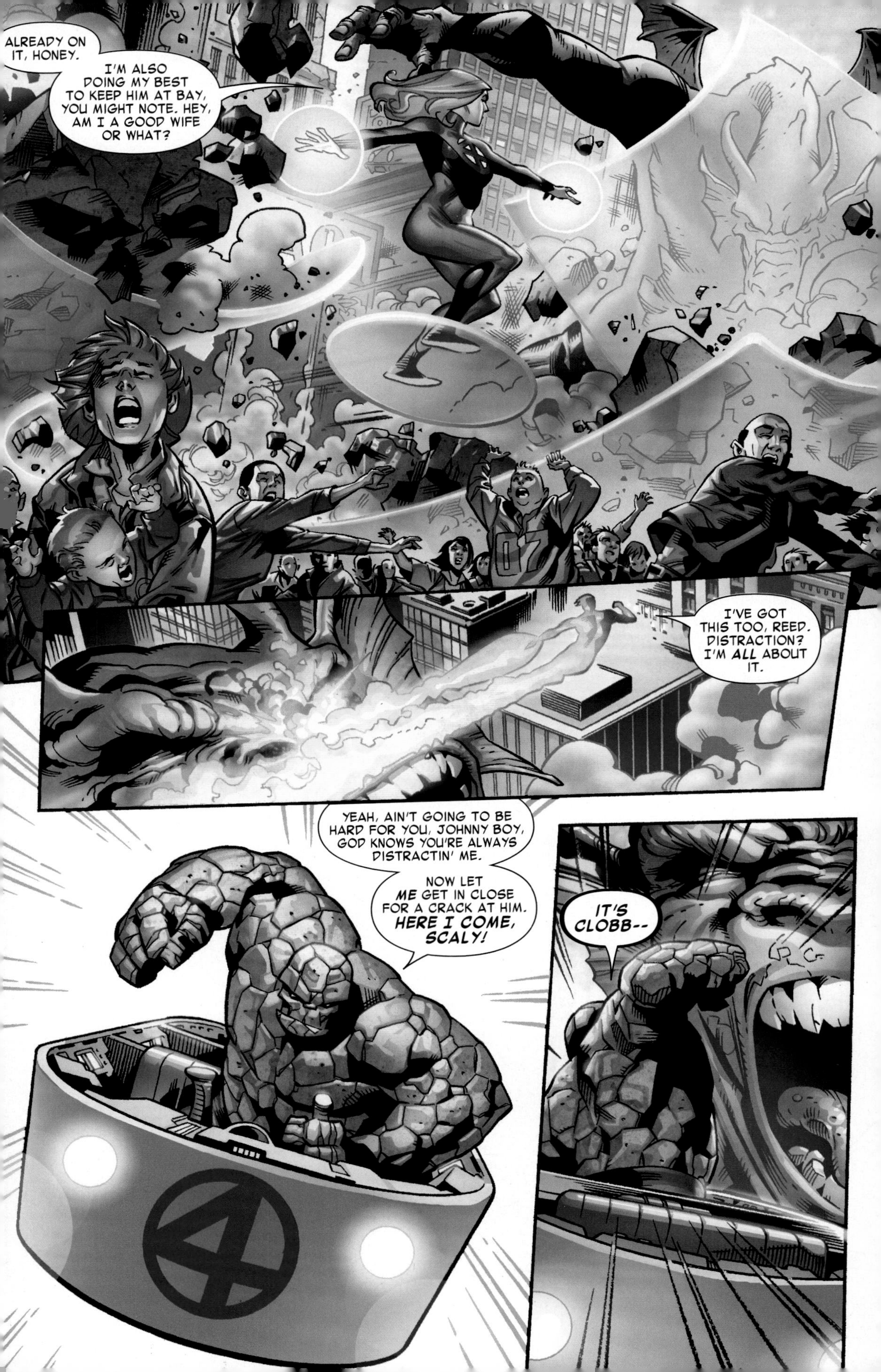
ALREADY ON IT, HONEY.
I'M ALSO DOING MY BEST TO KEEP HIM AT BAY, YOU MIGHT NOTE. HEY, AM I A GOOD WIFE OR WHAT?
I'VE GOT THIS TOO, REED. DISTRACTION? I'M ALL ABOUT IT.
YEAH, AIN'T GOING TO BE HARD FOR YOU, JOHNNY BOY, GOD KNOWS YOU'RE ALWAYS DISTRACTIN' ME.
NOW LET ME GET IN CLOSE FOR A CRACK AT HIM. HERE I COME, SCALY!
IT'S CLOBB--

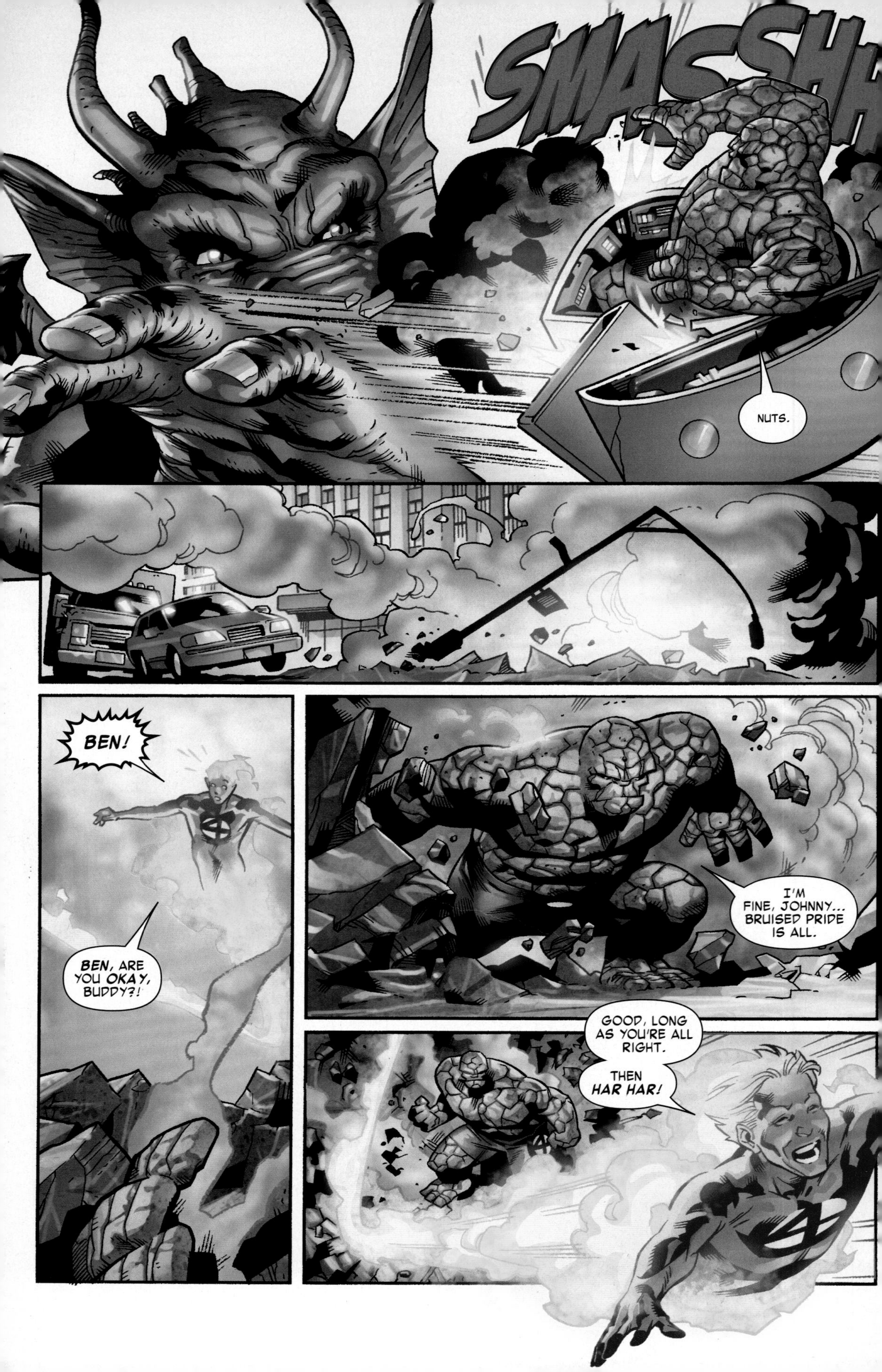
SMASSHH
NUTS.
BEN!
BEN, ARE YOU OKAY, BUDDY?!
I'M FINE, JOHNNY... BRUISED PRIDE IS ALL.
GOOD, LONG AS YOU'RE ALL RIGHT.
THEN HAR HAR!

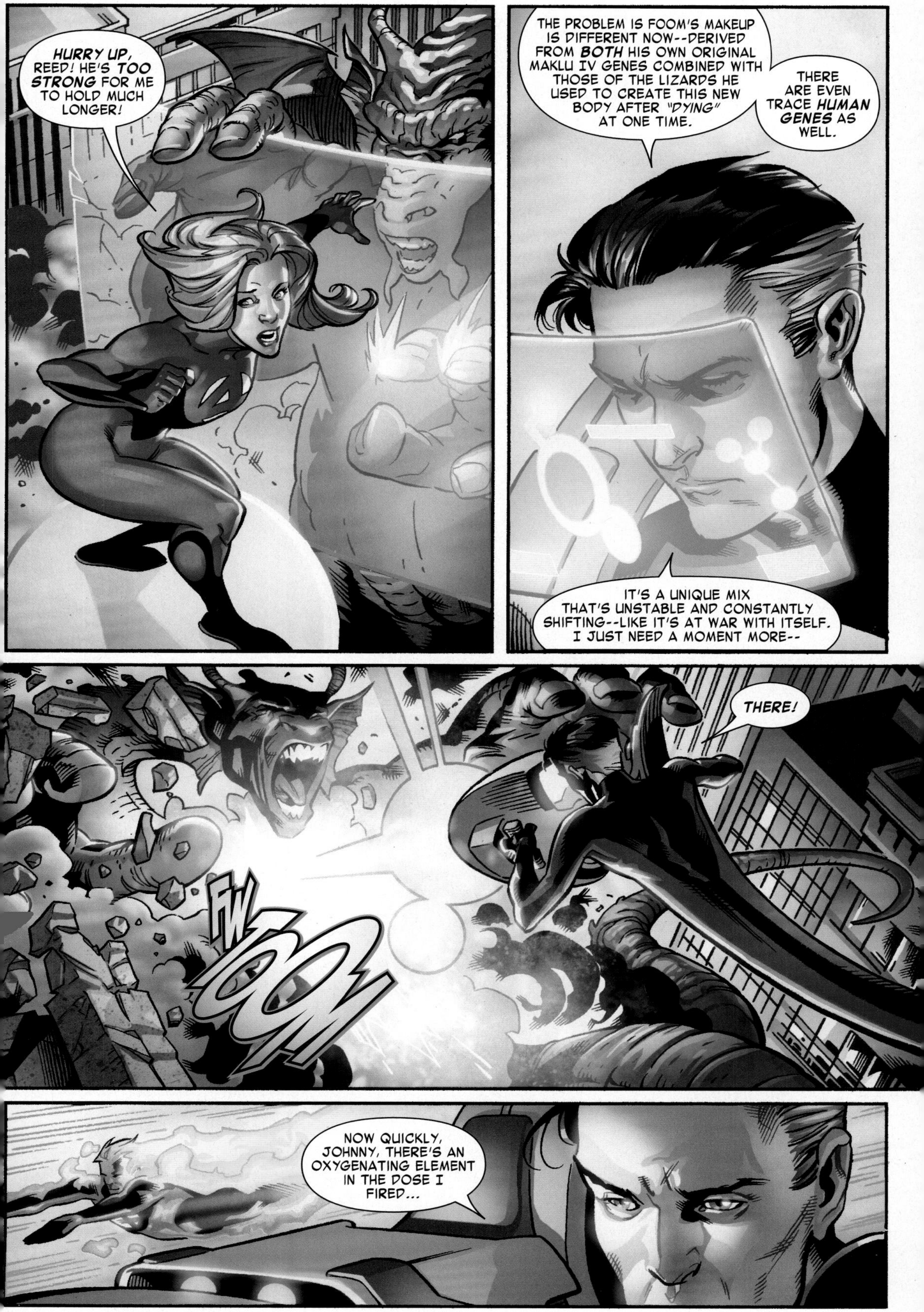
HURRY UP, REED! HE'S TOO STRONG FOR ME TO HOLD MUCH LONGER!
THE PROBLEM IS FOOM'S MAKEUP IS DIFFERENT NOW--DERIVED FROM BOTH HIS OWN ORIGINAL MAKLU IV GENES COMBINED WITH THOSE OF THE LIZARDS HE USED TO CREATE THIS NEW BODY AFTER "DYING" AT ONE TIME.
THERE ARE EVEN TRACE HUMAN GENES AS WELL.
IT'S A UNIQUE MIX THAT'S UNSTABLE AND CONSTANTLY SHIFTING--LIKE IT'S AT WAR WITH ITSELF. I JUST NEED A MOMENT MORE--
THERE!
FWOOM
NOW QUICKLY, JOHNNY, THERE'S AN OXYGENATING ELEMENT IN THE DOSE I FIRED...

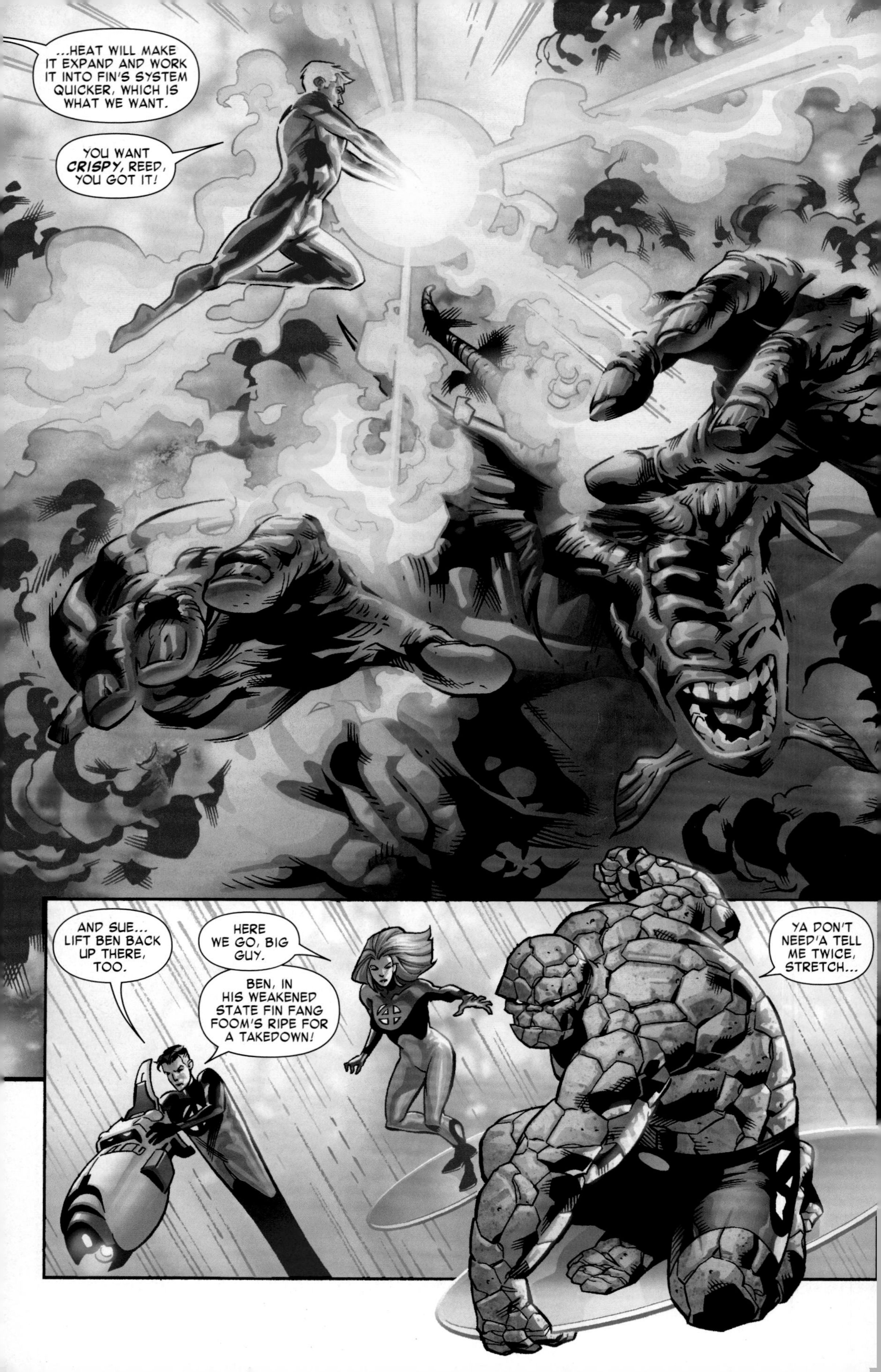
...HEAT WILL MAKE IT EXPAND AND WORK IT INTO FIN'S SYSTEM QUICKER, WHICH IS WHAT WE WANT.
YOU WANT CRISPY, REED, YOU GOT IT!
AND SUE... LIFT BEN BACK UP THERE, TOO.
HERE WE GO, BIG GUY.
BEN, IN HIS WEAKENED STATE FIN FANG FOOM'S RIPE FOR A TAKEDOWN!
YA DON'T NEED'A TELL ME TWICE, STRETCH...

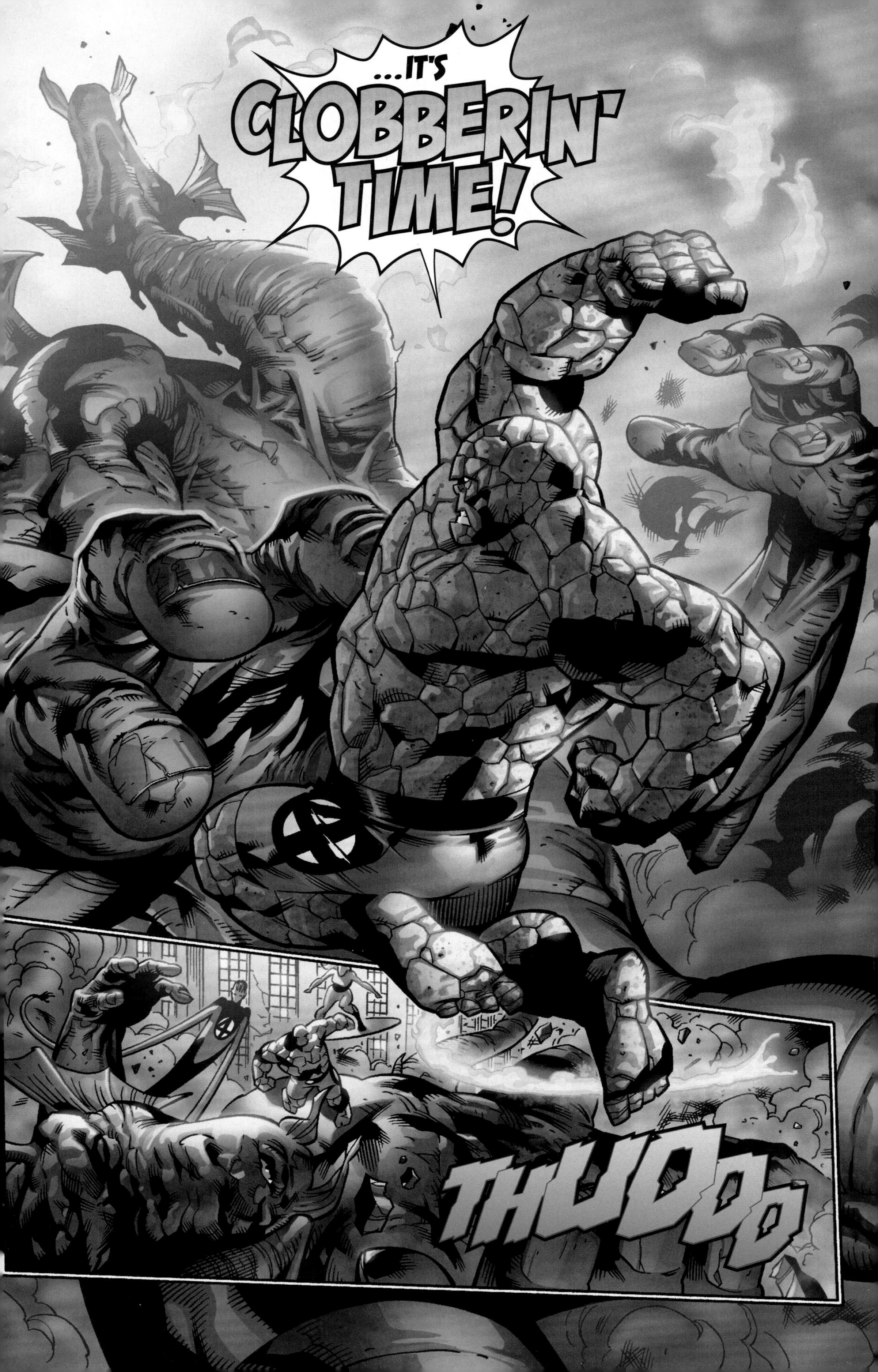
...IT'S CLOBBERIN' TIME!
THUDDD

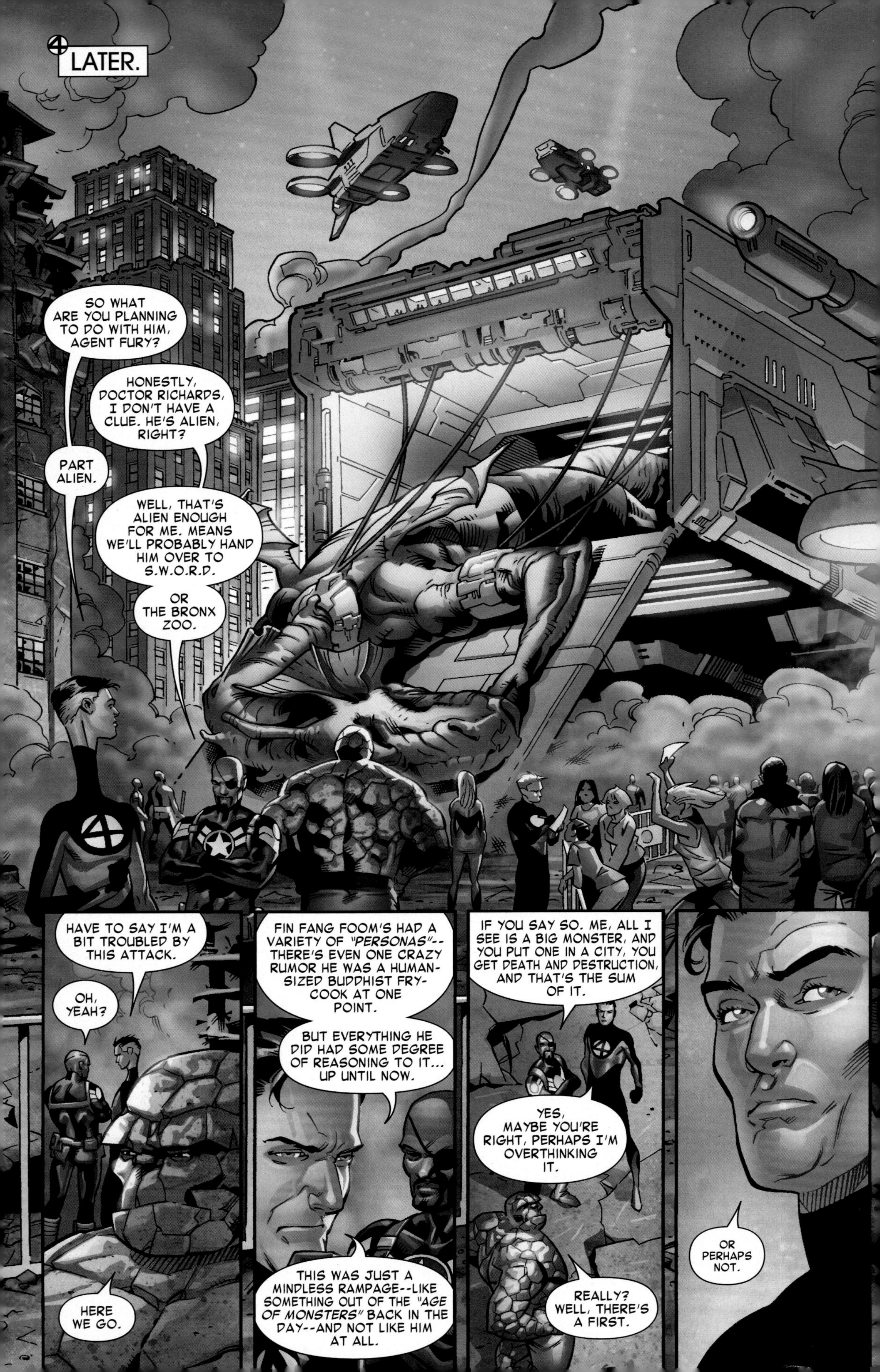

LATER.
SO WHAT ARE YOU PLANNING TO DO WITH HIM, AGENT FURY?
HONESTLY, DOCTOR RICHARDS, I DON'T HAVE A CLUE. HE'S ALIEN, RIGHT?
PART ALIEN.
WELL, THAT'S ALIEN ENOUGH FOR ME. MEANS WE'LL PROBABLY HAND HIM OVER TO S.W.O.R.D.
OR THE BRONX ZOO.
HAVE TO SAY I'M A BIT TROUBLED BY THIS ATTACK.
OH, YEAH?
HERE WE GO.
FIN FANG FOOM'S HAD A VARIETY OF "PERSONAS"--THERE'S EVEN ONE CRAZY RUMOR HE WAS A HUMAN-SIZED BUDDHIST FRY-COOK AT ONE POINT.
BUT EVERYTHING HE DID HAD SOME DEGREE OF REASONING TO IT... UP UNTIL NOW.
THIS WAS JUST A MINDLESS RAMPAGE--LIKE SOMETHING OUT OF THE "AGE OF MONSTERS" BACK IN THE DAY--AND NOT LIKE HIM AT ALL.
IF YOU SAY SO. ME, ALL I SEE IS A BIG MONSTER, AND YOU PUT ONE IN A CITY, YOU GET DEATH AND DESTRUCTION, AND THAT'S THE SUM OF IT.
YES, MAYBE YOU'RE RIGHT, PERHAPS I'M OVERTHINKING IT.
REALLY? WELL, THERE'S A FIRST.
OR PERHAPS NOT.

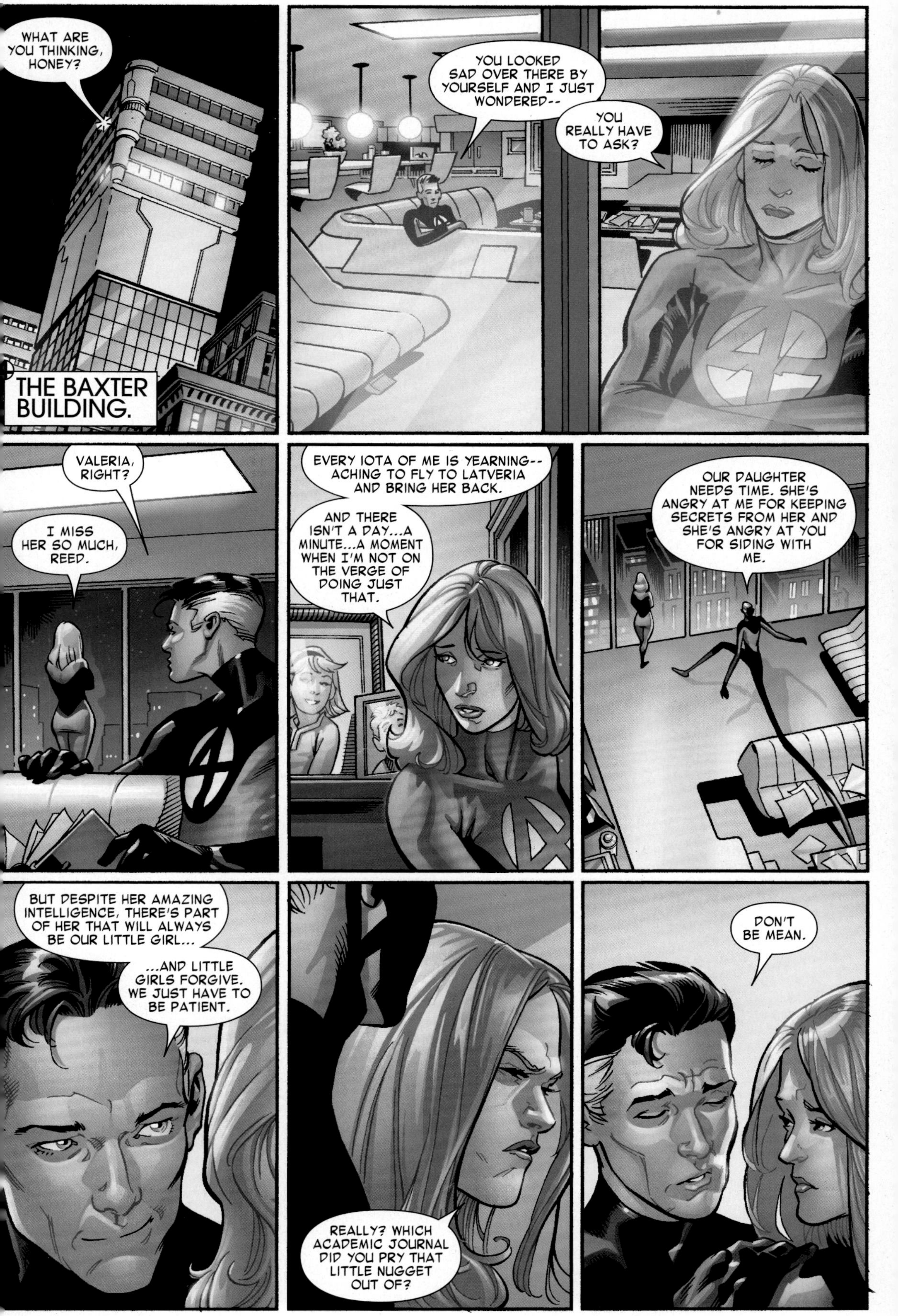
WHAT ARE YOU THINKING, HONEY?
THE BAXTER BUILDING.
YOU LOOKED SAD OVER THERE BY YOURSELF AND I JUST WONDERED--
YOU REALLY HAVE TO ASK?
VALERIA, RIGHT?
I MISS HER SO MUCH, REED.
EVERY IOTA OF ME IS YEARNING--ACHING TO FLY TO LATVERIA AND BRING HER BACK.
AND THERE ISN'T A DAY...A MINUTE...A MOMENT WHEN I'M NOT ON THE VERGE OF DOING JUST THAT.
OUR DAUGHTER NEEDS TIME. SHE'S ANGRY AT ME FOR KEEPING SECRETS FROM HER AND SHE'S ANGRY AT YOU FOR SIDING WITH ME.
BUT DESPITE HER AMAZING INTELLIGENCE, THERE'S PART OF HER THAT WILL ALWAYS BE OUR LITTLE GIRL...
...AND LITTLE GIRLS FORGIVE. WE JUST HAVE TO BE PATIENT.
REALLY? WHICH ACADEMIC JOURNAL DID YOU PRY THAT LITTLE NUGGET OUT OF?
DON'T BE MEAN.

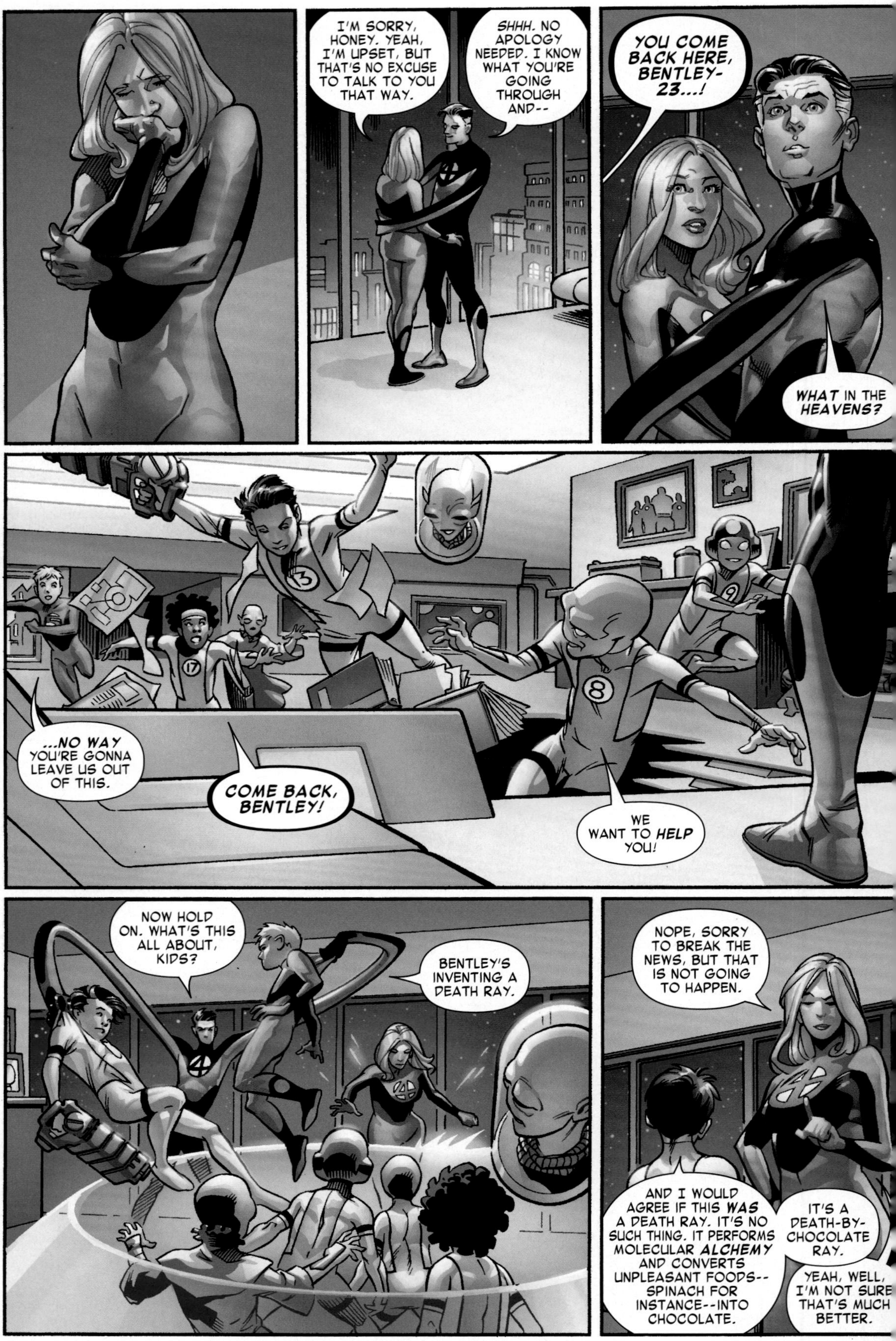
I'M SORRY, HONEY. YEAH, I'M UPSET, BUT THAT'S NO EXCUSE TO TALK TO YOU THAT WAY.
SHHH. NO APOLOGY NEEDED. I KNOW WHAT YOU'RE GOING THROUGH AND--
YOU COME BACK HERE, BENTLEY-23...!
WHAT IN THE HEAVENS?
...NO WAY YOU'RE GONNA LEAVE US OUT OF THIS.
COME BACK, BENTLEY!
WE WANT TO HELP YOU!
NOW HOLD ON. WHAT'S THIS ALL ABOUT, KIDS?
BENTLEY'S INVENTING A DEATH RAY.
NOPE, SORRY TO BREAK THE NEWS, BUT THAT IS NOT GOING TO HAPPEN.
AND I WOULD AGREE IF THIS WAS A DEATH RAY. IT'S NO SUCH THING. IT PERFORMS MOLECULAR ALCHEMY AND CONVERTS UNPLEASANT FOODS--SPINACH FOR INSTANCE--INTO CHOCOLATE.
IT'S A DEATH-BY-CHOCOLATE RAY.
YEAH, WELL, I'M NOT SURE THAT'S MUCH BETTER.

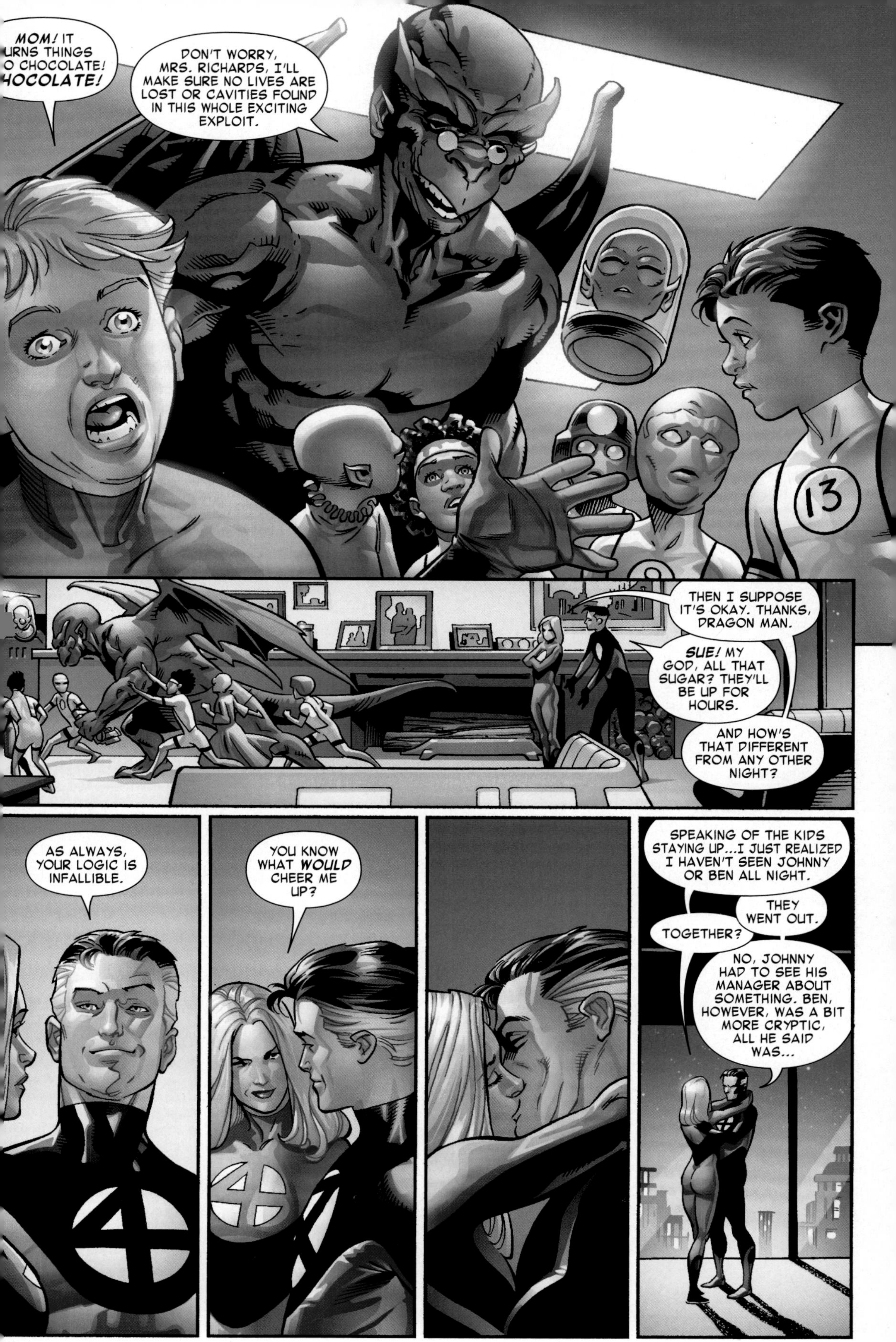
MOM! IT URNS THINGS O CHOCOLATE! HOCOLATE!
DON'T WORRY, MRS. RICHARDS, I'LL MAKE SURE NO LIVES ARE LOST OR CAVITIES FOUND IN THIS WHOLE EXCITING EXPLOIT.
13
THEN I SUPPOSE IT'S OKAY. THANKS, DRAGON MAN.
SUE! MY GOD, ALL THAT SUGAR? THEY'LL BE UP FOR HOURS.
AND HOW'S THAT DIFFERENT FROM ANY OTHER NIGHT?
AS ALWAYS, YOUR LOGIC IS INFALLIBLE.
YOU KNOW WHAT WOULD CHEER ME UP?
SPEAKING OF THE KIDS STAYING UP...I JUST REALIZED I HAVEN'T SEEN JOHNNY OR BEN ALL NIGHT.
THEY WENT OUT.
TOGETHER?
NO, JOHNNY HAD TO SEE HIS MANAGER ABOUT SOMETHING. BEN, HOWEVER, WAS A BIT MORE CRYPTIC, ALL HE SAID WAS...

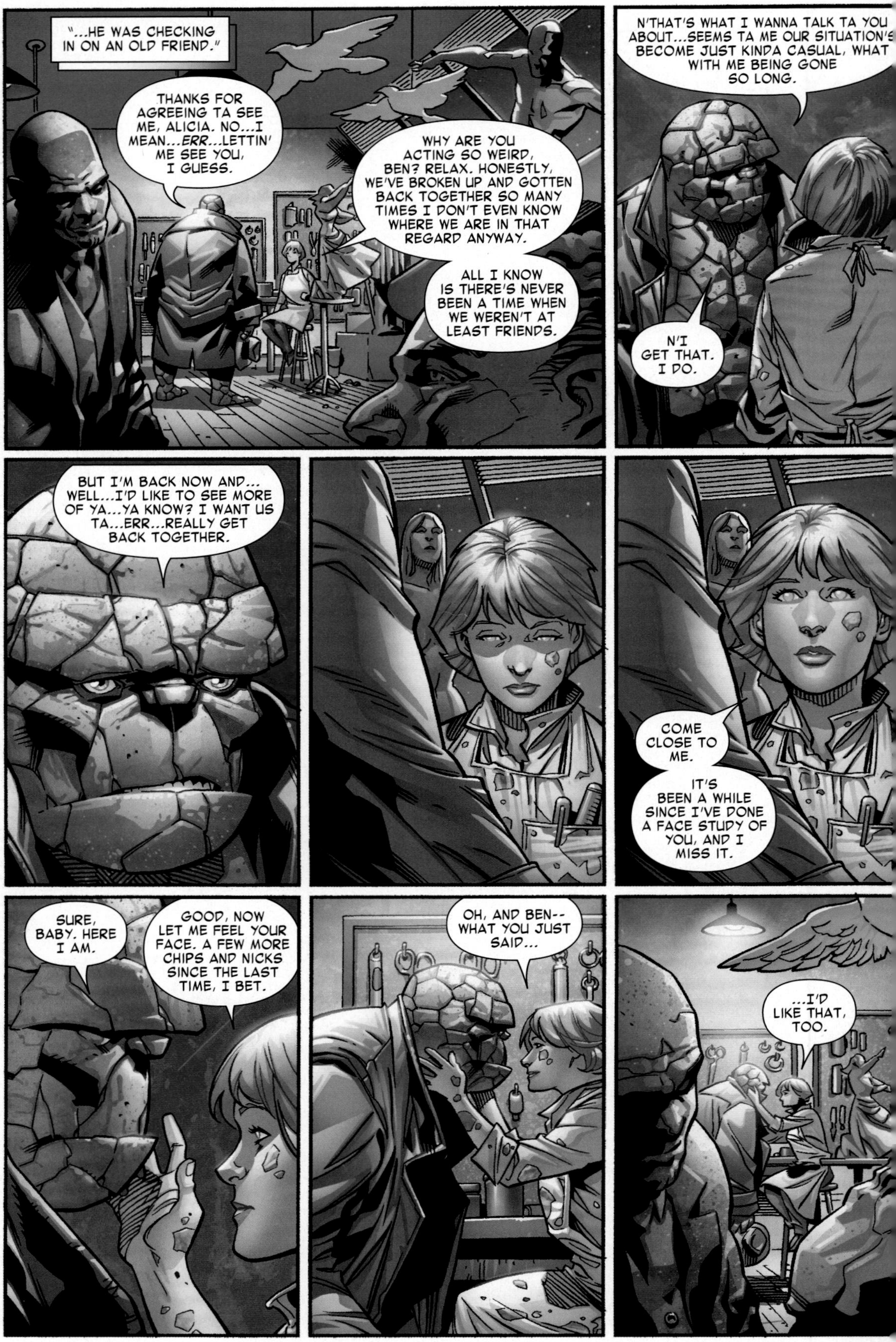
"...HE WAS CHECKING IN ON AN OLD FRIEND."
THANKS FOR AGREEING TA SEE ME, ALICIA. NO...I MEAN...ERR...LETTIN' ME SEE YOU, I GUESS.
WHY ARE YOU ACTING SO WEIRD, BEN? RELAX. HONESTLY, WE'VE BROKEN UP AND GOTTEN BACK TOGETHER SO MANY TIMES I DON'T EVEN KNOW WHERE WE ARE IN THAT REGARD ANYWAY.
ALL I KNOW IS THERE'S NEVER BEEN A TIME WHEN WE WEREN'T AT LEAST FRIENDS.
N'THAT'S WHAT I WANNA TALK TA YOU ABOUT...SEEMS TA ME OUR SITUATION'S BECOME JUST KINDA CASUAL, WHAT WITH ME BEING GONE SO LONG.
N'I GET THAT. I DO.
BUT I'M BACK NOW AND... WELL...I'D LIKE TO SEE MORE OF YA...YA KNOW? I WANT US TA...ERR...REALLY GET BACK TOGETHER.
COME CLOSE TO ME.
IT'S BEEN A WHILE SINCE I'VE DONE A FACE STUDY OF YOU, AND I MISS IT.
SURE, BABY. HERE I AM.
GOOD, NOW LET ME FEEL YOUR FACE. A FEW MORE CHIPS AND NICKS SINCE THE LAST TIME, I BET.
OH, AND BEN-- WHAT YOU JUST SAID...
...I'D LIKE THAT, TOO.

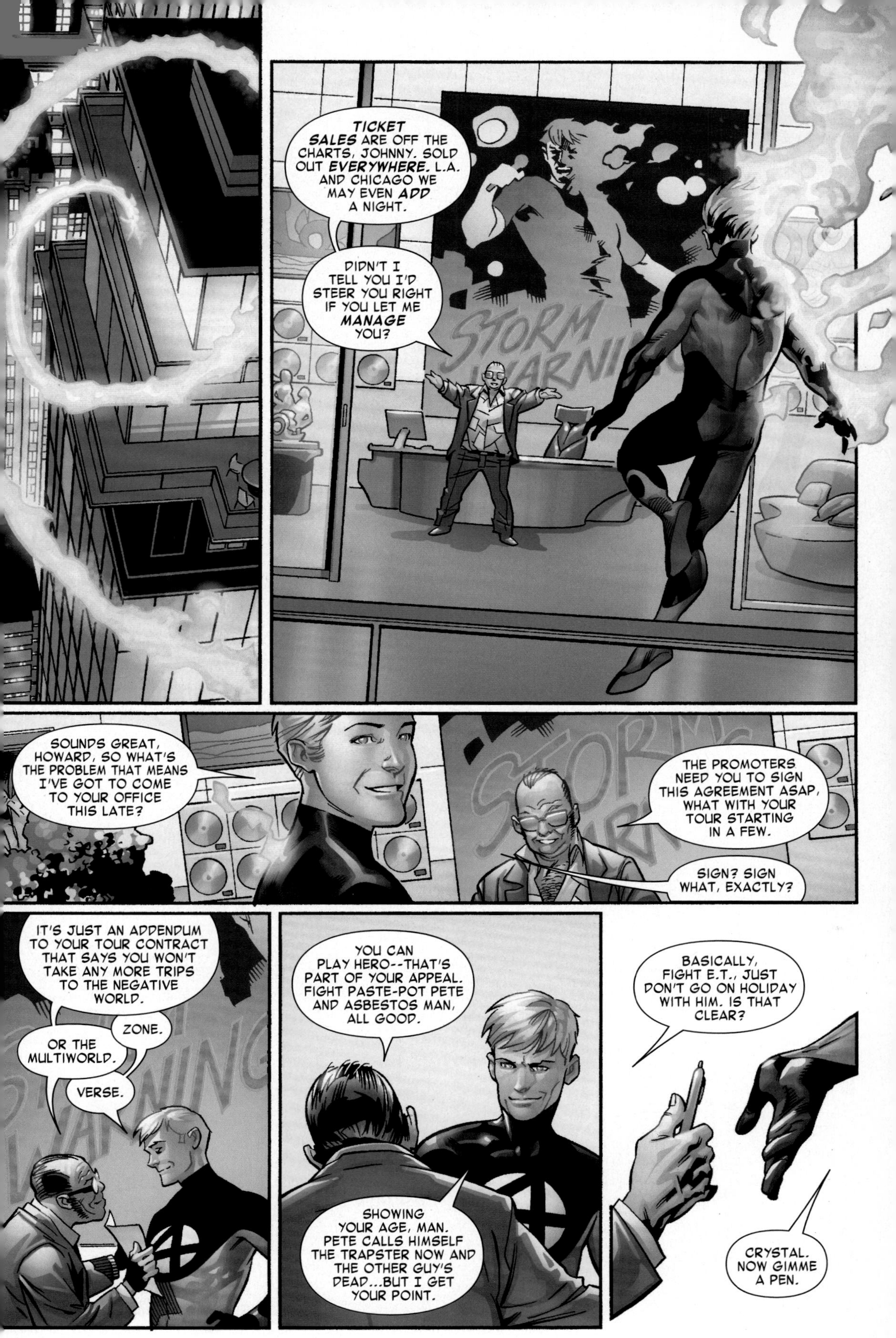

TICKET SALES ARE OFF THE CHARTS, JOHNNY. SOLD OUT EVERYWHERE. L.A. AND CHICAGO WE MAY EVEN ADD A NIGHT.
DIDN'T I TELL YOU I'D STEER YOU RIGHT IF YOU LET ME MANAGE YOU?
STORM WARNING
SOUNDS GREAT, HOWARD, SO WHAT'S THE PROBLEM THAT MEANS I'VE GOT TO COME TO YOUR OFFICE THIS LATE?
THE PROMOTERS NEED YOU TO SIGN THIS AGREEMENT ASAP, WHAT WITH YOUR TOUR STARTING IN A FEW.
SIGN? SIGN WHAT, EXACTLY?
IT'S JUST AN ADDENDUM TO YOUR TOUR CONTRACT THAT SAYS YOU WON'T TAKE ANY MORE TRIPS TO THE NEGATIVE WORLD.
ZONE.
OR THE MULTIWORLD.
VERSE.
YOU CAN PLAY HERO--THAT'S PART OF YOUR APPEAL. FIGHT PASTE-POT PETE AND ASBESTOS MAN, ALL GOOD.
SHOWING YOUR AGE, MAN. PETE CALLS HIMSELF THE TRAPSTER NOW AND THE OTHER GUY'S DEAD...BUT I GET YOUR POINT.
BASICALLY, FIGHT E.T., JUST DON'T GO ON HOLIDAY WITH HIM. IS THAT CLEAR?
CRYSTAL. NOW GIMME A PEN.

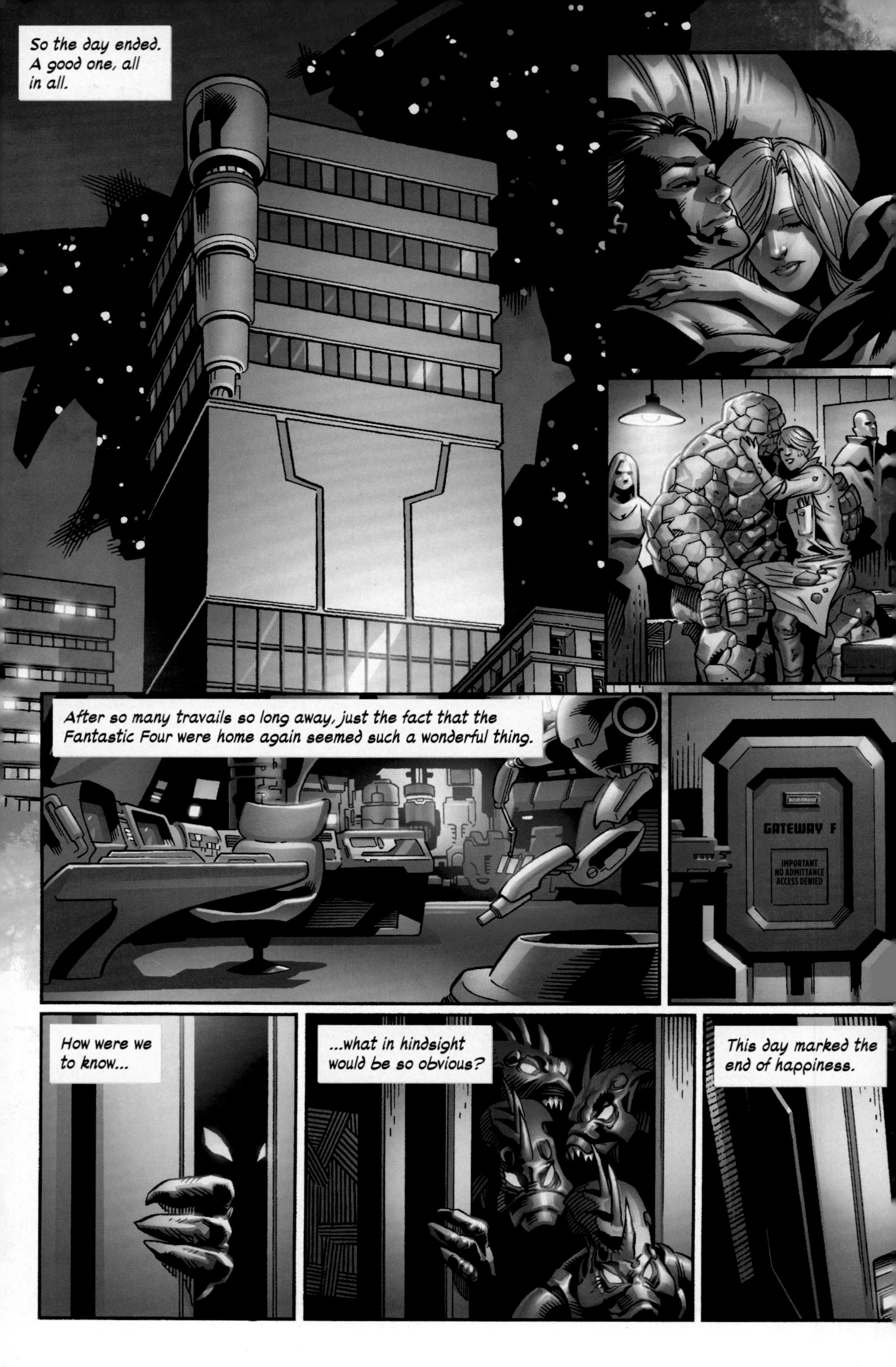

So the day ended. A good one, all in all.
After so many travails so long away, just the fact that the Fantastic Four were home again seemed such a wonderful thing.
GATEWAY F
IMPORTANT
NO ADMITTANCE
ACCESS DENIED
How were we to know...
...what in hindsight would be so obvious?
This day marked the end of happiness.

And yes, I may have been brokenhearted about you, Val—your choice to be apart from us...

...but even I had to admit that in so many other ways...

...the future seemed so positive...

...so bright and alive.

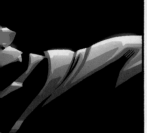

SEALED

ATEWAY F

IMPORTANT
NO ADMITTANCE
ACCESS DENIED

SEALED

ATEWAY

UNSEALED

ITEWAY

The end of hope.

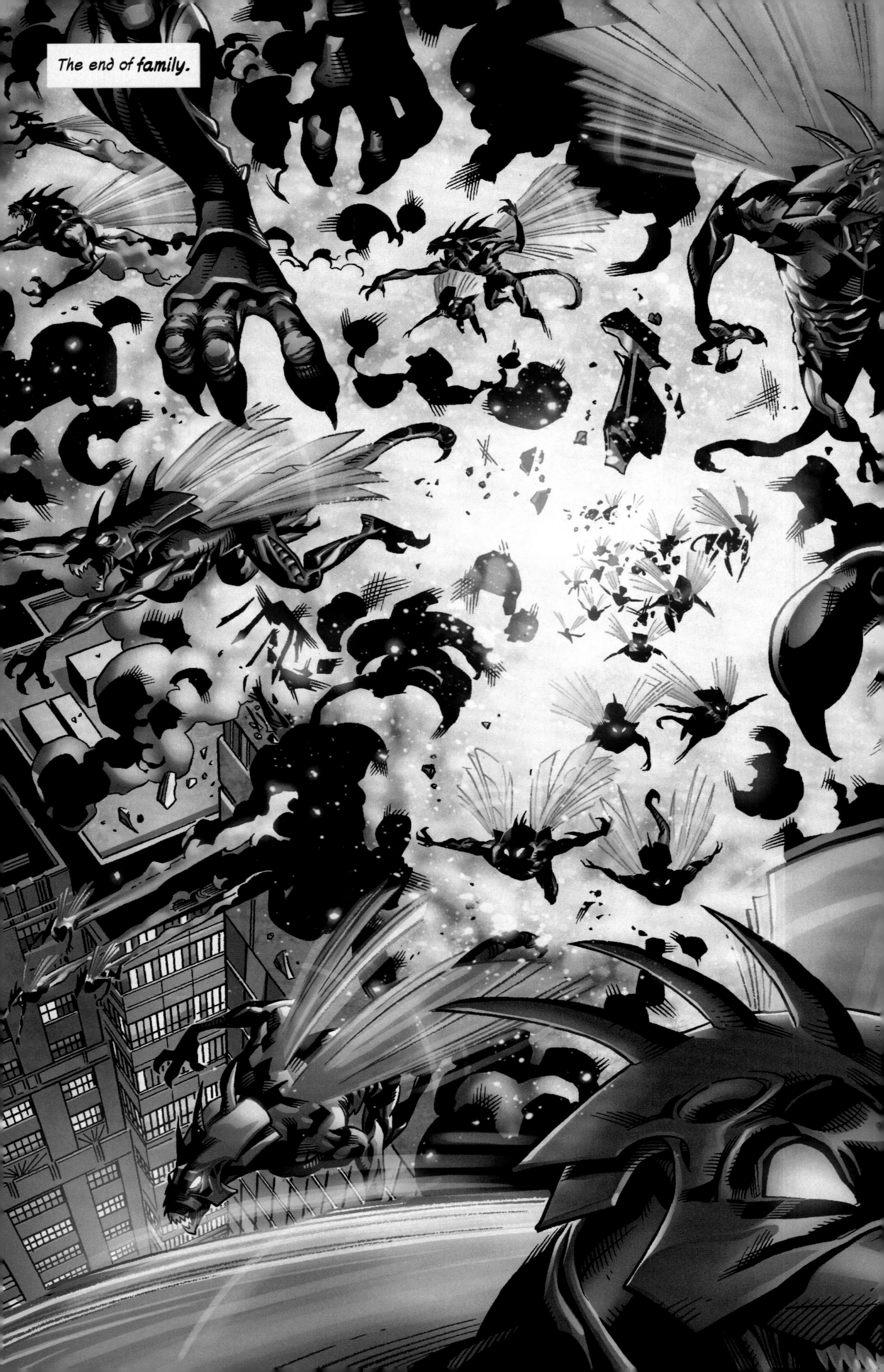
The end of family.

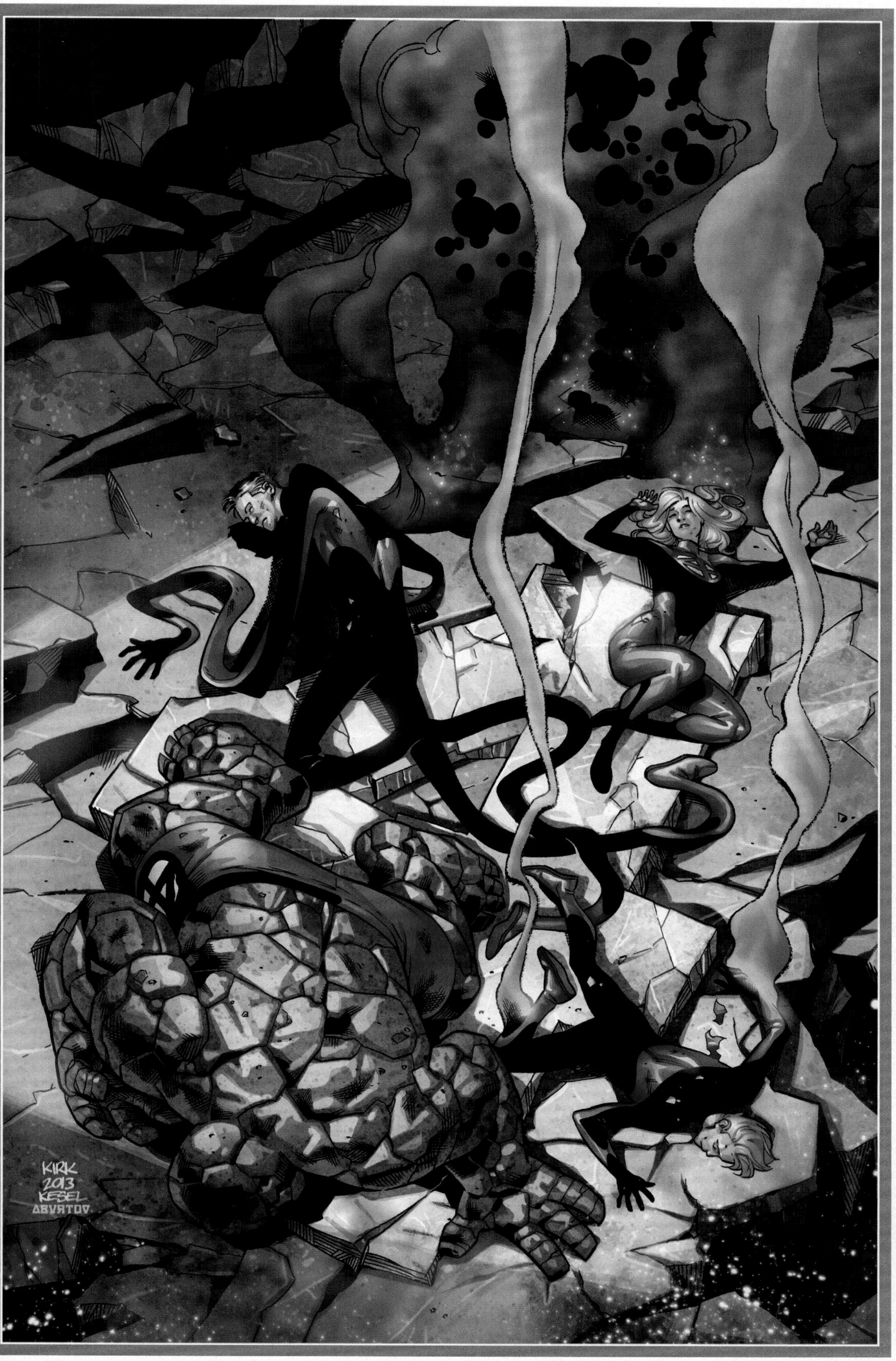
KIRK
2013
KESEL
AVARTOV

TWO

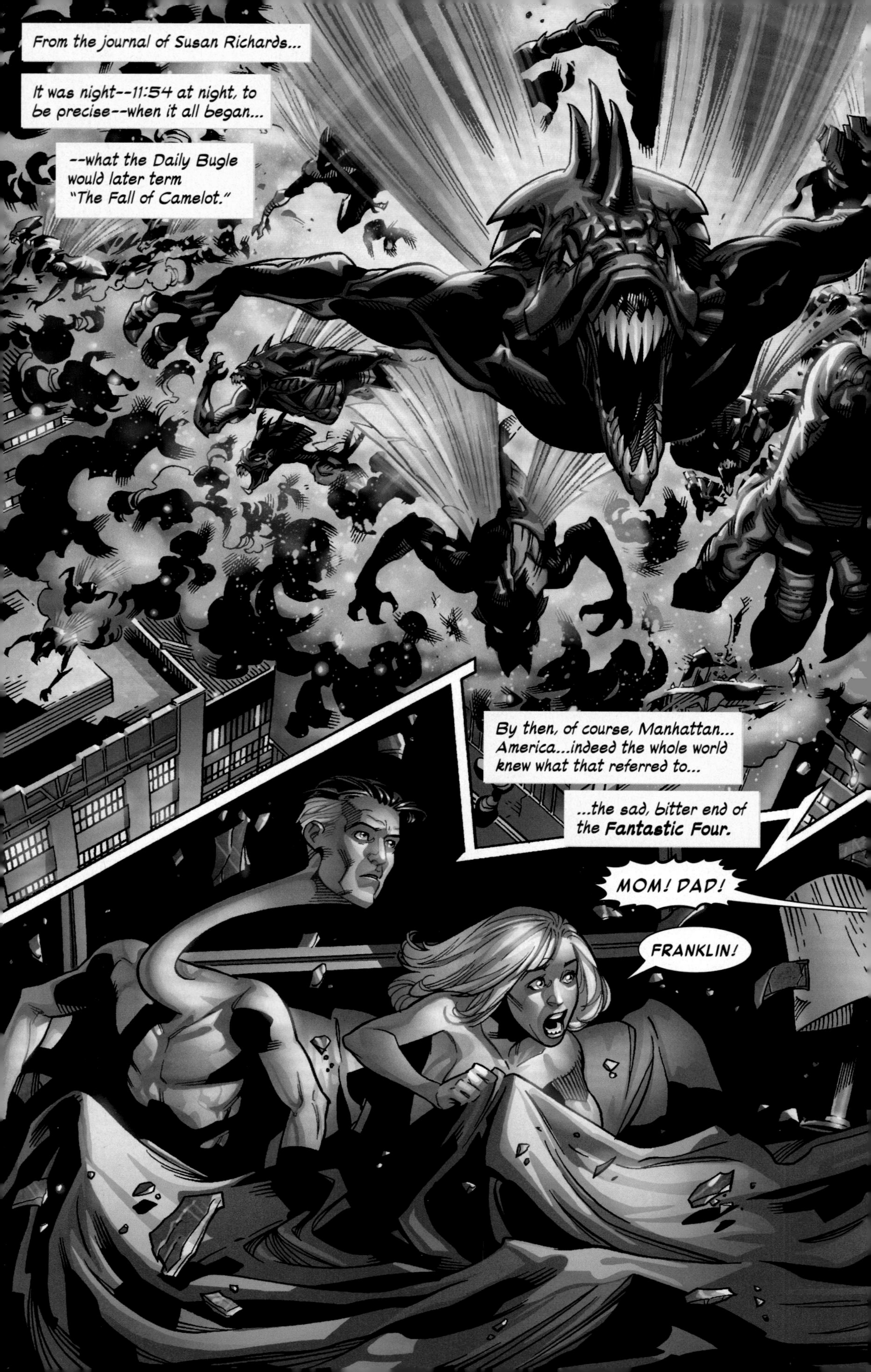
From the journal of Susan Richards...
It was night--11:54 at night, to be precise--when it all began...
--what the Daily Bugle would later term "The Fall of Camelot."
By then, of course, Manhattan... America...indeed the whole world knew what that referred to...
...the sad, bitter end of the Fantastic Four.
MOM! DAD!
FRANKLIN!

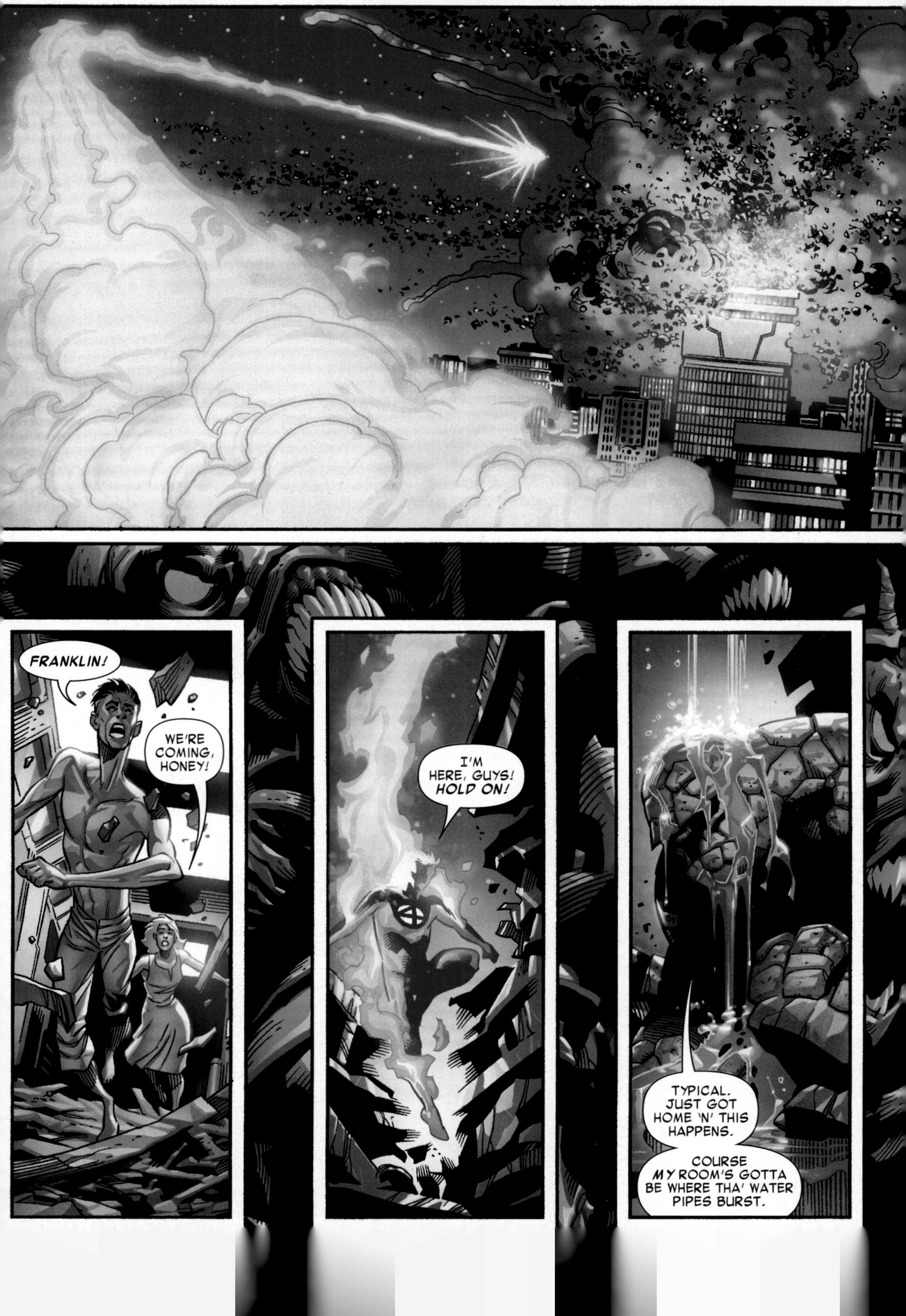
FRANKLIN!
WE'RE COMING, HONEY!
I'M HERE, GUYS! HOLD ON!
TYPICAL. JUST GOT HOME 'N' THIS HAPPENS.
COURSE MY ROOM'S GOTTA BE WHERE THA' WATER PIPES BURST.

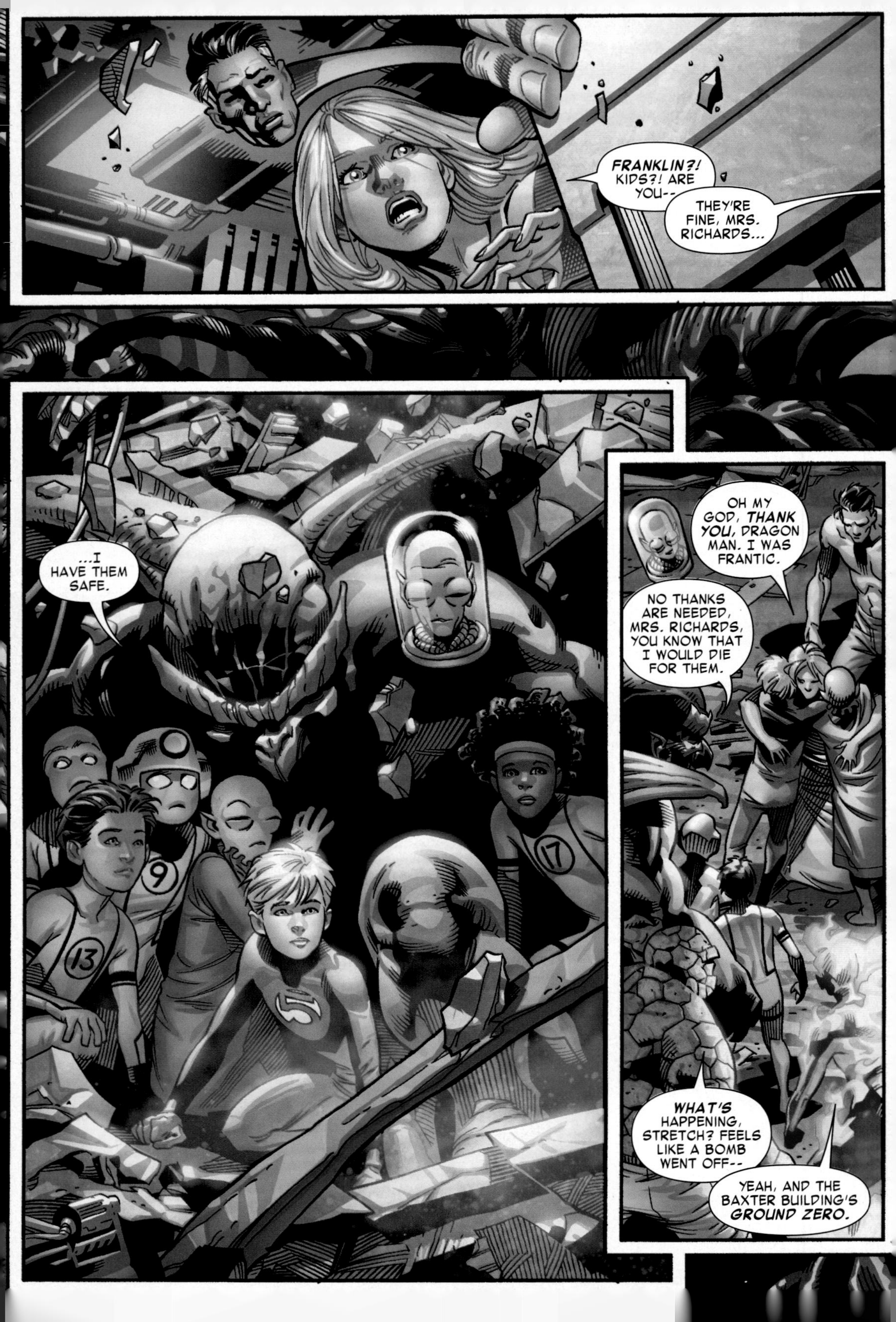
FRANKLIN?! KIDS?! ARE YOU--
THEY'RE FINE, MRS. RICHARDS...
...I HAVE THEM SAFE.
OH MY GOD, THANK YOU, DRAGON MAN. I WAS FRANTIC.
NO THANKS ARE NEEDED, MRS. RICHARDS, YOU KNOW THAT I WOULD DIE FOR THEM.
WHAT'S HAPPENING, STRETCH? FEELS LIKE A BOMB WENT OFF--
YEAH, AND THE BAXTER BUILDING'S GROUND ZERO.

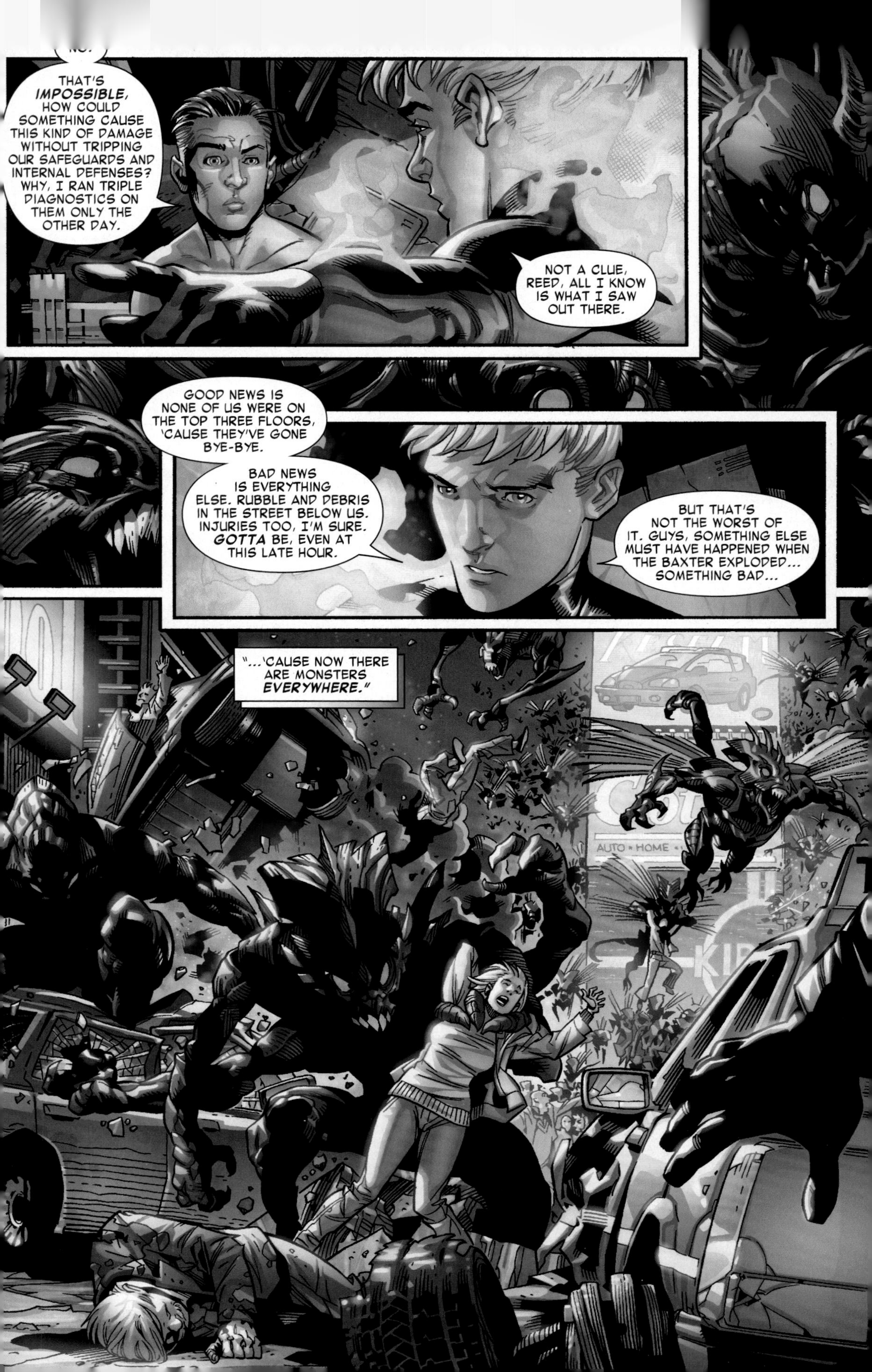
NO?
THAT'S IMPOSSIBLE, HOW COULD SOMETHING CAUSE THIS KIND OF DAMAGE WITHOUT TRIPPING OUR SAFEGUARDS AND INTERNAL DEFENSES? WHY, I RAN TRIPLE DIAGNOSTICS ON THEM ONLY THE OTHER DAY.
NOT A CLUE, REED, ALL I KNOW IS WHAT I SAW OUT THERE.
GOOD NEWS IS NONE OF US WERE ON THE TOP THREE FLOORS, 'CAUSE THEY'VE GONE BYE-BYE.
BAD NEWS IS EVERYTHING ELSE. RUBBLE AND DEBRIS IN THE STREET BELOW US. INJURIES TOO, I'M SURE. GOTTA BE, EVEN AT THIS LATE HOUR.
BUT THAT'S NOT THE WORST OF IT. GUYS, SOMETHING ELSE MUST HAVE HAPPENED WHEN THE BAXTER EXPLODED... SOMETHING BAD...
"...'CAUSE NOW THERE ARE MONSTERS EVERYWHERE."
AUTO • HOME

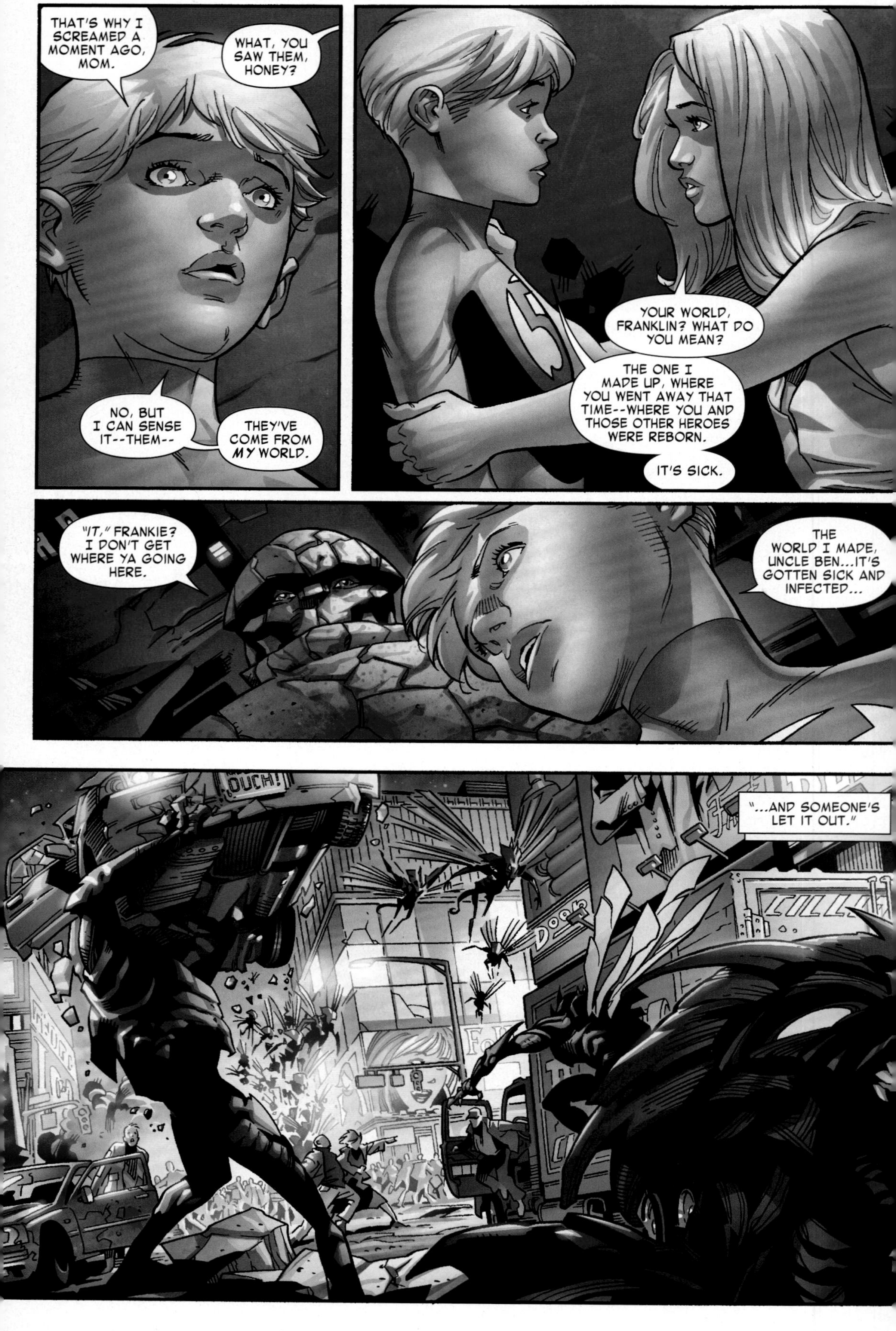
THAT'S WHY I SCREAMED A MOMENT AGO, MOM.
WHAT, YOU SAW THEM, HONEY?
NO, BUT I CAN SENSE IT--THEM--
THEY'VE COME FROM *MY* WORLD.
YOUR WORLD, FRANKLIN? WHAT DO YOU MEAN?
THE ONE I MADE UP, WHERE YOU WENT AWAY THAT TIME--WHERE YOU AND THOSE OTHER HEROES WERE REBORN.
IT'S SICK.
"*IT*," FRANKIE? I DON'T GET WHERE YA GOING HERE.
THE WORLD I MADE, UNCLE BEN...IT'S GOTTEN SICK AND INFECTED...
"...AND SOMEONE'S LET IT OUT."
OUCH!

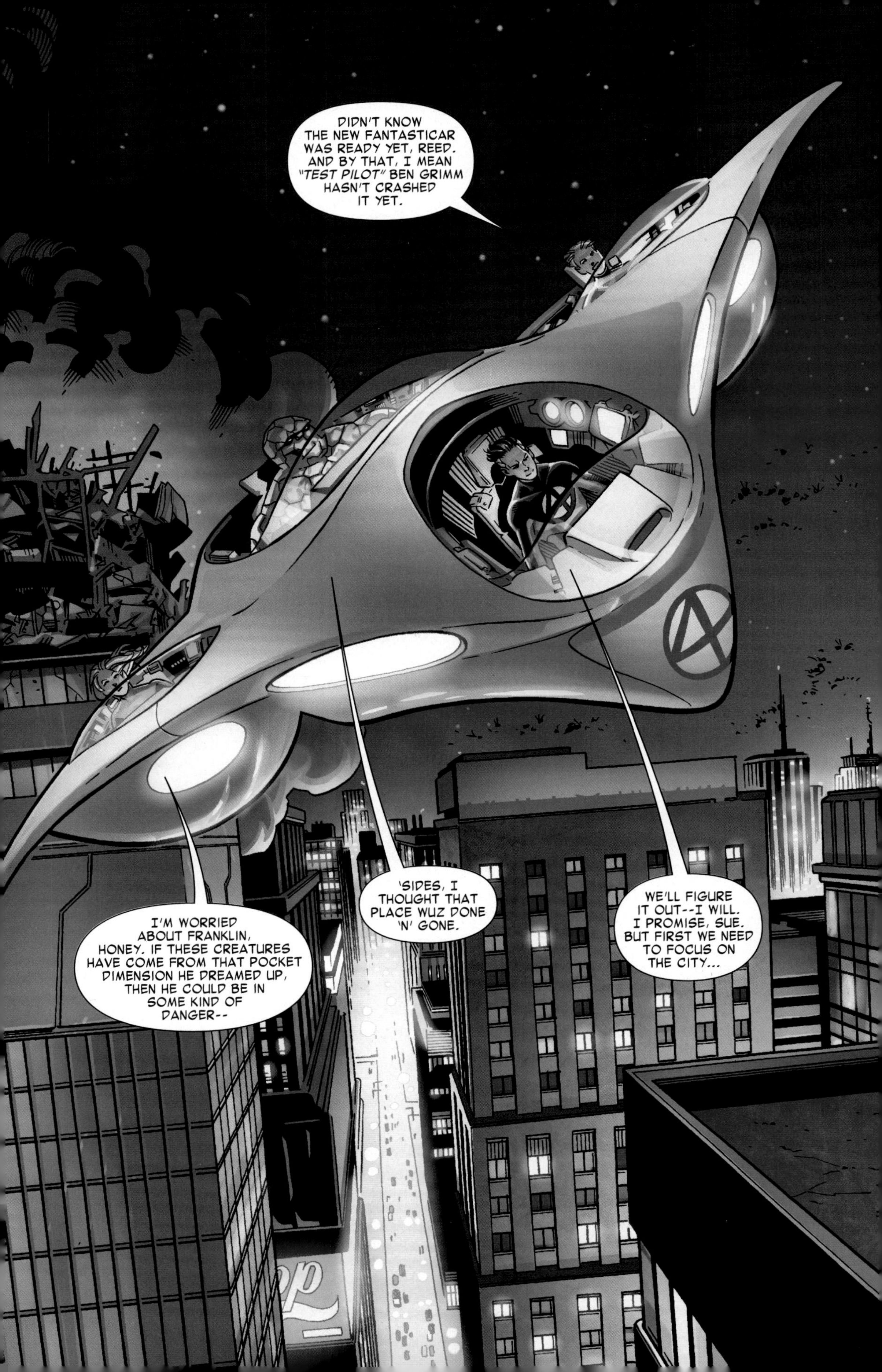
DIDN'T KNOW THE NEW FANTASTICAR WAS READY YET, REED. AND BY THAT, I MEAN "TEST PILOT" BEN GRIMM HASN'T CRASHED IT YET.
I'M WORRIED ABOUT FRANKLIN, HONEY. IF THESE CREATURES HAVE COME FROM THAT POCKET DIMENSION HE DREAMED UP, THEN HE COULD BE IN SOME KIND OF DANGER--
'SIDES, I THOUGHT THAT PLACE WUZ DONE 'N' GONE.
WE'LL FIGURE IT OUT--I WILL. I PROMISE, SUE. BUT FIRST WE NEED TO FOCUS ON THE CITY...

...AND WITH THIS THREAT SO FAR-REACHING, WE'LL BE MORE EFFECTIVE BY SPLITTING UP.

TIME TO FIELD-TEST THE NEW QUADRANT COUPLINGS.

WELL, I'M LEAVING MY POD HERE, BUT SURE, LET'S DO THIS!

BEN, AS YOU ARE INDEED OUR "TEAM PILOT," YOU CAN HAVE THE HONOR.

OR IN "BEN GRIMM SPEAK," PUSH THE BIG BUTTON, DUMMY.

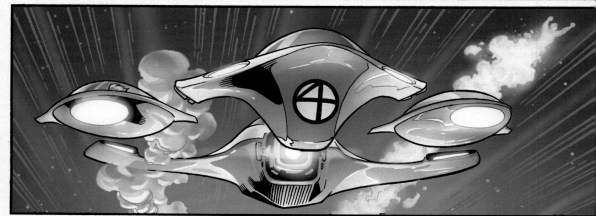

I WONDER IF THEY SEE IT...

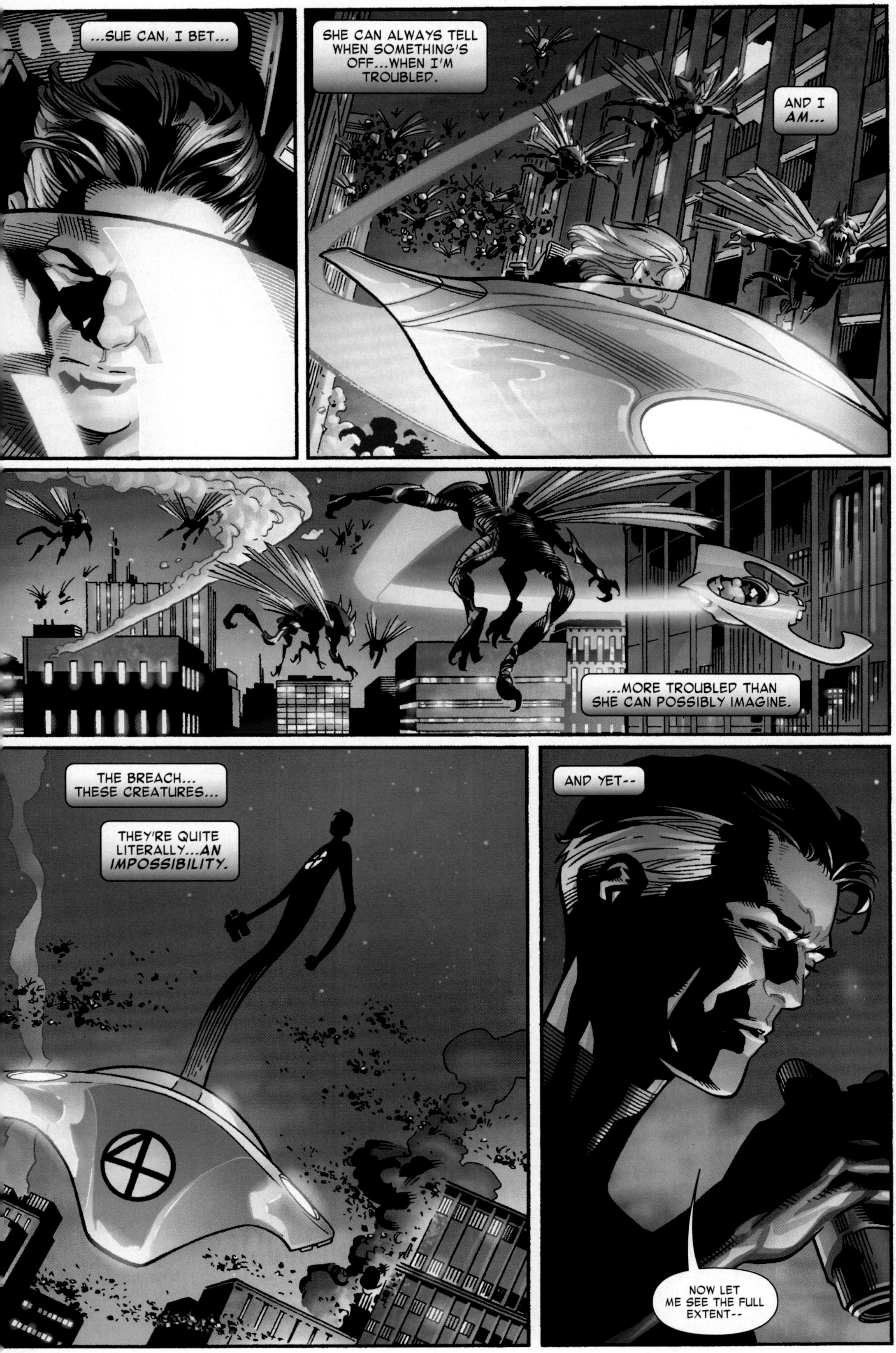
...SUE CAN, I BET...
SHE CAN ALWAYS TELL WHEN SOMETHING'S OFF...WHEN I'M TROUBLED.
AND I AM...
...MORE TROUBLED THAN SHE CAN POSSIBLY IMAGINE.
THE BREACH... THESE CREATURES...
THEY'RE QUITE LITERALLY...AN IMPOSSIBILITY.
AND YET--
NOW LET ME SEE THE FULL EXTENT--

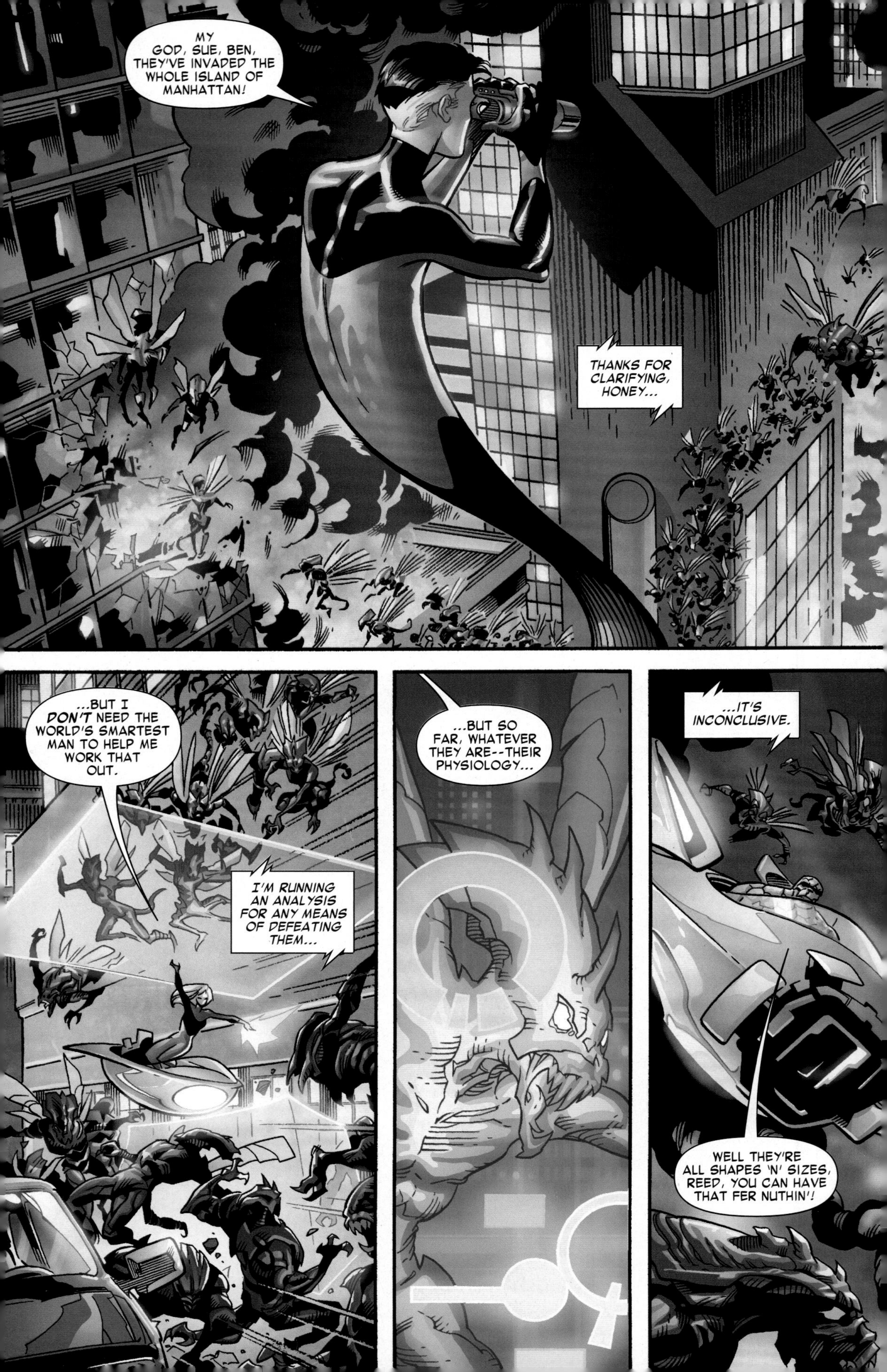
MY GOD, SUE, BEN, THEY'VE INVADED THE WHOLE ISLAND OF MANHATTAN!
THANKS FOR CLARIFYING, HONEY...
...BUT I DON'T NEED THE WORLD'S SMARTEST MAN TO HELP ME WORK THAT OUT.
I'M RUNNING AN ANALYSIS FOR ANY MEANS OF DEFEATING THEM...
...BUT SO FAR, WHATEVER THEY ARE--THEIR PHYSIOLOGY...
...IT'S INCONCLUSIVE.
WELL THEY'RE ALL SHAPES 'N' SIZES, REED, YOU CAN HAVE THAT FER NUTHIN'!

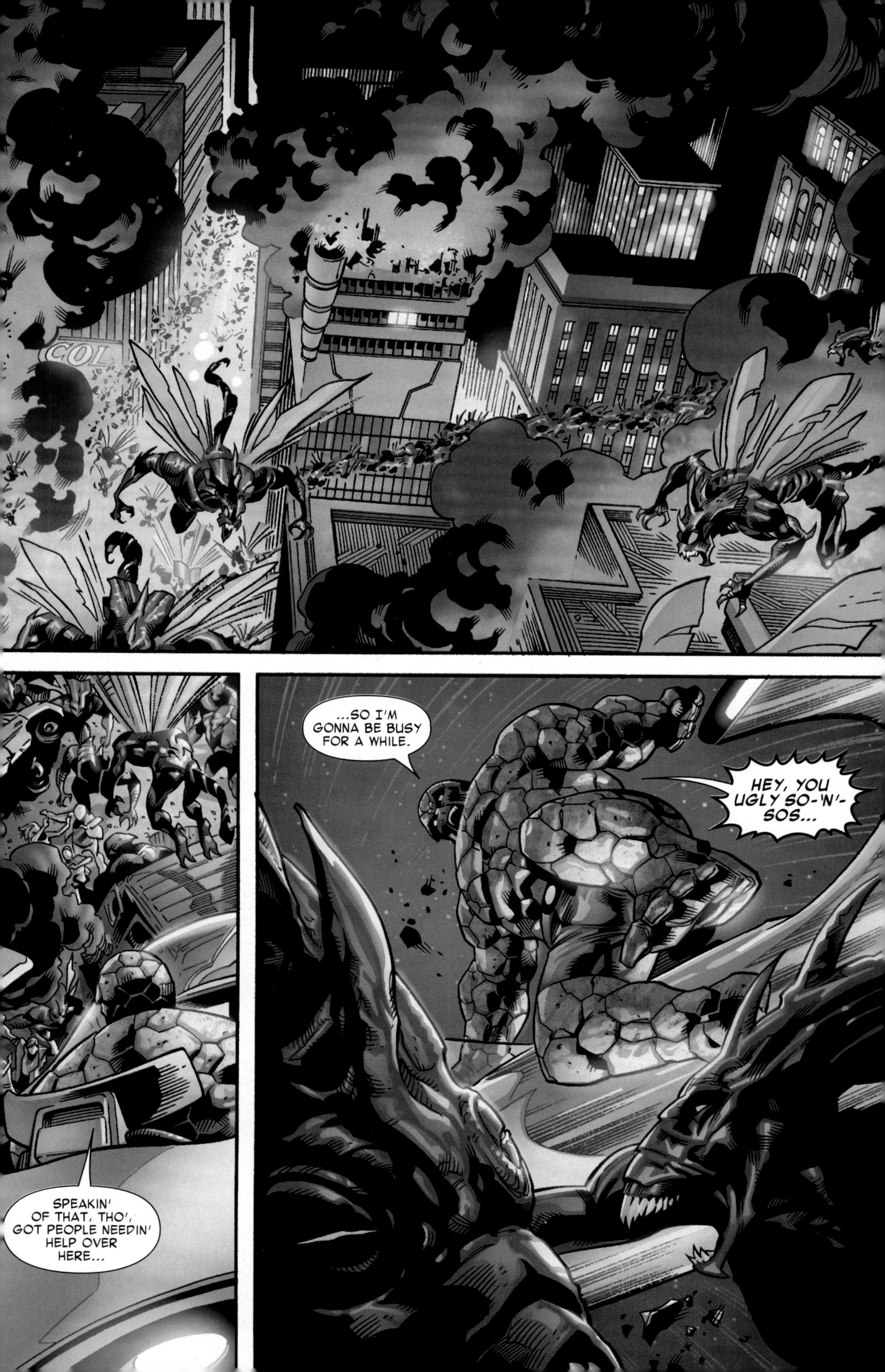
COL
SPEAKIN' OF THAT, THO', GOT PEOPLE NEEDIN' HELP OVER HERE...
...SO I'M GONNA BE BUSY FOR A WHILE.
HEY, YOU UGLY SO-'N'-SOS...

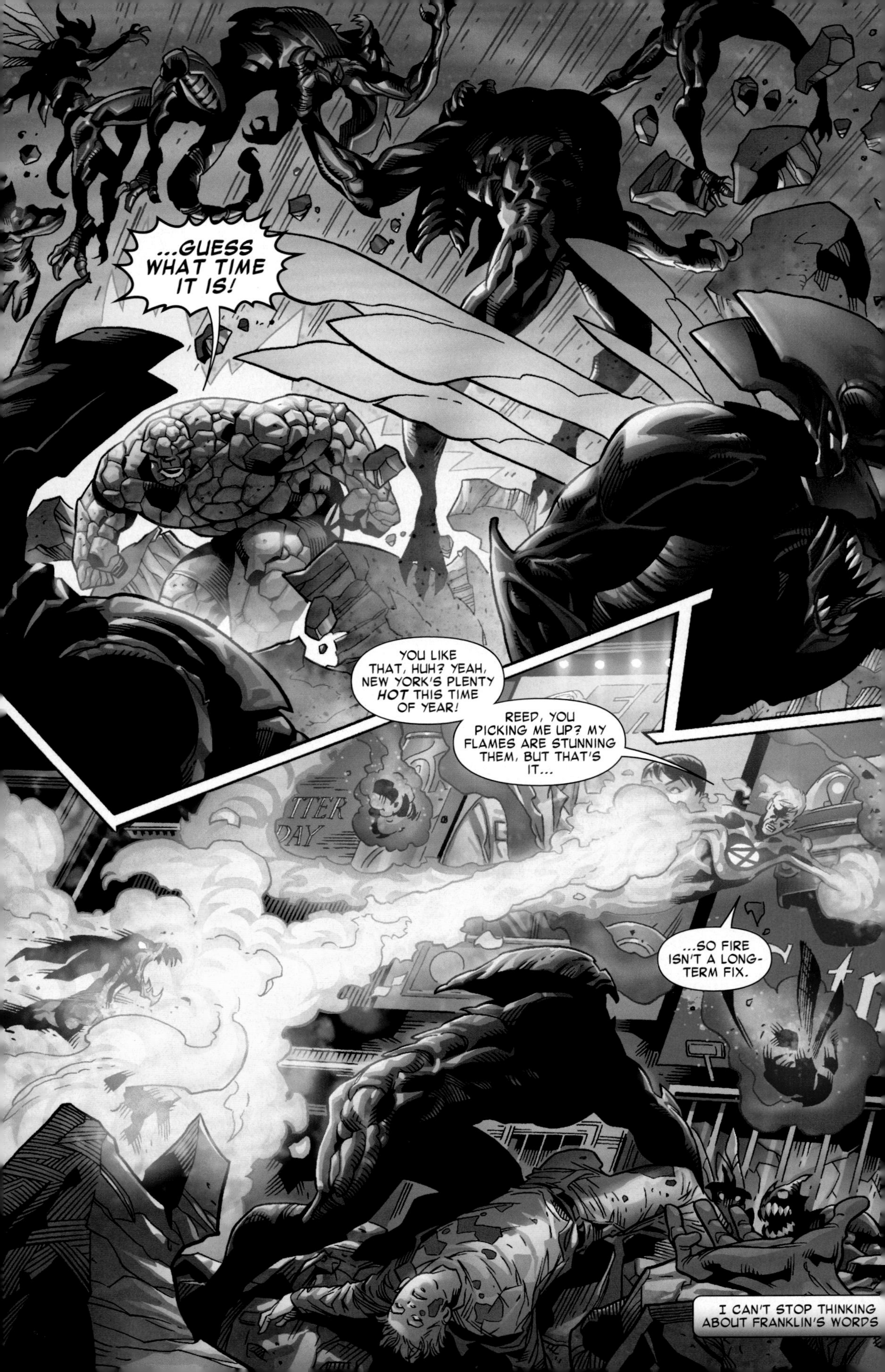
...GUESS WHAT TIME IT IS!
YOU LIKE THAT, HUH? YEAH, NEW YORK'S PLENTY HOT THIS TIME OF YEAR!
REED, YOU PICKING ME UP? MY FLAMES ARE STUNNING THEM, BUT THAT'S IT...
...SO FIRE ISN'T A LONG-TERM FIX.
I CAN'T STOP THINKING ABOUT FRANKLIN'S WORDS

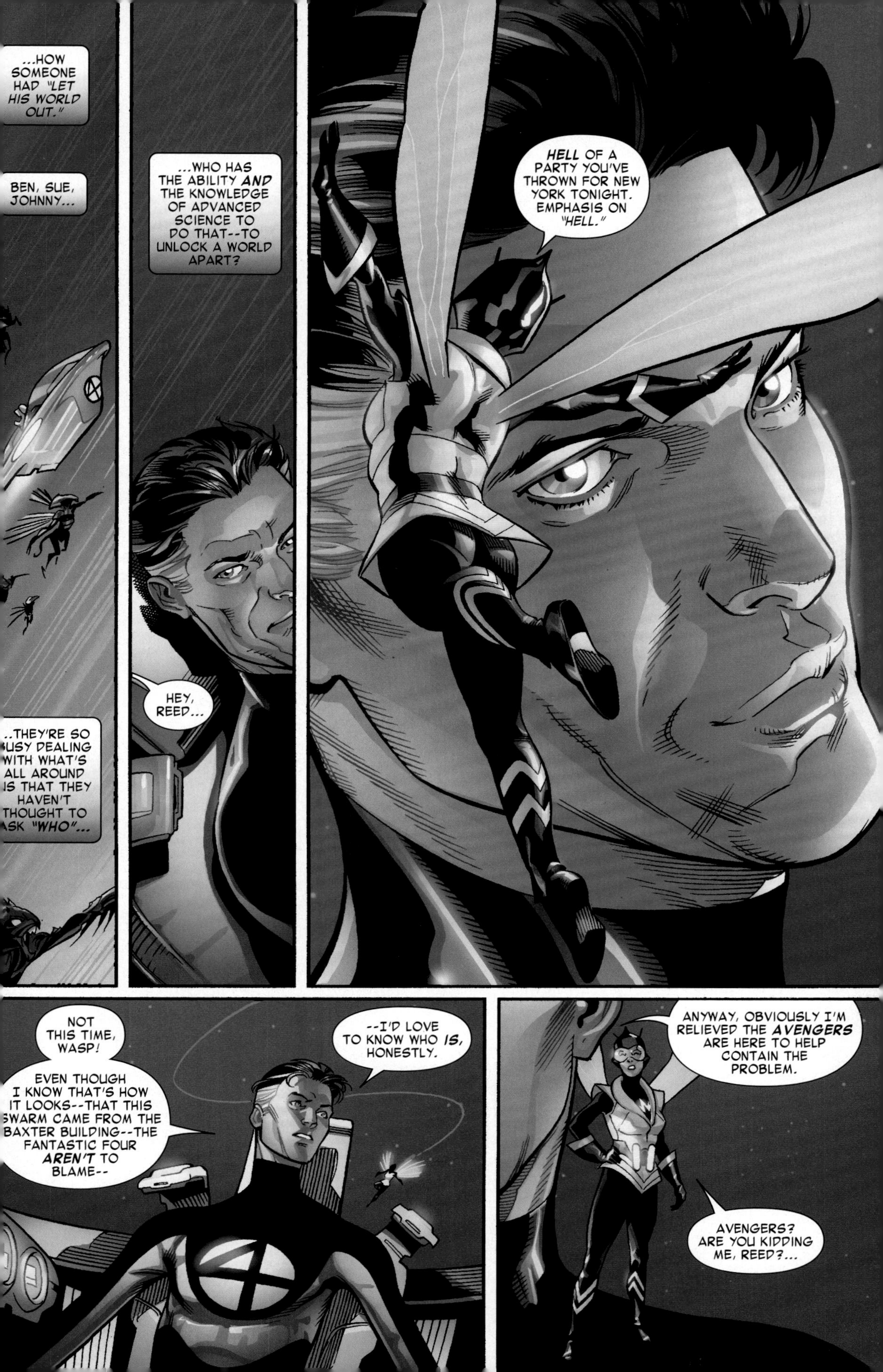
...HOW SOMEONE HAD "LET HIS WORLD OUT."
BEN, SUE, JOHNNY...
..THEY'RE SO BUSY DEALING WITH WHAT'S ALL AROUND US THAT THEY HAVEN'T THOUGHT TO ASK "WHO"...
...WHO HAS THE ABILITY AND THE KNOWLEDGE OF ADVANCED SCIENCE TO DO THAT--TO UNLOCK A WORLD APART?
HEY, REED...
HELL OF A PARTY YOU'VE THROWN FOR NEW YORK TONIGHT. EMPHASIS ON "HELL."
NOT THIS TIME, WASP!
EVEN THOUGH I KNOW THAT'S HOW IT LOOKS--THAT THIS SWARM CAME FROM THE BAXTER BUILDING--THE FANTASTIC FOUR AREN'T TO BLAME--
--I'D LOVE TO KNOW WHO IS, HONESTLY.
ANYWAY, OBVIOUSLY I'M RELIEVED THE AVENGERS ARE HERE TO HELP CONTAIN THE PROBLEM.
AVENGERS? ARE YOU KIDDING ME, REED?...

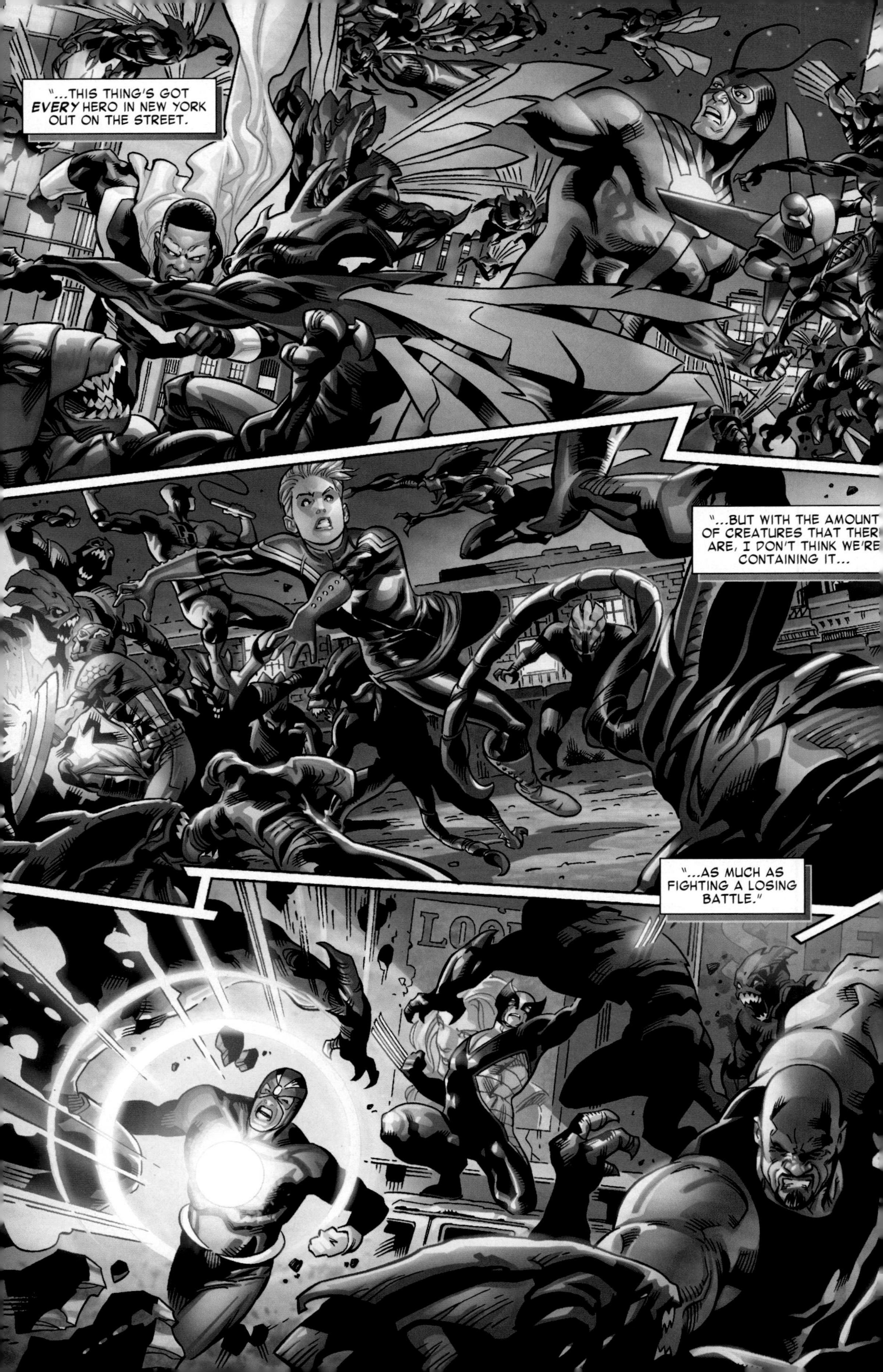
"...THIS THING'S GOT EVERY HERO IN NEW YORK OUT ON THE STREET.
"...BUT WITH THE AMOUNT OF CREATURES THAT THER ARE, I DON'T THINK WE'RE CONTAINING IT...
"...AS MUCH AS FIGHTING A LOSING BATTLE."

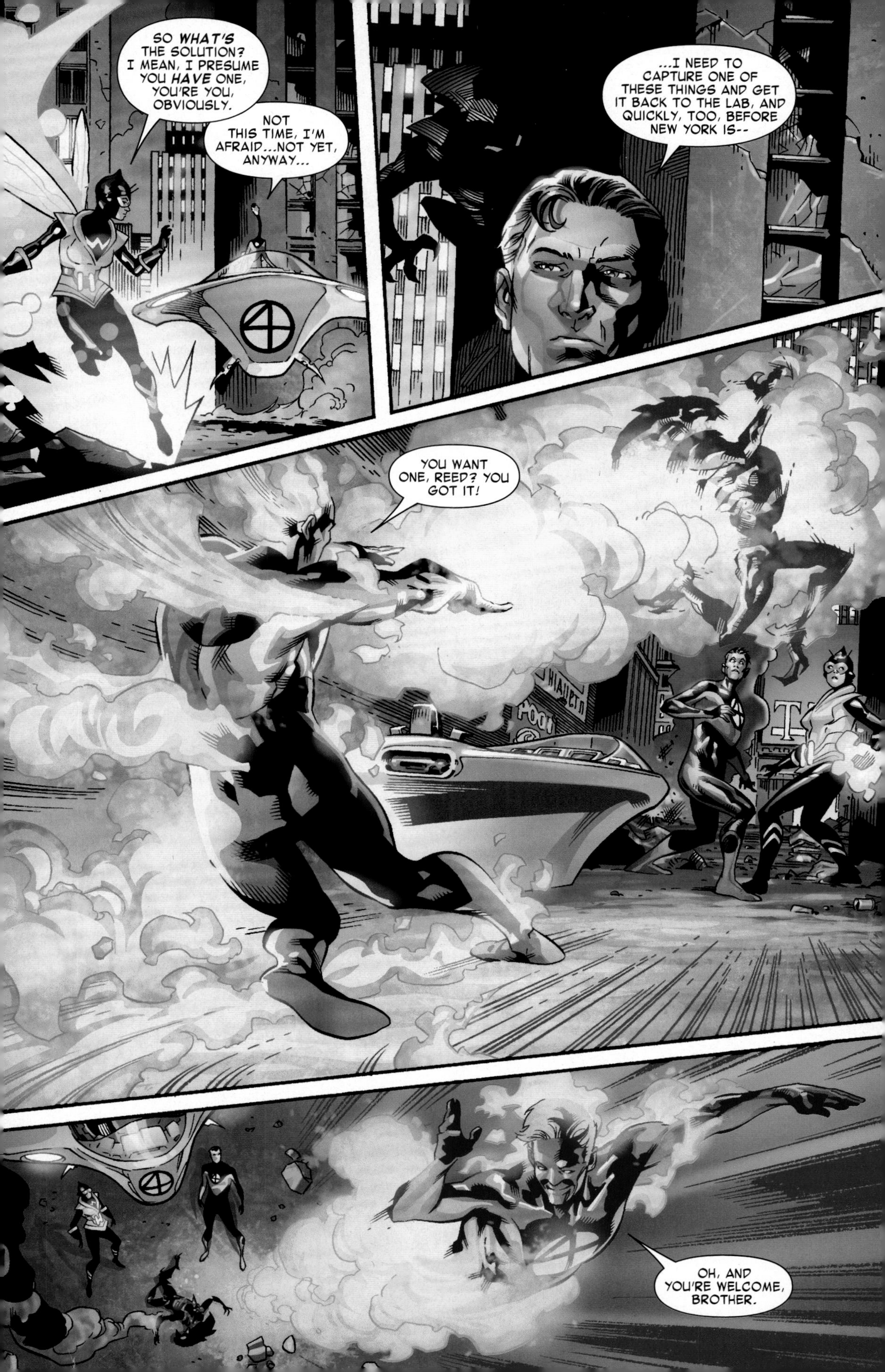
SO WHAT'S THE SOLUTION? I MEAN, I PRESUME YOU HAVE ONE, YOU'RE YOU, OBVIOUSLY.
NOT THIS TIME, I'M AFRAID...NOT YET, ANYWAY...
...I NEED TO CAPTURE ONE OF THESE THINGS AND GET IT BACK TO THE LAB, AND QUICKLY, TOO, BEFORE NEW YORK IS--
YOU WANT ONE, REED? YOU GOT IT!
OH, AND YOU'RE WELCOME, BROTHER.

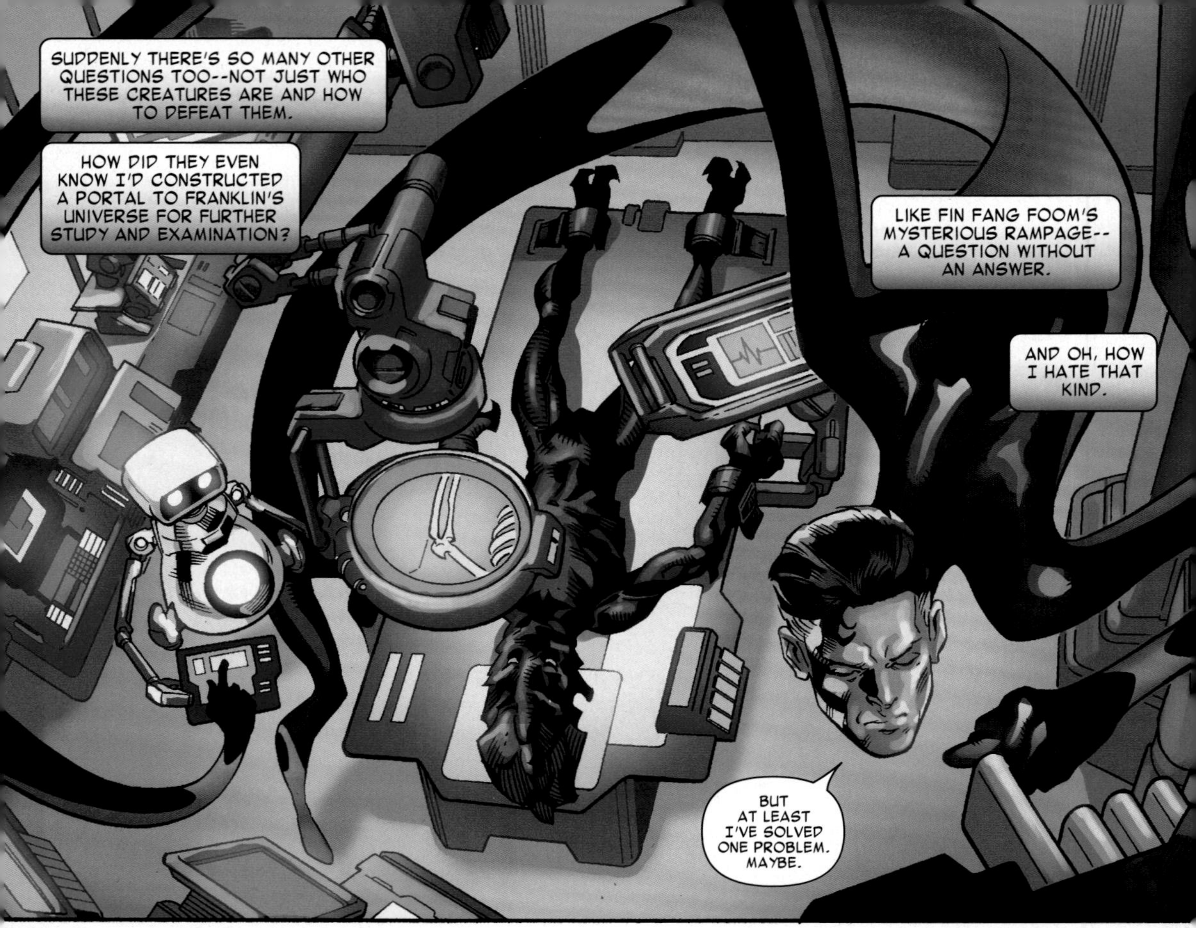
SUDDENLY THERE'S SO MANY OTHER QUESTIONS TOO--NOT JUST WHO THESE CREATURES ARE AND HOW TO DEFEAT THEM.
HOW DID THEY EVEN KNOW I'D CONSTRUCTED A PORTAL TO FRANKLIN'S UNIVERSE FOR FURTHER STUDY AND EXAMINATION?
LIKE FIN FANG FOOM'S MYSTERIOUS RAMPAGE-- A QUESTION WITHOUT AN ANSWER.
AND OH, HOW I HATE THAT KIND.
BUT AT LEAST I'VE SOLVED ONE PROBLEM. MAYBE.

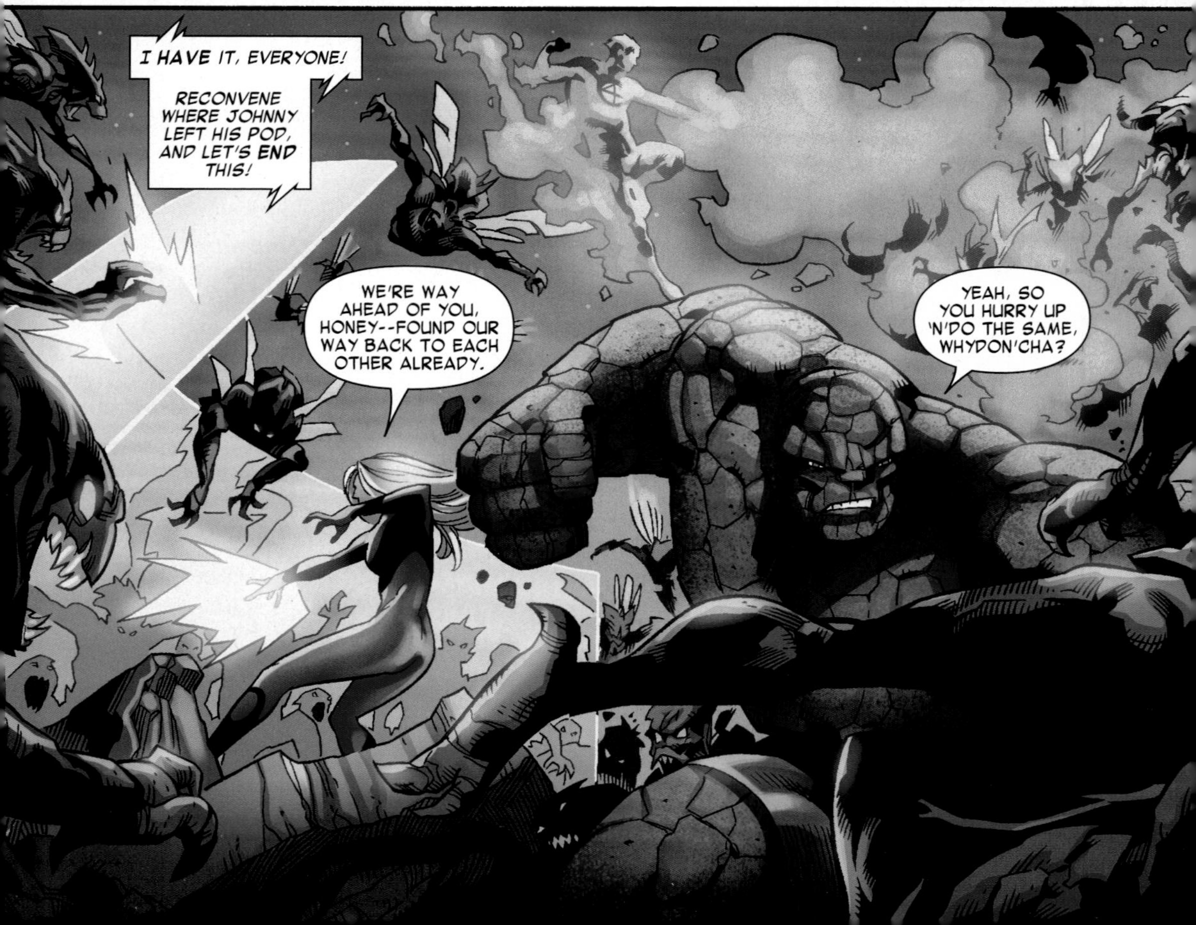
I HAVE IT, EVERYONE!
RECONVENE WHERE JOHNNY LEFT HIS POD, AND LET'S END THIS!
WE'RE WAY AHEAD OF YOU, HONEY--FOUND OUR WAY BACK TO EACH OTHER ALREADY.
YEAH, SO YOU HURRY UP 'N'DO THE SAME, WHYDON'CHA?

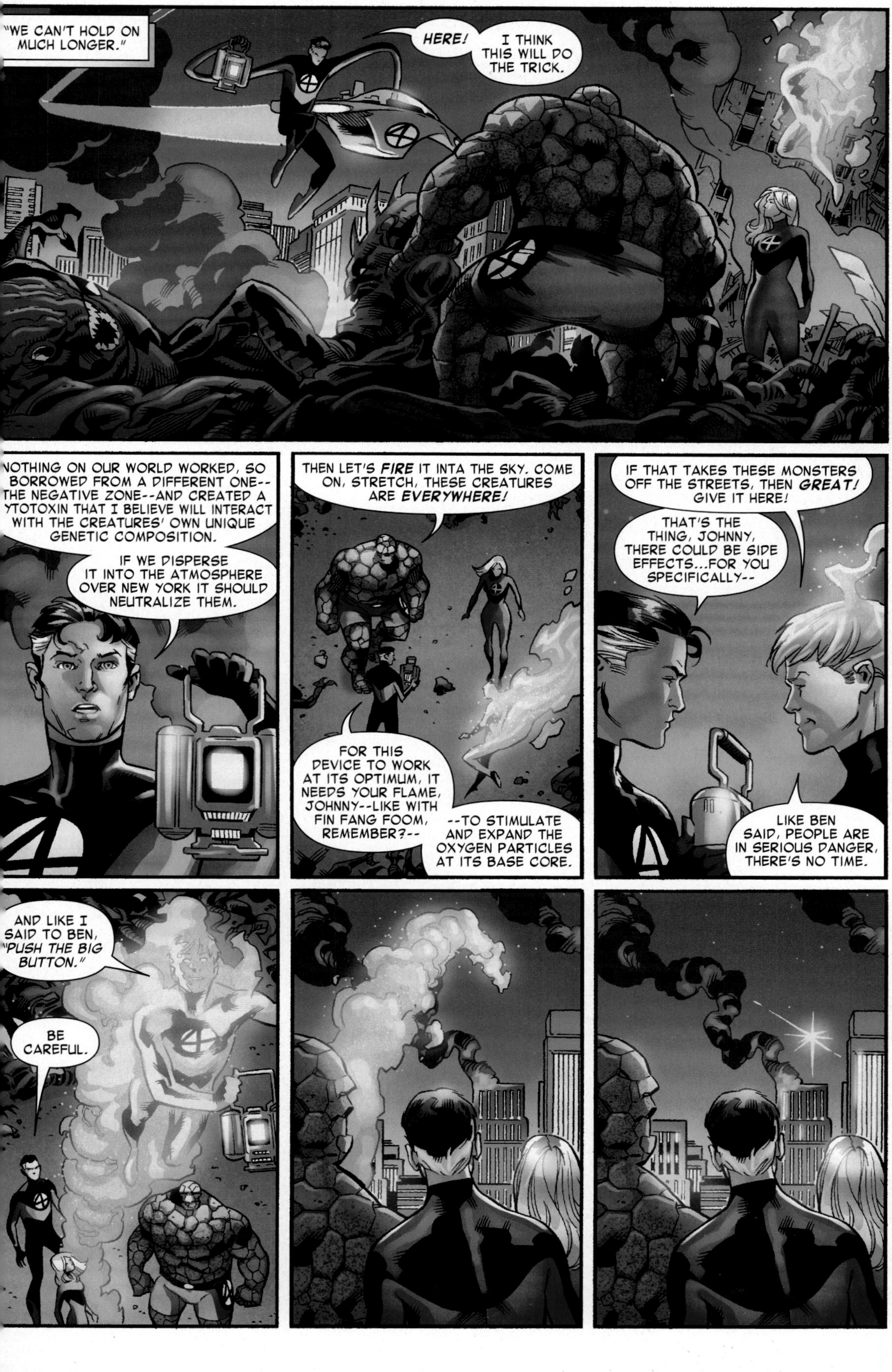
"WE CAN'T HOLD ON MUCH LONGER."
HERE! I THINK THIS WILL DO THE TRICK.
NOTHING ON OUR WORLD WORKED, SO I BORROWED FROM A DIFFERENT ONE--THE NEGATIVE ZONE--AND CREATED A CYTOTOXIN THAT I BELIEVE WILL INTERACT WITH THE CREATURES' OWN UNIQUE GENETIC COMPOSITION.
IF WE DISPERSE IT INTO THE ATMOSPHERE OVER NEW YORK IT SHOULD NEUTRALIZE THEM.
THEN LET'S FIRE IT INTA THE SKY. COME ON, STRETCH, THESE CREATURES ARE EVERYWHERE!
FOR THIS DEVICE TO WORK AT ITS OPTIMUM, IT NEEDS YOUR FLAME, JOHNNY--LIKE WITH FIN FANG FOOM, REMEMBER?--
--TO STIMULATE AND EXPAND THE OXYGEN PARTICLES AT ITS BASE CORE.
IF THAT TAKES THESE MONSTERS OFF THE STREETS, THEN GREAT! GIVE IT HERE!
THAT'S THE THING, JOHNNY, THERE COULD BE SIDE EFFECTS...FOR YOU SPECIFICALLY--
LIKE BEN SAID, PEOPLE ARE IN SERIOUS DANGER, THERE'S NO TIME.
AND LIKE I SAID TO BEN, "PUSH THE BIG BUTTON."
BE CAREFUL.

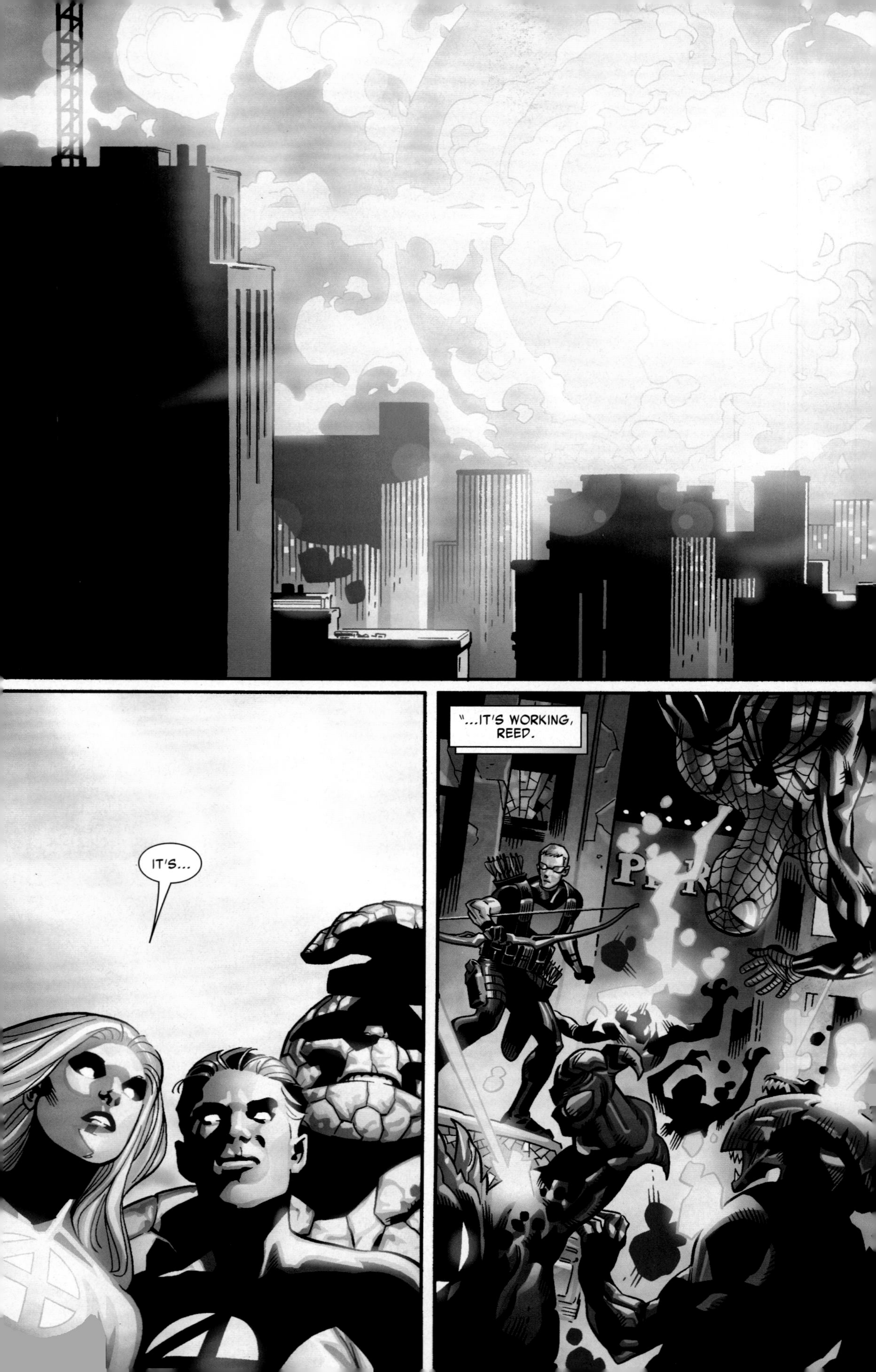
IT'S...
"...IT'S WORKING, REED.

"THEY'RE DROPPING... ALL OF THEM.

"FALLING--"

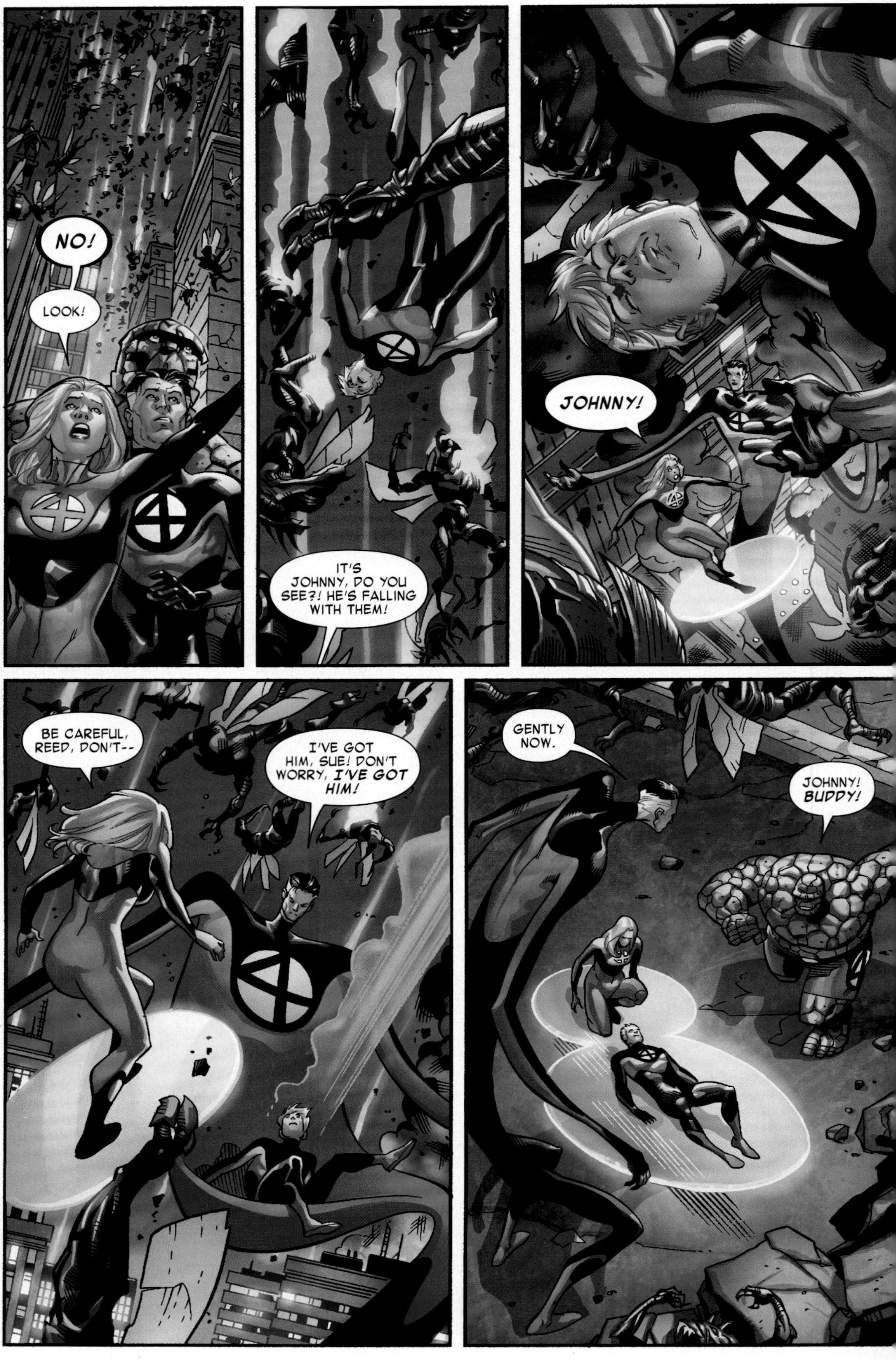
NO!
LOOK!
IT'S JOHNNY, DO YOU SEE?! HE'S FALLING WITH THEM!
JOHNNY!
BE CAREFUL, REED, DON'T--
I'VE GOT HIM, SUE! DON'T WORRY, *I'VE GOT HIM!*
GENTLY NOW.
JOHNNY! *BUDDY!*

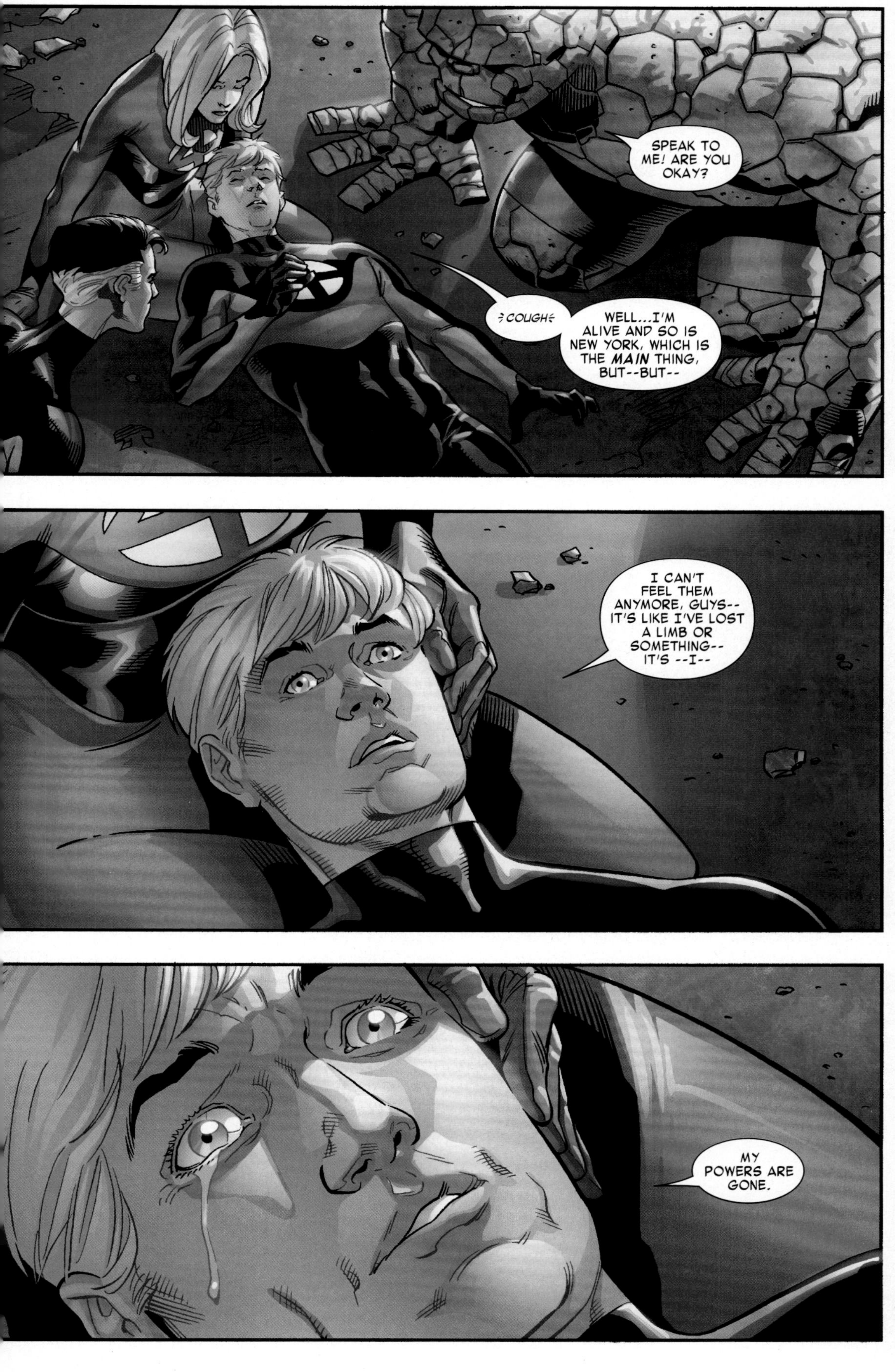
SPEAK TO ME! ARE YOU OKAY?
≠COUGH≠
WELL...I'M ALIVE AND SO IS NEW YORK, WHICH IS THE MAIN THING, BUT--BUT--
I CAN'T FEEL THEM ANYMORE, GUYS--IT'S LIKE I'VE LOST A LIMB OR SOMETHING--IT'S --I--
MY POWERS ARE GONE.

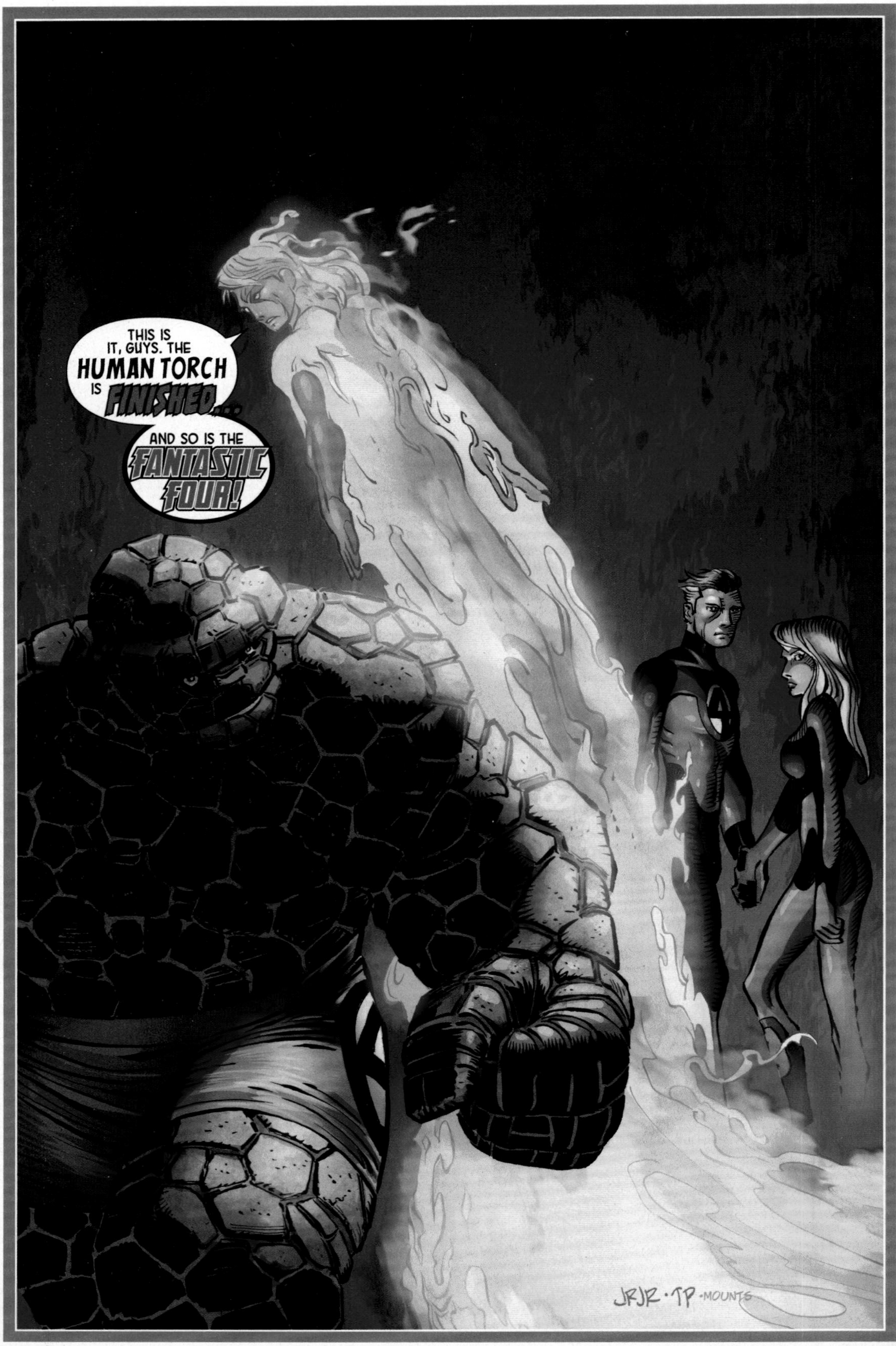
THIS IS IT, GUYS. THE HUMAN TORCH IS FINISHED...
AND SO IS THE FANTASTIC FOUR!
JRJR · TP · MOUNTS

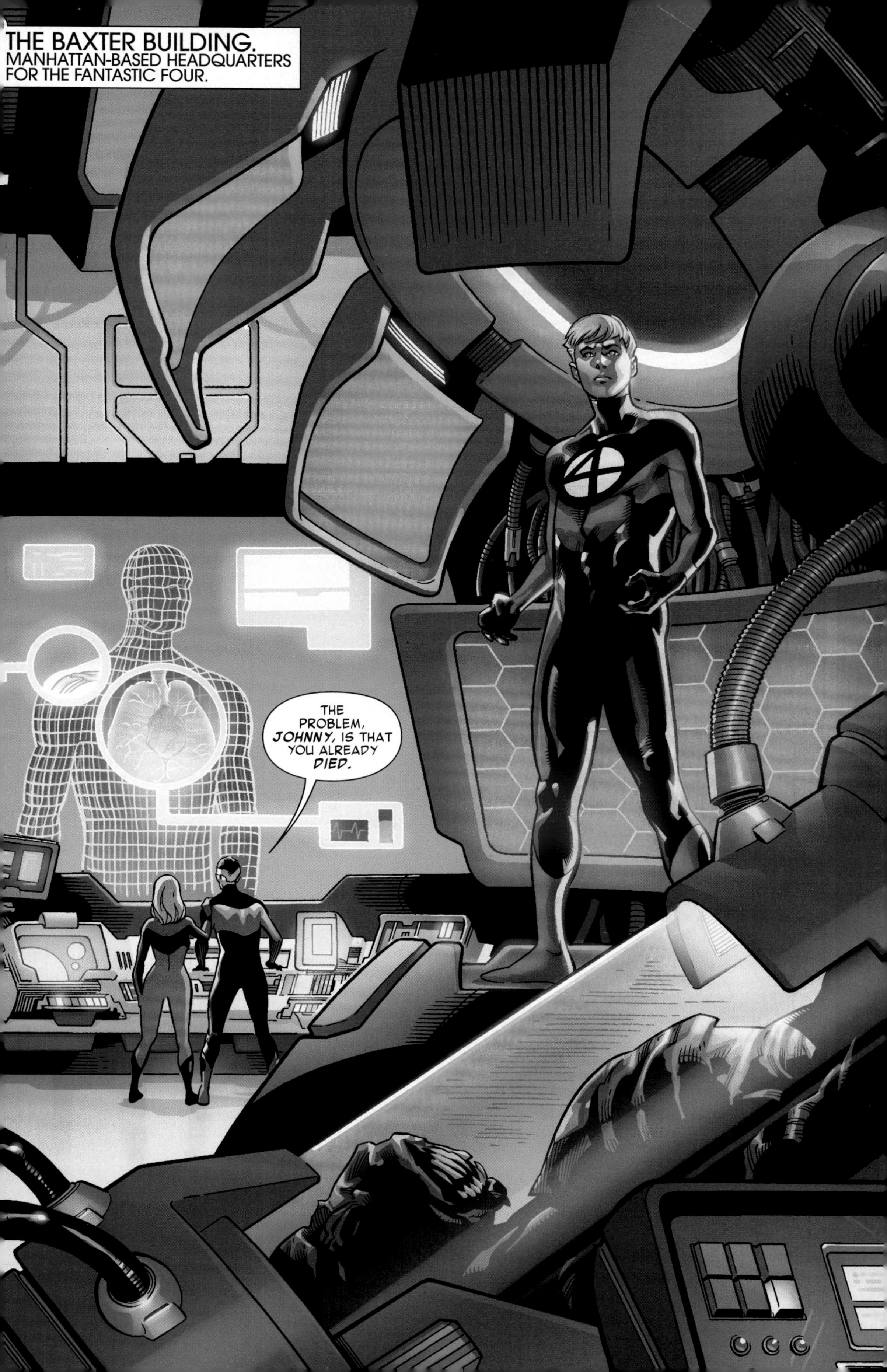
THE BAXTER BUILDING. MANHATTAN-BASED HEADQUARTERS FOR THE FANTASTIC FOUR.
THE PROBLEM, JOHNNY, IS THAT YOU ALREADY DIED.

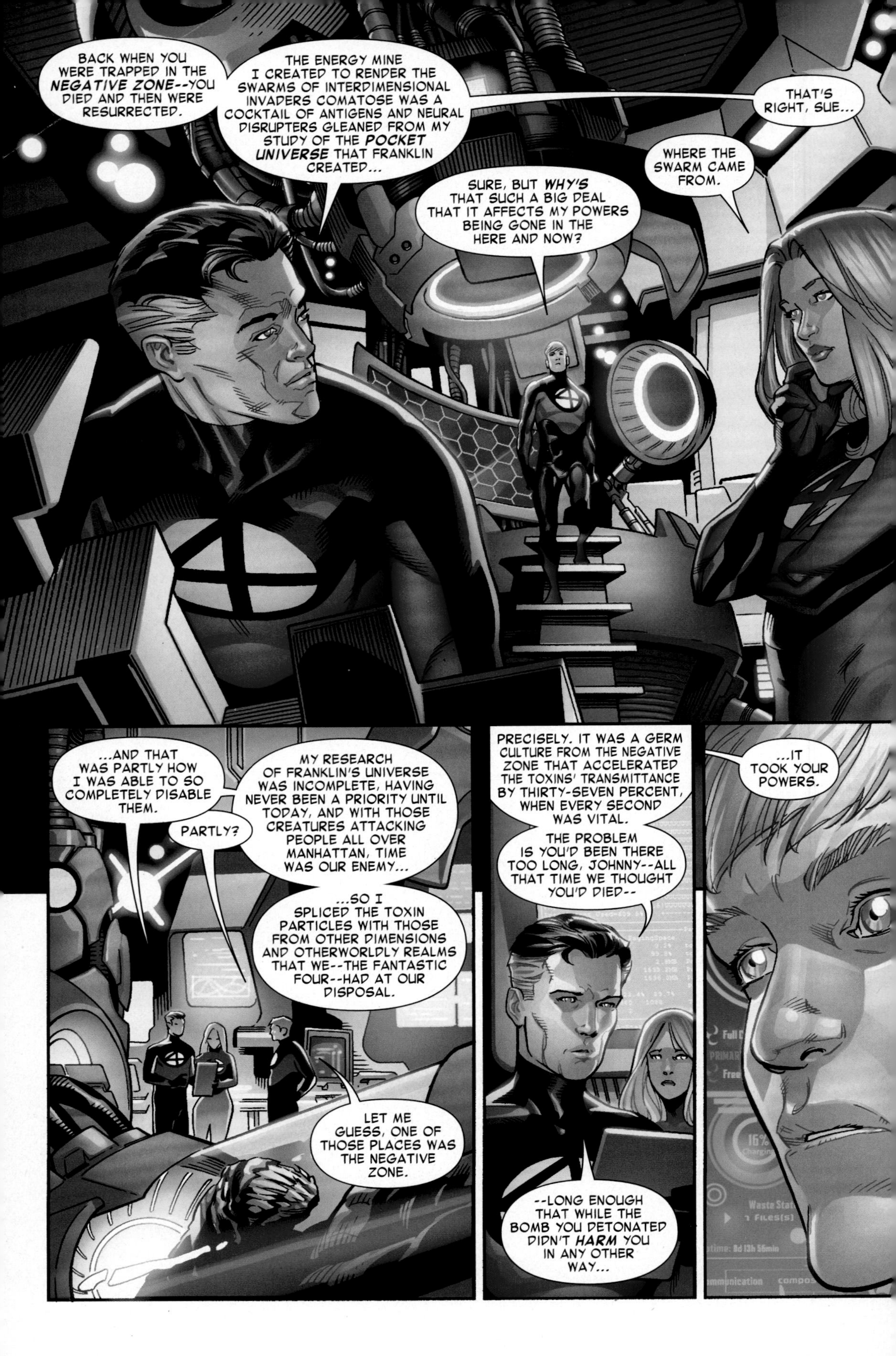

BACK WHEN YOU WERE TRAPPED IN THE NEGATIVE ZONE--YOU DIED AND THEN WERE RESURRECTED.
THE ENERGY MINE I CREATED TO RENDER THE SWARMS OF INTERDIMENSIONAL INVADERS COMATOSE WAS A COCKTAIL OF ANTIGENS AND NEURAL DISRUPTERS GLEANED FROM MY STUDY OF THE POCKET UNIVERSE THAT FRANKLIN CREATED...
THAT'S RIGHT, SUE...
WHERE THE SWARM CAME FROM.
SURE, BUT WHY'S THAT SUCH A BIG DEAL THAT IT AFFECTS MY POWERS BEING GONE IN THE HERE AND NOW?
...AND THAT WAS PARTLY HOW I WAS ABLE TO SO COMPLETELY DISABLE THEM.
PARTLY?
MY RESEARCH OF FRANKLIN'S UNIVERSE WAS INCOMPLETE, HAVING NEVER BEEN A PRIORITY UNTIL TODAY, AND WITH THOSE CREATURES ATTACKING PEOPLE ALL OVER MANHATTAN, TIME WAS OUR ENEMY...
...SO I SPLICED THE TOXIN PARTICLES WITH THOSE FROM OTHER DIMENSIONS AND OTHERWORLDLY REALMS THAT WE--THE FANTASTIC FOUR--HAD AT OUR DISPOSAL.
LET ME GUESS, ONE OF THOSE PLACES WAS THE NEGATIVE ZONE.
PRECISELY. IT WAS A GERM CULTURE FROM THE NEGATIVE ZONE THAT ACCELERATED THE TOXINS' TRANSMITTANCE BY THIRTY-SEVEN PERCENT, WHEN EVERY SECOND WAS VITAL.
THE PROBLEM IS YOU'D BEEN THERE TOO LONG, JOHNNY--ALL THAT TIME WE THOUGHT YOU'D DIED--
--LONG ENOUGH THAT WHILE THE BOMB YOU DETONATED DIDN'T HARM YOU IN ANY OTHER WAY...
...IT TOOK YOUR POWERS.

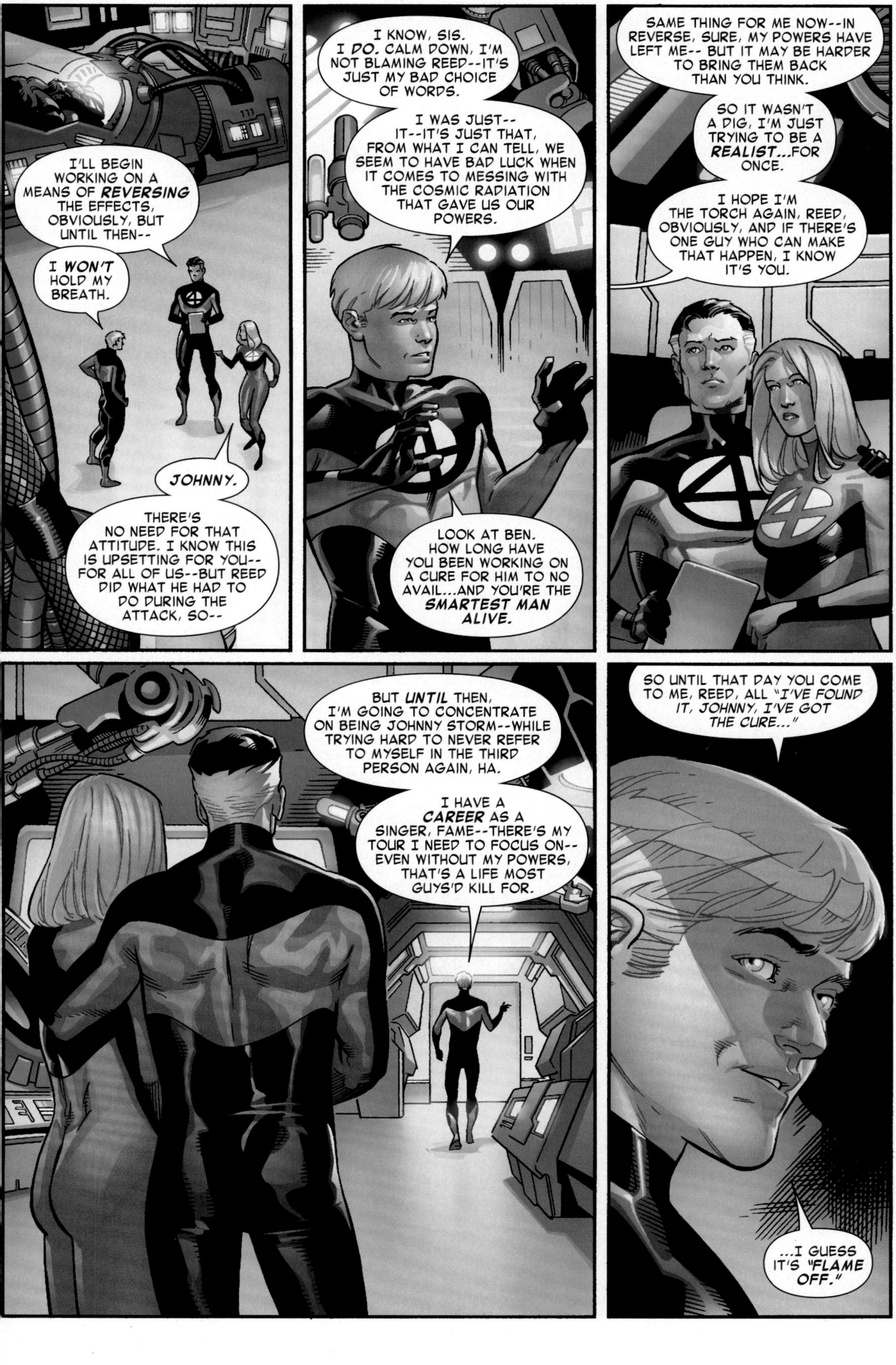
I'LL BEGIN WORKING ON A MEANS OF **REVERSING** THE EFFECTS, OBVIOUSLY, BUT UNTIL THEN--
I ***WON'T*** HOLD MY BREATH.
JOHNNY.
THERE'S NO NEED FOR THAT ATTITUDE. I KNOW THIS IS UPSETTING FOR YOU--FOR ALL OF US--BUT REED DID WHAT HE HAD TO DO DURING THE ATTACK, SO--
I KNOW, SIS. I *DO.* CALM DOWN, I'M NOT BLAMING REED--IT'S JUST MY BAD CHOICE OF WORDS.
I WAS JUST-- IT--IT'S JUST THAT, FROM WHAT I CAN TELL, WE SEEM TO HAVE BAD LUCK WHEN IT COMES TO MESSING WITH THE COSMIC RADIATION THAT GAVE US OUR POWERS.
LOOK AT BEN. HOW LONG HAVE YOU BEEN WORKING ON A CURE FOR HIM TO NO AVAIL...AND YOU'RE THE ***SMARTEST MAN ALIVE.***
SAME THING FOR ME NOW--IN REVERSE, SURE, MY POWERS HAVE LEFT ME-- BUT IT MAY BE HARDER TO BRING THEM BACK THAN YOU THINK.
SO IT WASN'T A DIG, I'M JUST TRYING TO BE A ***REALIST...***FOR ONCE.
I HOPE I'M THE TORCH AGAIN, REED, OBVIOUSLY, AND IF THERE'S ONE GUY WHO CAN MAKE THAT HAPPEN, I KNOW IT'S YOU.
BUT ***UNTIL*** THEN, I'M GOING TO CONCENTRATE ON BEING JOHNNY STORM--WHILE TRYING HARD TO NEVER REFER TO MYSELF IN THE THIRD PERSON AGAIN, HA.
I HAVE A ***CAREER*** AS A SINGER, FAME--THERE'S MY TOUR I NEED TO FOCUS ON--EVEN WITHOUT MY POWERS, THAT'S A LIFE MOST GUYS'D KILL FOR.
SO UNTIL THAT DAY YOU COME TO ME, REED, ALL *"I'VE FOUND IT, JOHNNY, I'VE GOT THE CURE..."*
...I GUESS IT'S ***"FLAME OFF."***

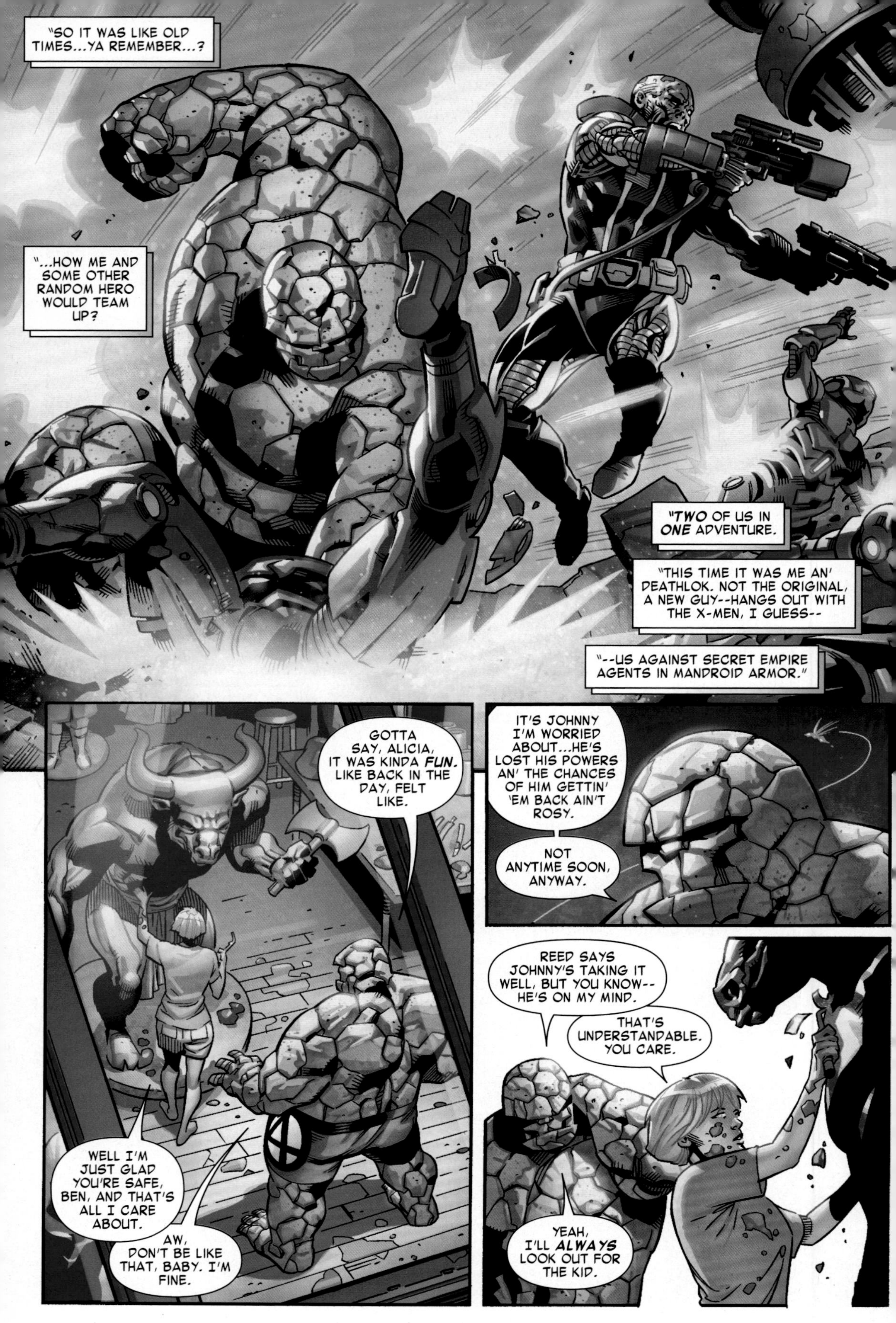

"SO IT WAS LIKE OLD TIMES...YA REMEMBER...?
"...HOW ME AND SOME OTHER RANDOM HERO WOULD TEAM UP?
"TWO OF US IN ONE ADVENTURE.
"THIS TIME IT WAS ME AN' DEATHLOK. NOT THE ORIGINAL, A NEW GUY--HANGS OUT WITH THE X-MEN, I GUESS--
"--US AGAINST SECRET EMPIRE AGENTS IN MANDROID ARMOR."
GOTTA SAY, ALICIA, IT WAS KINDA FUN. LIKE BACK IN THE DAY, FELT LIKE.
WELL I'M JUST GLAD YOU'RE SAFE, BEN, AND THAT'S ALL I CARE ABOUT.
AW, DON'T BE LIKE THAT, BABY. I'M FINE.
IT'S JOHNNY I'M WORRIED ABOUT...HE'S LOST HIS POWERS AN' THE CHANCES OF HIM GETTIN' 'EM BACK AIN'T ROSY.
NOT ANYTIME SOON, ANYWAY.
REED SAYS JOHNNY'S TAKING IT WELL, BUT YOU KNOW--HE'S ON MY MIND.
THAT'S UNDERSTANDABLE. YOU CARE.
YEAH, I'LL ALWAYS LOOK OUT FOR THE KID.

WELL I WORRY ABOUT *ALL* OF YOU...WHENEVER I USED TO HEAR ON THE RADIO HOW SOME MENACE WAS ATTACKING YOU, BEN...EVEN DURING THE TIMES WHEN WE WEREN'T A COUPLE--

--EVEN TODAY-- A DEATHLOK? THAT SOUNDS *TERRIFYING*, NOT FUN.

I KNOW I SEEM SELFISH, BUT NOW THAT YOU'RE BACK IN MY LIFE--WELL-- IN MY EXPERIENCE IT'S WHEN WE'RE HAPPIEST THAT SOMETHING EVIL OR COSMIC OR *BOTH* RAMPAGES INTO OUR LIVES, INTENT ON TEARING EVERYTHING DOWN.

NO, BABY...

...NOT THIS TIME. I'LL PROTECT YOU, I PROMISE...

...*YOU* AND WHAT *WE* HAVE TOGETHER.

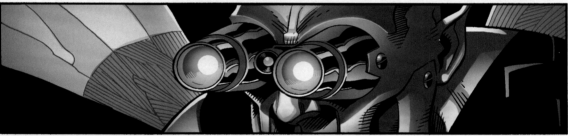

--I'LL PROTECT YOU, I PROMISE...

...*YOU* AND WHAT *WE* HAVE TOGETHER.

OH, I *DOUBT* THAT, YOU MONSTROSITY. I DOUBT THAT *SINCERELY.*

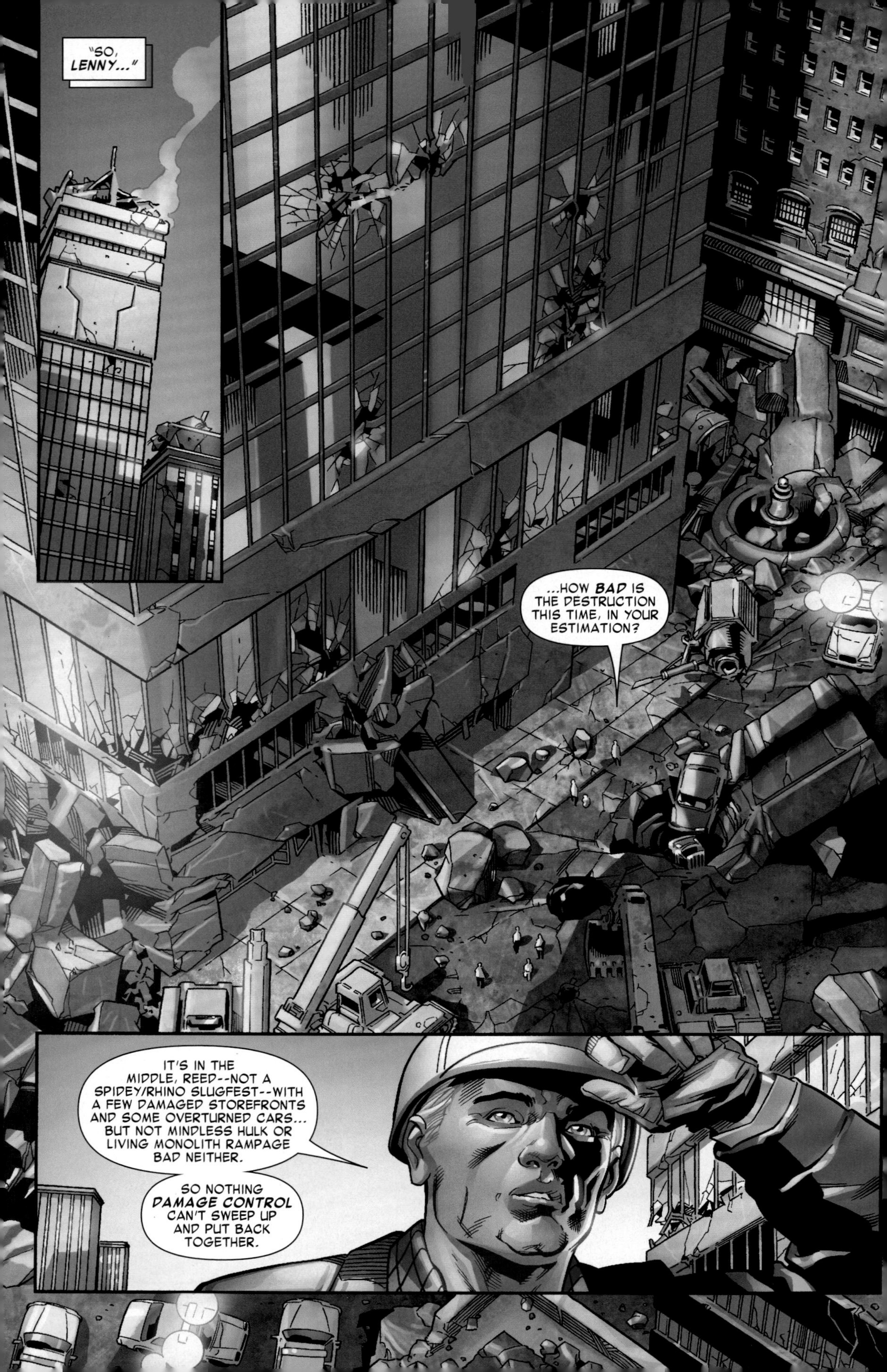
"SO, LENNY..."
...HOW BAD IS THE DESTRUCTION THIS TIME, IN YOUR ESTIMATION?
IT'S IN THE MIDDLE, REED--NOT A SPIDEY/RHINO SLUGFEST--WITH A FEW DAMAGED STOREFRONTS AND SOME OVERTURNED CARS... BUT NOT MINDLESS HULK OR LIVING MONOLITH RAMPAGE BAD NEITHER.
SO NOTHING DAMAGE CONTROL CAN'T SWEEP UP AND PUT BACK TOGETHER.

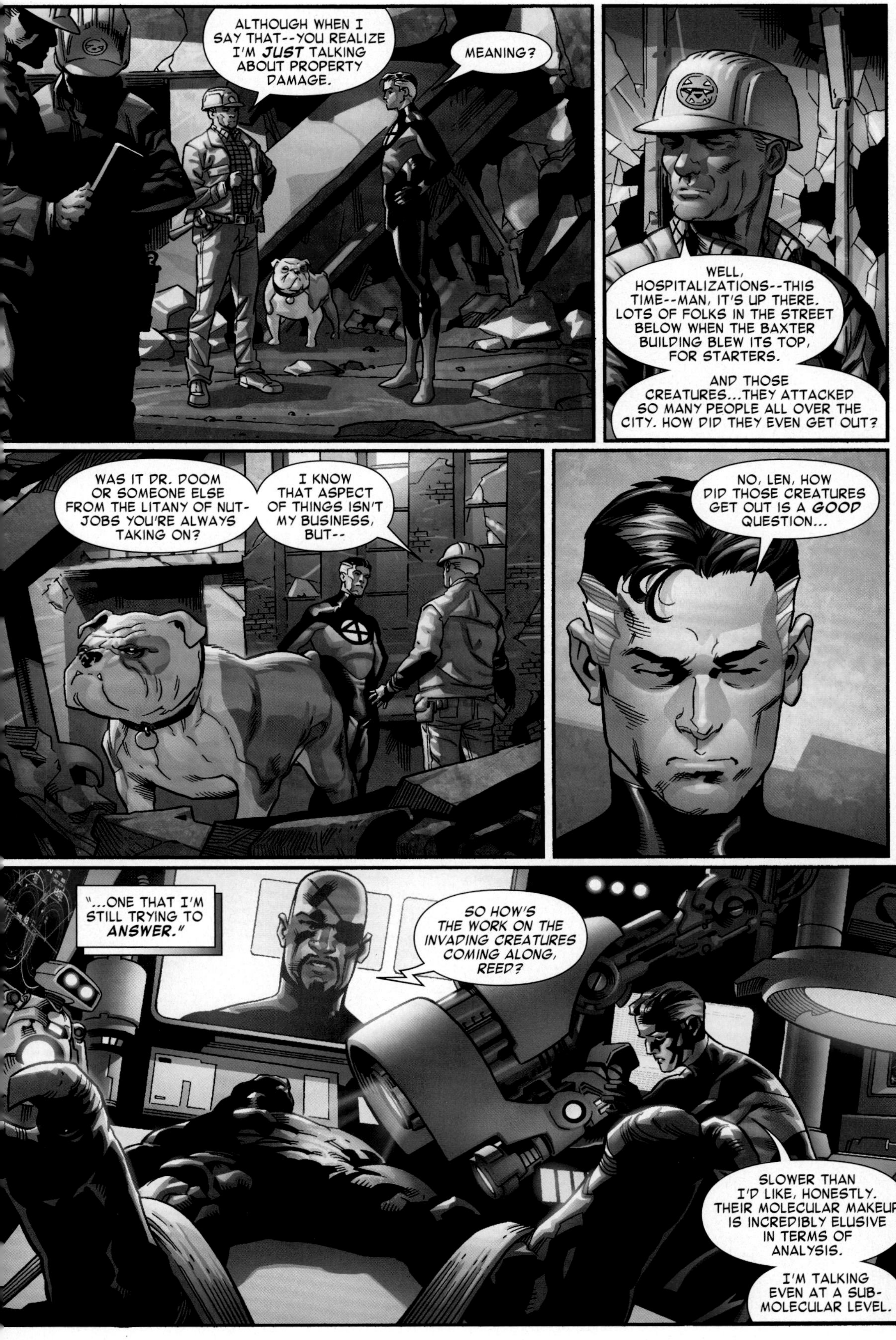
ALTHOUGH WHEN I SAY THAT--YOU REALIZE I'M *JUST* TALKING ABOUT PROPERTY DAMAGE.
MEANING?
WELL, HOSPITALIZATIONS--THIS TIME--MAN, IT'S UP THERE. LOTS OF FOLKS IN THE STREET BELOW WHEN THE BAXTER BUILDING BLEW ITS TOP, FOR STARTERS.
AND THOSE CREATURES...THEY ATTACKED SO MANY PEOPLE ALL OVER THE CITY. HOW DID THEY EVEN GET OUT?
WAS IT DR. DOOM OR SOMEONE ELSE FROM THE LITANY OF NUT-JOBS YOU'RE ALWAYS TAKING ON?
I KNOW THAT ASPECT OF THINGS ISN'T MY BUSINESS, BUT--
NO, LEN, HOW DID THOSE CREATURES GET OUT IS A *GOOD* QUESTION...
"...ONE THAT I'M STILL TRYING TO *ANSWER.*"
SO HOW'S THE WORK ON THE INVADING CREATURES COMING ALONG, REED?
SLOWER THAN I'D LIKE, HONESTLY. THEIR MOLECULAR MAKEUP IS INCREDIBLY ELUSIVE IN TERMS OF ANALYSIS.
I'M TALKING EVEN AT A SUB-MOLECULAR LEVEL.

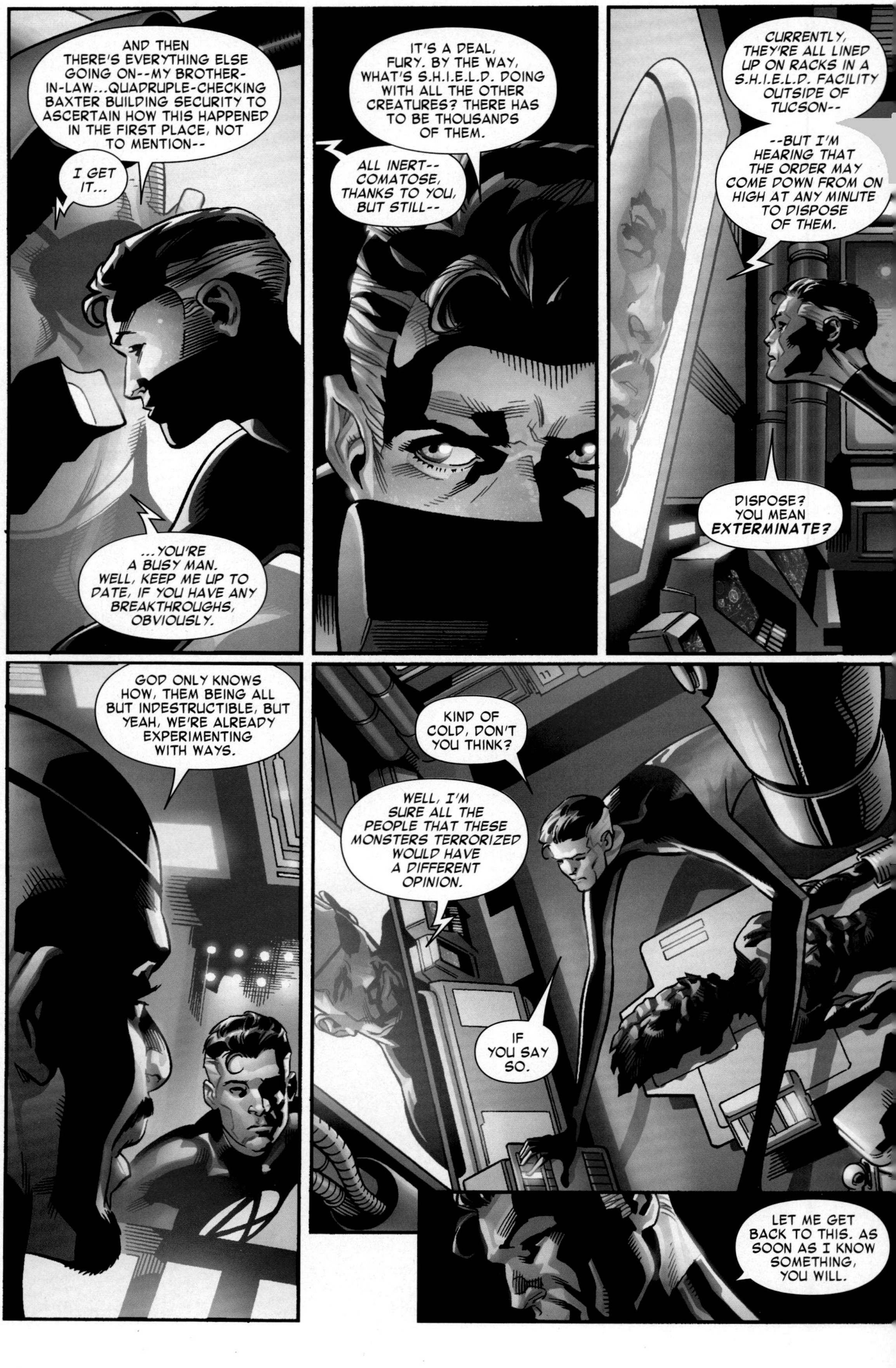
AND THEN THERE'S EVERYTHING ELSE GOING ON--MY BROTHER-IN-LAW...QUADRUPLE-CHECKING BAXTER BUILDING SECURITY TO ASCERTAIN HOW THIS HAPPENED IN THE FIRST PLACE, NOT TO MENTION--
I GET IT...
...YOU'RE A BUSY MAN. WELL, KEEP ME UP TO DATE, IF YOU HAVE ANY BREAKTHROUGHS, OBVIOUSLY.
IT'S A DEAL, FURY. BY THE WAY, WHAT'S S.H.I.E.L.D. DOING WITH ALL THE OTHER CREATURES? THERE HAS TO BE THOUSANDS OF THEM.
ALL INERT--COMATOSE, THANKS TO YOU, BUT STILL--
CURRENTLY, THEY'RE ALL LINED UP ON RACKS IN A S.H.I.E.L.D. FACILITY OUTSIDE OF TUCSON--
--BUT I'M HEARING THAT THE ORDER MAY COME DOWN FROM ON HIGH AT ANY MINUTE TO DISPOSE OF THEM.
DISPOSE? YOU MEAN *EXTERMINATE?*
GOD ONLY KNOWS HOW, THEM BEING ALL BUT INDESTRUCTIBLE, BUT YEAH, WE'RE ALREADY EXPERIMENTING WITH WAYS.
KIND OF COLD, DON'T YOU THINK?
WELL, I'M SURE ALL THE PEOPLE THAT THESE MONSTERS TERRORIZED WOULD HAVE A DIFFERENT OPINION.
IF YOU SAY SO.
LET ME GET BACK TO THIS. AS SOON AS I KNOW SOMETHING, YOU WILL.

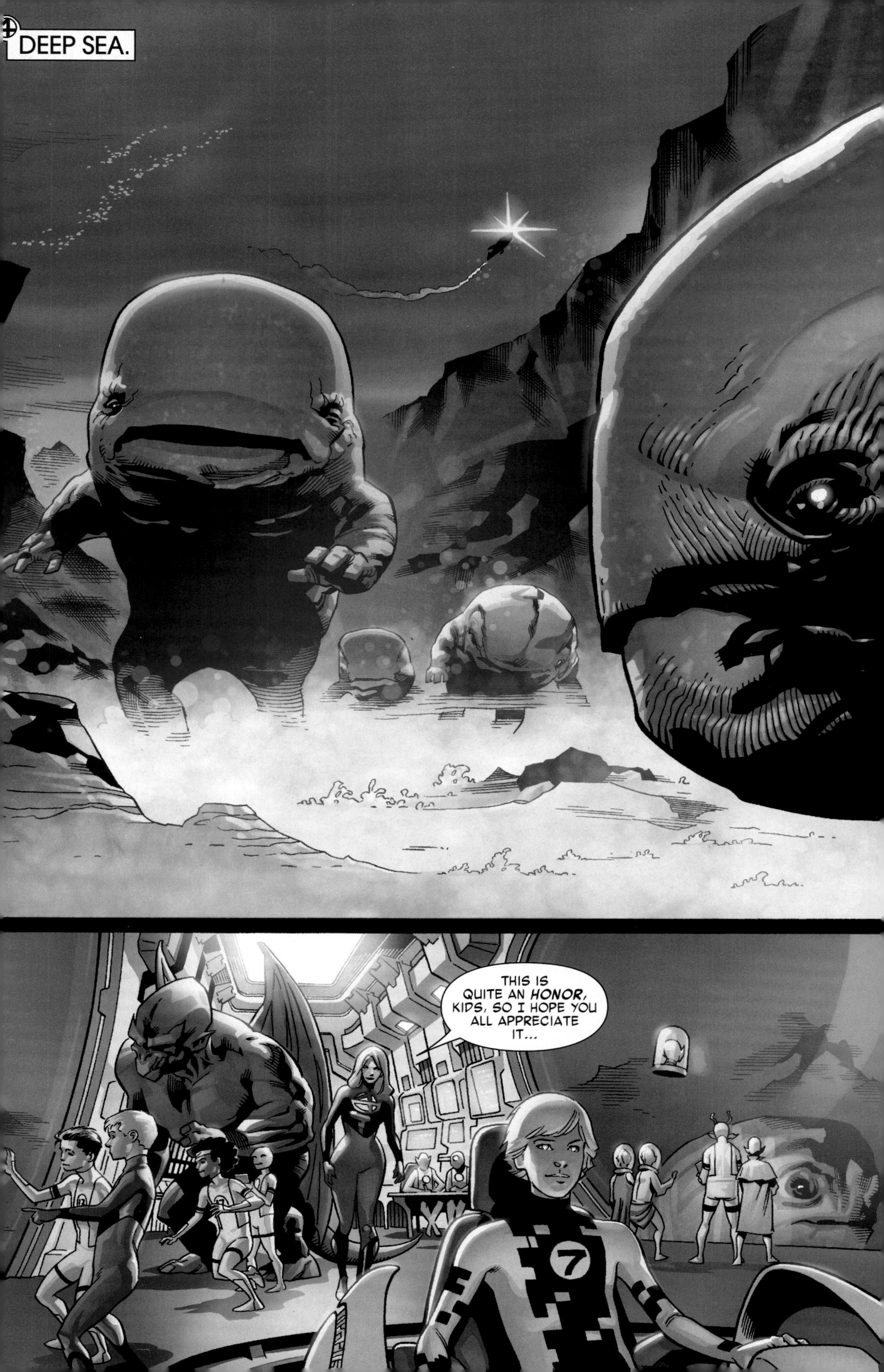
DEEP SEA.
THIS IS QUITE AN *HONOR*, KIDS, SO I HOPE YOU ALL APPRECIATE IT...

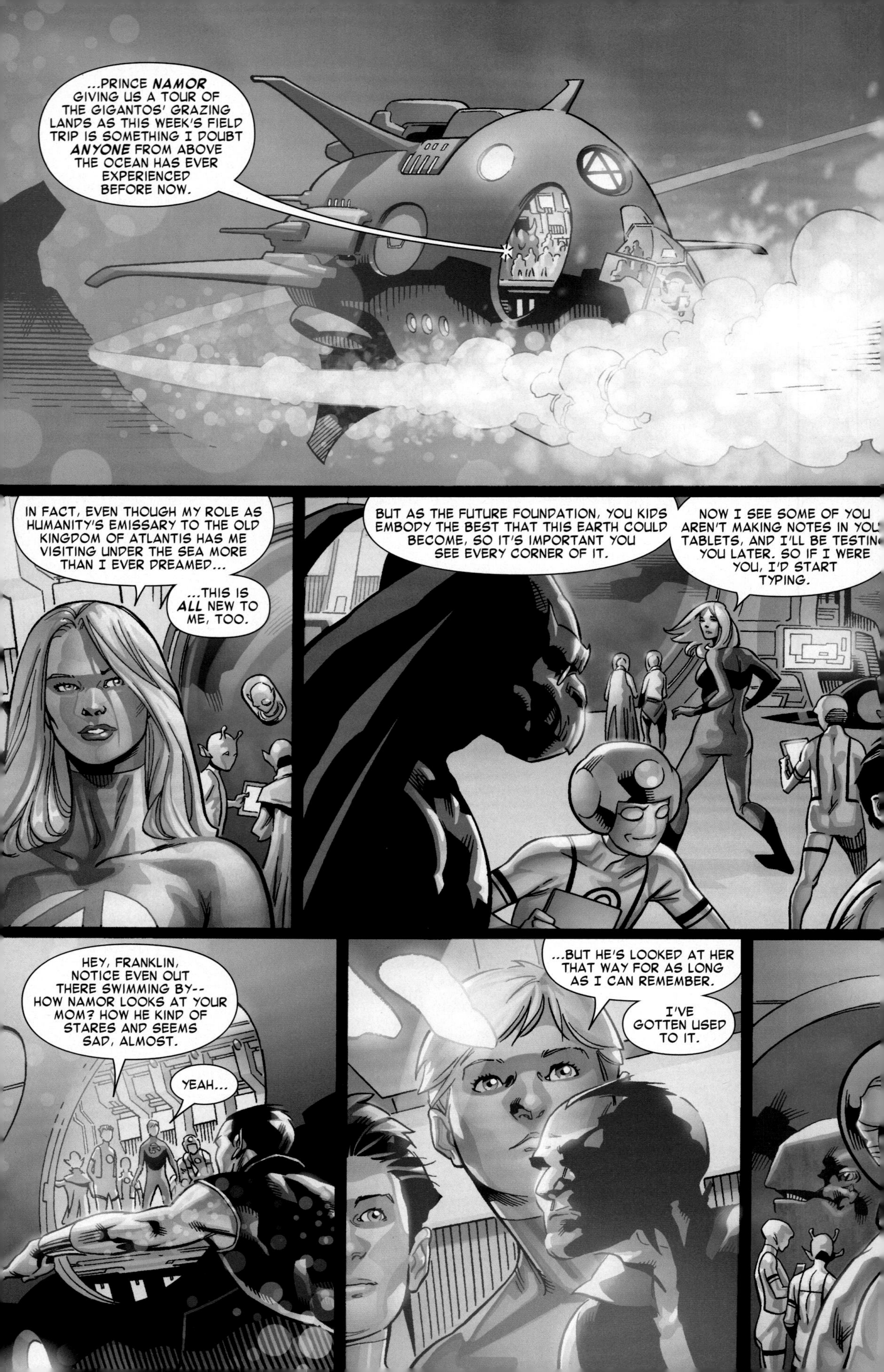
...PRINCE NAMOR GIVING US A TOUR OF THE GIGANTOS' GRAZING LANDS AS THIS WEEK'S FIELD TRIP IS SOMETHING I DOUBT ANYONE FROM ABOVE THE OCEAN HAS EVER EXPERIENCED BEFORE NOW.
IN FACT, EVEN THOUGH MY ROLE AS HUMANITY'S EMISSARY TO THE OLD KINGDOM OF ATLANTIS HAS ME VISITING UNDER THE SEA MORE THAN I EVER DREAMED...
...THIS IS ALL NEW TO ME, TOO.
BUT AS THE FUTURE FOUNDATION, YOU KIDS EMBODY THE BEST THAT THIS EARTH COULD BECOME, SO IT'S IMPORTANT YOU SEE EVERY CORNER OF IT.
NOW I SEE SOME OF YOU AREN'T MAKING NOTES IN YOU TABLETS, AND I'LL BE TESTIN YOU LATER. SO IF I WERE YOU, I'D START TYPING.
HEY, FRANKLIN, NOTICE EVEN OUT THERE SWIMMING BY-- HOW NAMOR LOOKS AT YOUR MOM? HOW HE KIND OF STARES AND SEEMS SAD, ALMOST.
YEAH...
...BUT HE'S LOOKED AT HER THAT WAY FOR AS LONG AS I CAN REMEMBER.
I'VE GOTTEN USED TO IT.

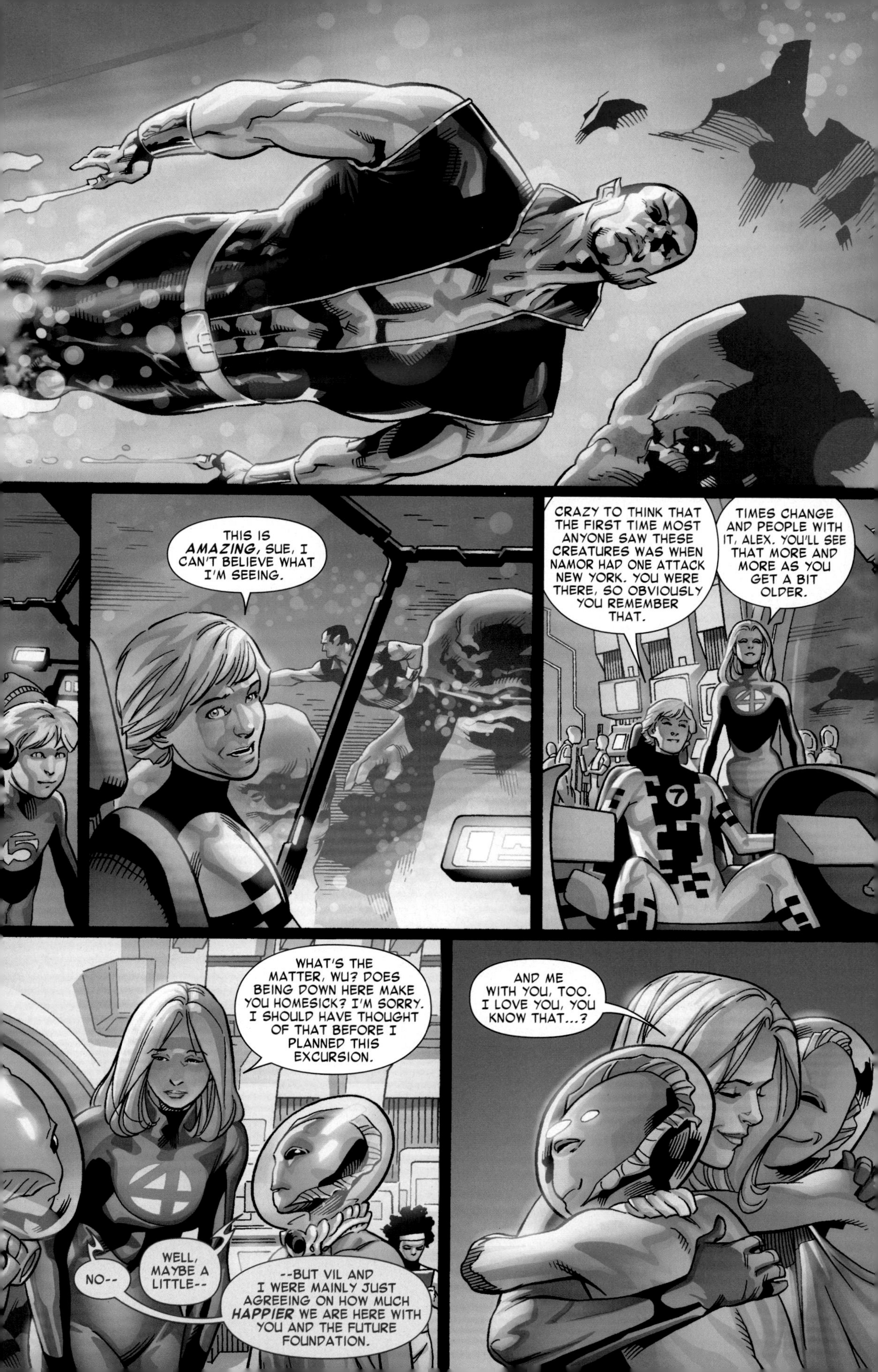
THIS IS AMAZING, SUE, I CAN'T BELIEVE WHAT I'M SEEING.
CRAZY TO THINK THAT THE FIRST TIME MOST ANYONE SAW THESE CREATURES WAS WHEN NAMOR HAD ONE ATTACK NEW YORK. YOU WERE THERE, SO OBVIOUSLY YOU REMEMBER THAT.
TIMES CHANGE AND PEOPLE WITH IT, ALEX. YOU'LL SEE THAT MORE AND MORE AS YOU GET A BIT OLDER.
WHAT'S THE MATTER, WU? DOES BEING DOWN HERE MAKE YOU HOMESICK? I'M SORRY. I SHOULD HAVE THOUGHT OF THAT BEFORE I PLANNED THIS EXCURSION.
NO--
WELL, MAYBE A LITTLE--
--BUT VIL AND I WERE MAINLY JUST AGREEING ON HOW MUCH HAPPIER WE ARE HERE WITH YOU AND THE FUTURE FOUNDATION.
AND ME WITH YOU, TOO. I LOVE YOU, YOU KNOW THAT...?

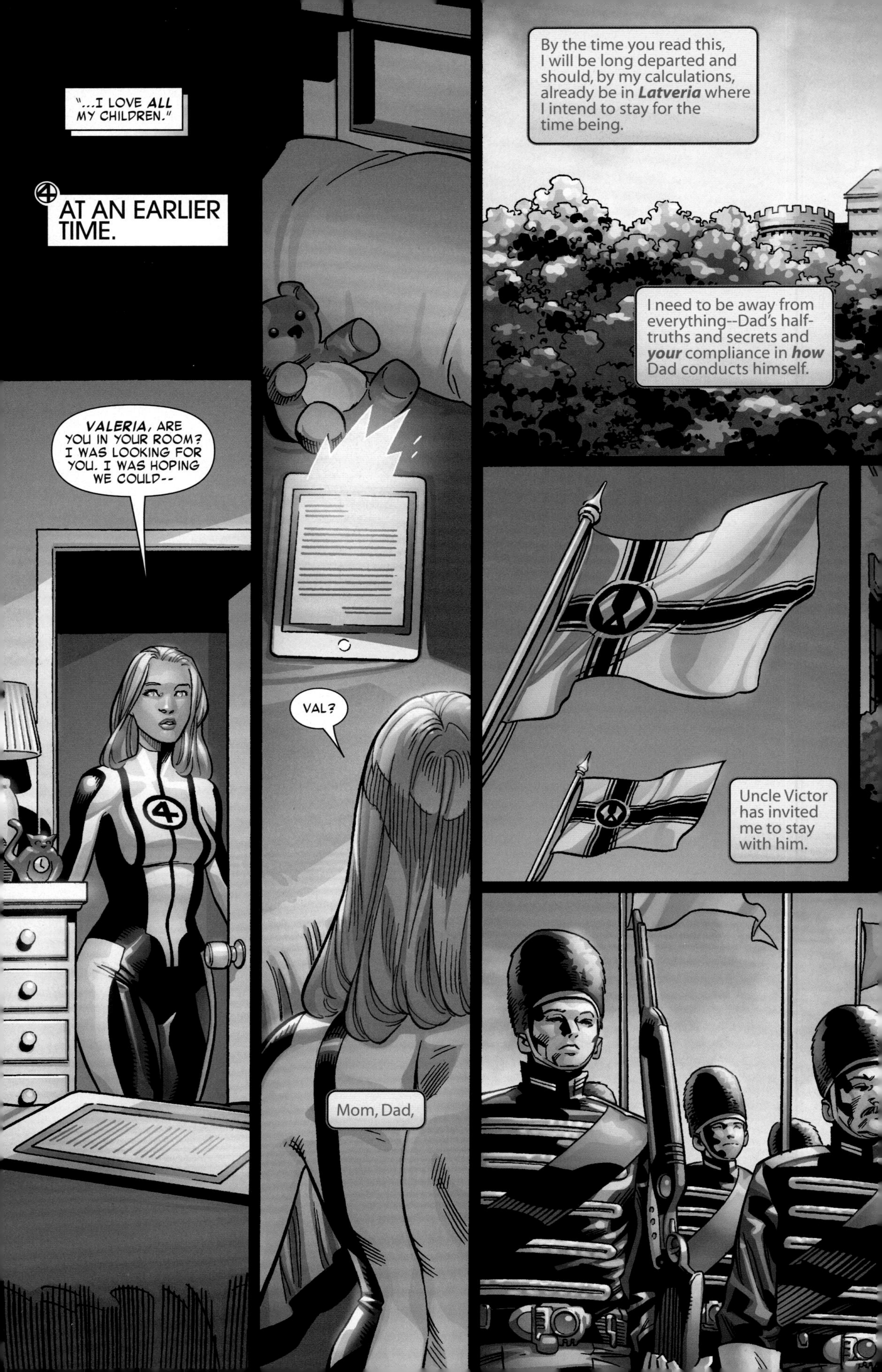
"...I LOVE ALL MY CHILDREN."
AT AN EARLIER TIME.
VALERIA, ARE YOU IN YOUR ROOM? I WAS LOOKING FOR YOU. I WAS HOPING WE COULD--
VAL?
Mom, Dad,
By the time you read this, I will be long departed and should, by my calculations, already be in Latveria where I intend to stay for the time being.
I need to be away from everything--Dad's half-truths and secrets and your compliance in how Dad conducts himself.
Uncle Victor has invited me to stay with him.

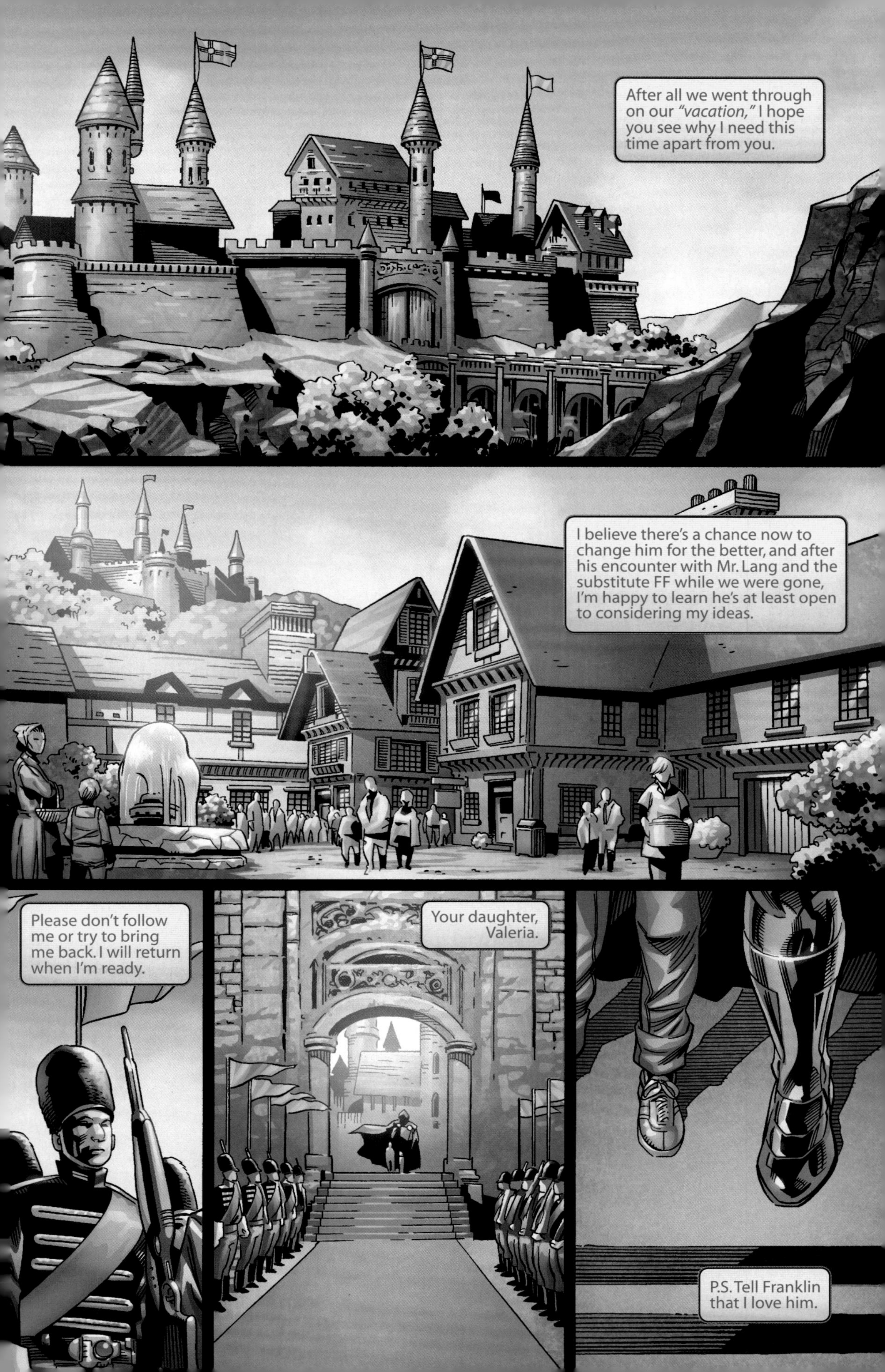

After all we went through on our *"vacation,"* I hope you see why I need this time apart from you.
I believe there's a chance now to change him for the better, and after his encounter with Mr. Lang and the substitute FF while we were gone, I'm happy to learn he's at least open to considering my ideas.
Please don't follow me or try to bring me back. I will return when I'm ready.
Your daughter, Valeria.
P.S. Tell Franklin that I love him.

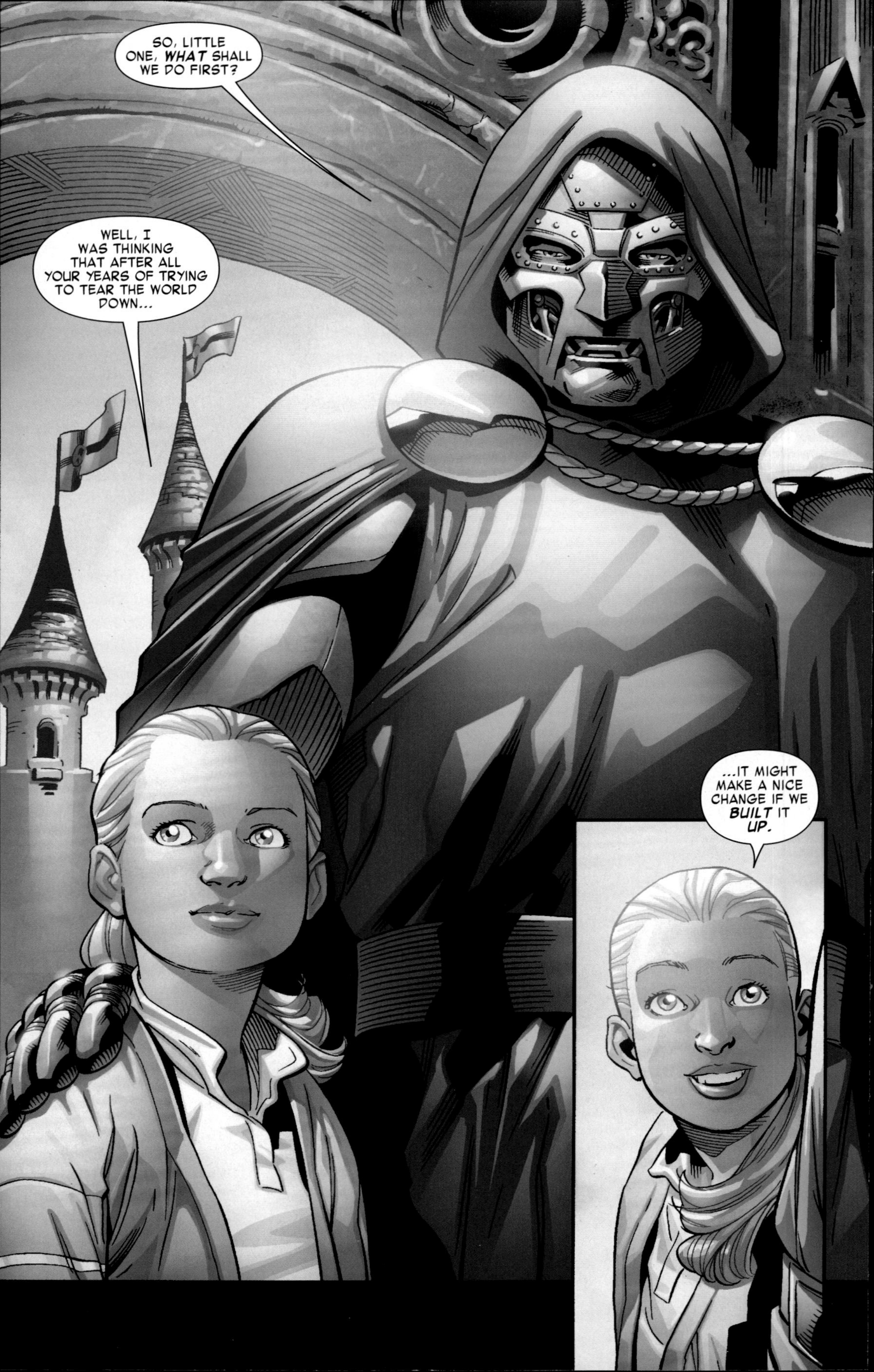
SO, LITTLE ONE, WHAT SHALL WE DO FIRST?
WELL, I WAS THINKING THAT AFTER ALL YOUR YEARS OF TRYING TO TEAR THE WORLD DOWN...
...IT MIGHT MAKE A NICE CHANGE IF WE BUILT IT UP.

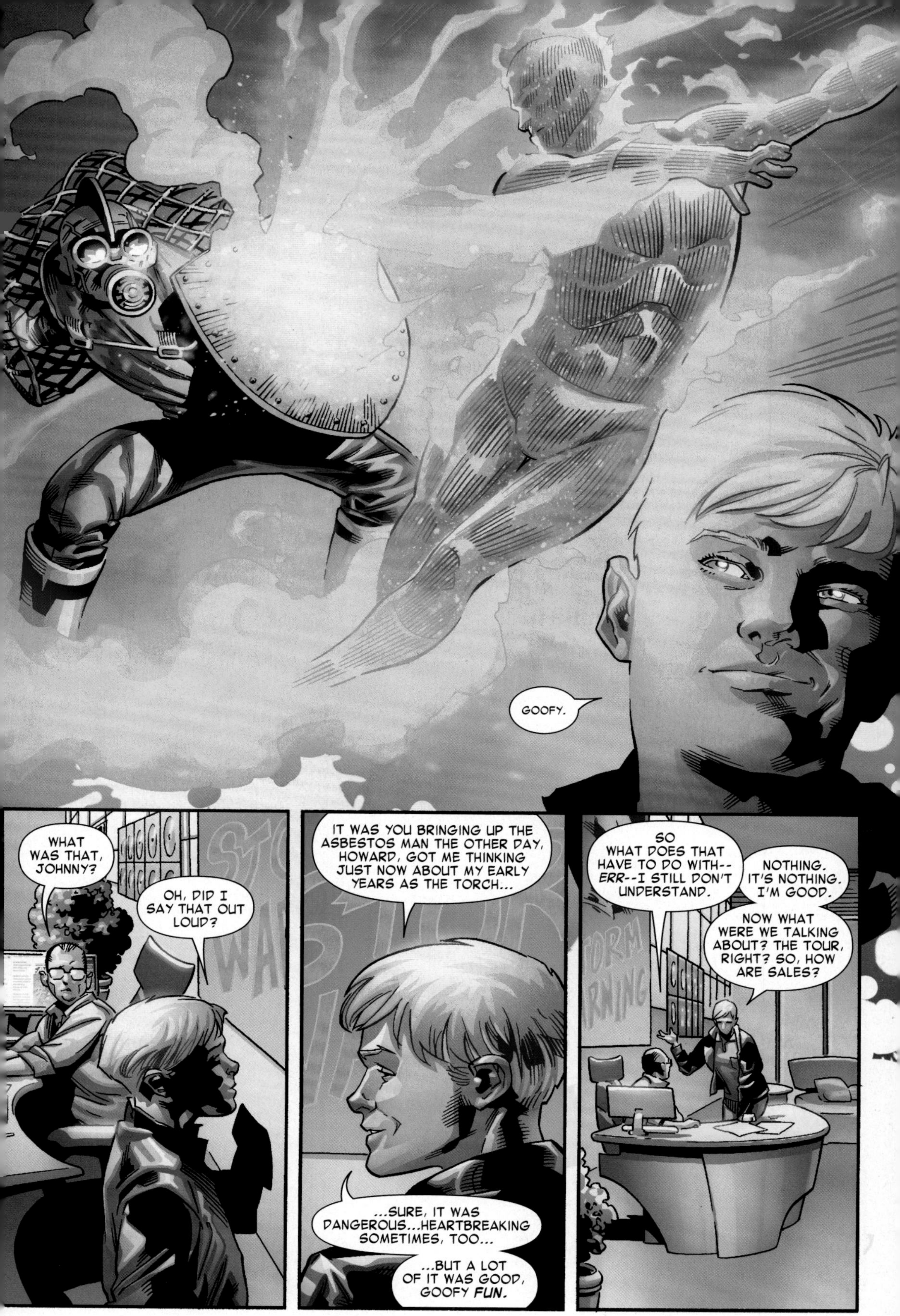
GOOFY.
WHAT WAS THAT, JOHNNY?
OH, DID I SAY THAT OUT LOUD?
IT WAS YOU BRINGING UP THE ASBESTOS MAN THE OTHER DAY, HOWARD, GOT ME THINKING JUST NOW ABOUT MY EARLY YEARS AS THE TORCH...
...SURE, IT WAS DANGEROUS...HEARTBREAKING SOMETIMES, TOO...
...BUT A LOT OF IT WAS GOOD, GOOFY *FUN.*
SO WHAT DOES THAT HAVE TO DO WITH-- *ERR*--I STILL DON'T UNDERSTAND.
NOTHING. IT'S NOTHING. I'M GOOD.
NOW WHAT WERE WE TALKING ABOUT? THE TOUR, RIGHT? SO, HOW ARE SALES?

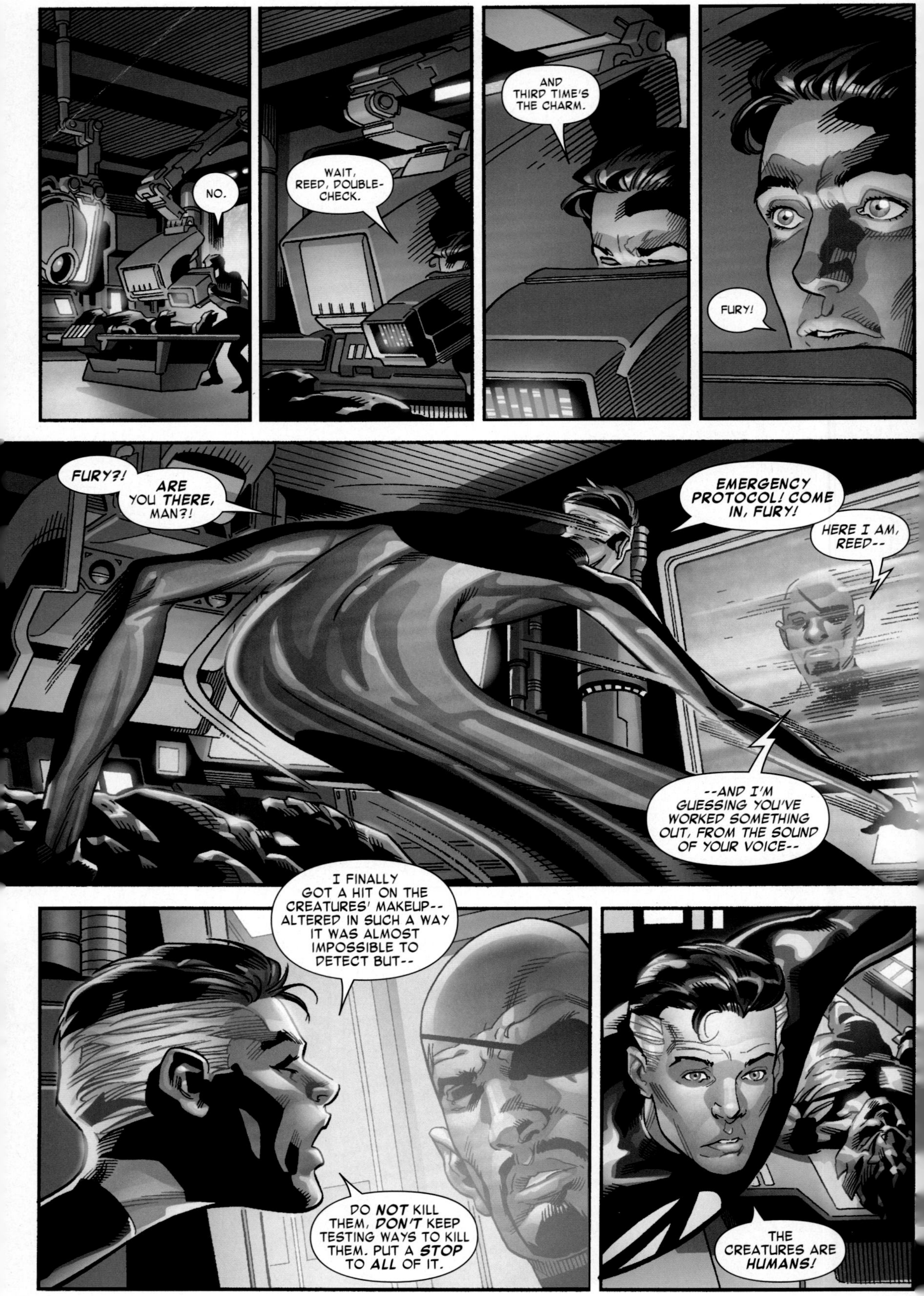
NO.
WAIT, REED, DOUBLE-CHECK.
AND THIRD TIME'S THE CHARM.
FURY!
FURY?!
ARE YOU THERE, MAN?!
EMERGENCY PROTOCOL! COME IN, FURY!
HERE I AM, REED--
--AND I'M GUESSING YOU'VE WORKED SOMETHING OUT, FROM THE SOUND OF YOUR VOICE--
I FINALLY GOT A HIT ON THE CREATURES' MAKEUP--ALTERED IN SUCH A WAY IT WAS ALMOST IMPOSSIBLE TO DETECT BUT--
DO NOT KILL THEM, DON'T KEEP TESTING WAYS TO KILL THEM. PUT A STOP TO ALL OF IT.
THE CREATURES ARE HUMANS!

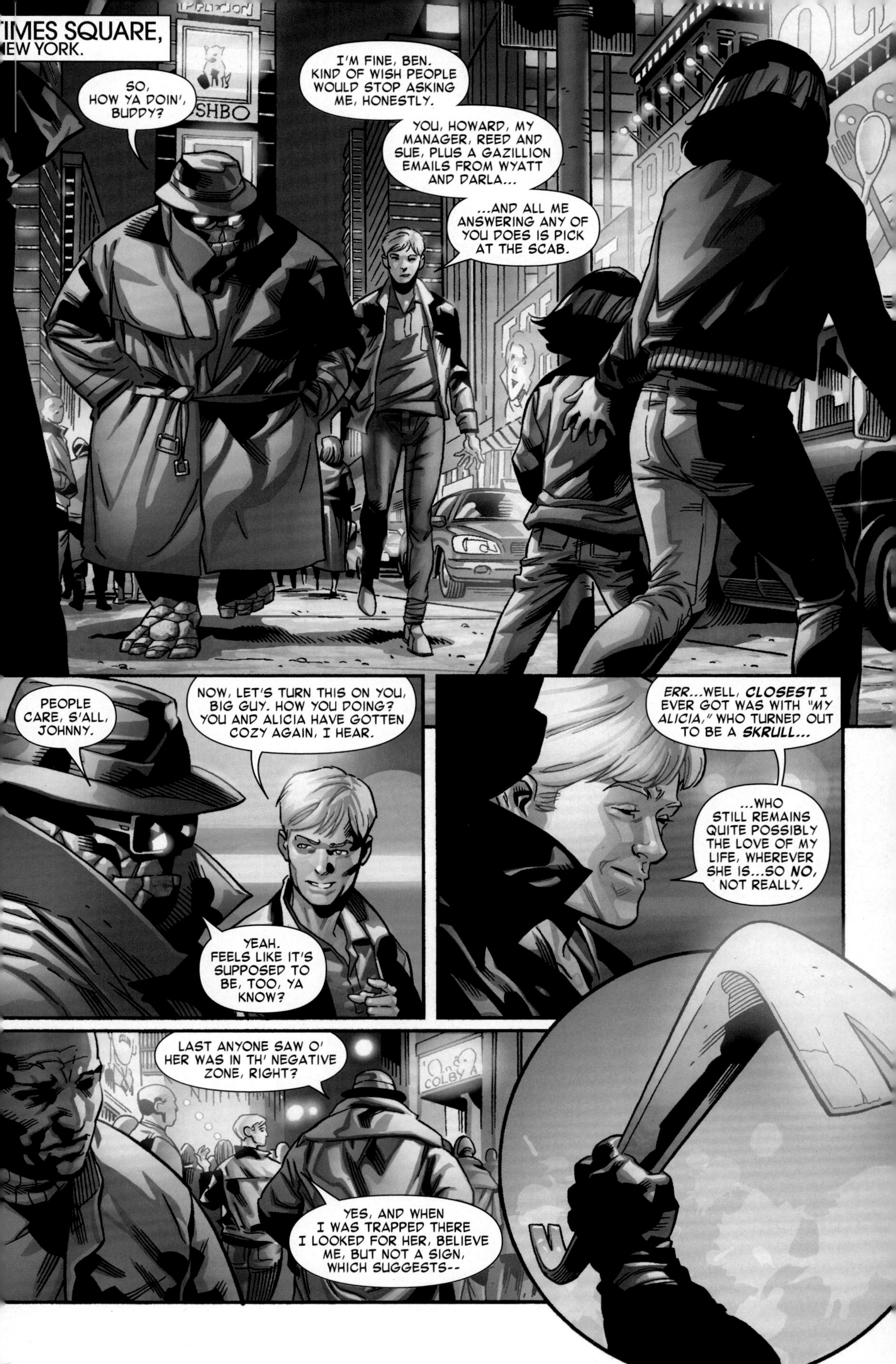
TIMES SQUARE,
NEW YORK.
SO, HOW YA DOIN', BUDDY?
I'M FINE, BEN. KIND OF WISH PEOPLE WOULD STOP ASKING ME, HONESTLY.
YOU, HOWARD, MY MANAGER, REED AND SUE, PLUS A GAZILLION EMAILS FROM WYATT AND DARLA...
...AND ALL ME ANSWERING ANY OF YOU DOES IS PICK AT THE SCAB.
PEOPLE CARE, S'ALL, JOHNNY.
NOW, LET'S TURN THIS ON YOU, BIG GUY. HOW YOU DOING? YOU AND ALICIA HAVE GOTTEN COZY AGAIN, I HEAR.
YEAH. FEELS LIKE IT'S SUPPOSED TO BE, TOO, YA KNOW?
ERR...WELL, CLOSEST I EVER GOT WAS WITH "MY ALICIA," WHO TURNED OUT TO BE A SKRULL...
...WHO STILL REMAINS QUITE POSSIBLY THE LOVE OF MY LIFE, WHEREVER SHE IS...SO NO, NOT REALLY.
LAST ANYONE SAW O' HER WAS IN TH' NEGATIVE ZONE, RIGHT?
YES, AND WHEN I WAS TRAPPED THERE I LOOKED FOR HER, BELIEVE ME, BUT NOT A SIGN, WHICH SUGGESTS--

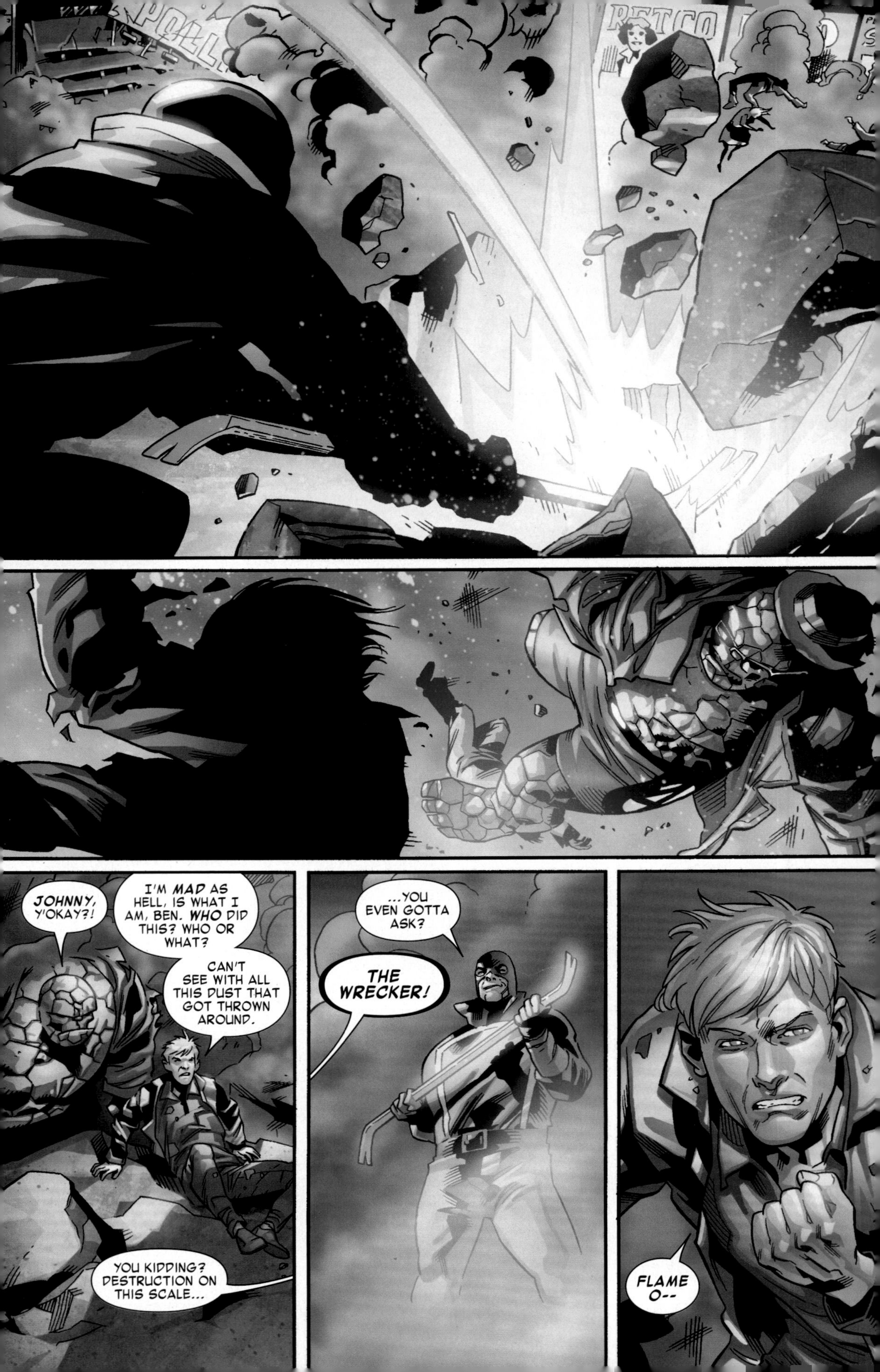

RETCO
JOHNNY, Y'OKAY?!
I'M MAD AS HELL, IS WHAT I AM, BEN. WHO DID THIS? WHO OR WHAT?
CAN'T SEE WITH ALL THIS DUST THAT GOT THROWN AROUND.
YOU KIDDING? DESTRUCTION ON THIS SCALE...
...YOU EVEN GOTTA ASK?
THE WRECKER!
FLAME O--

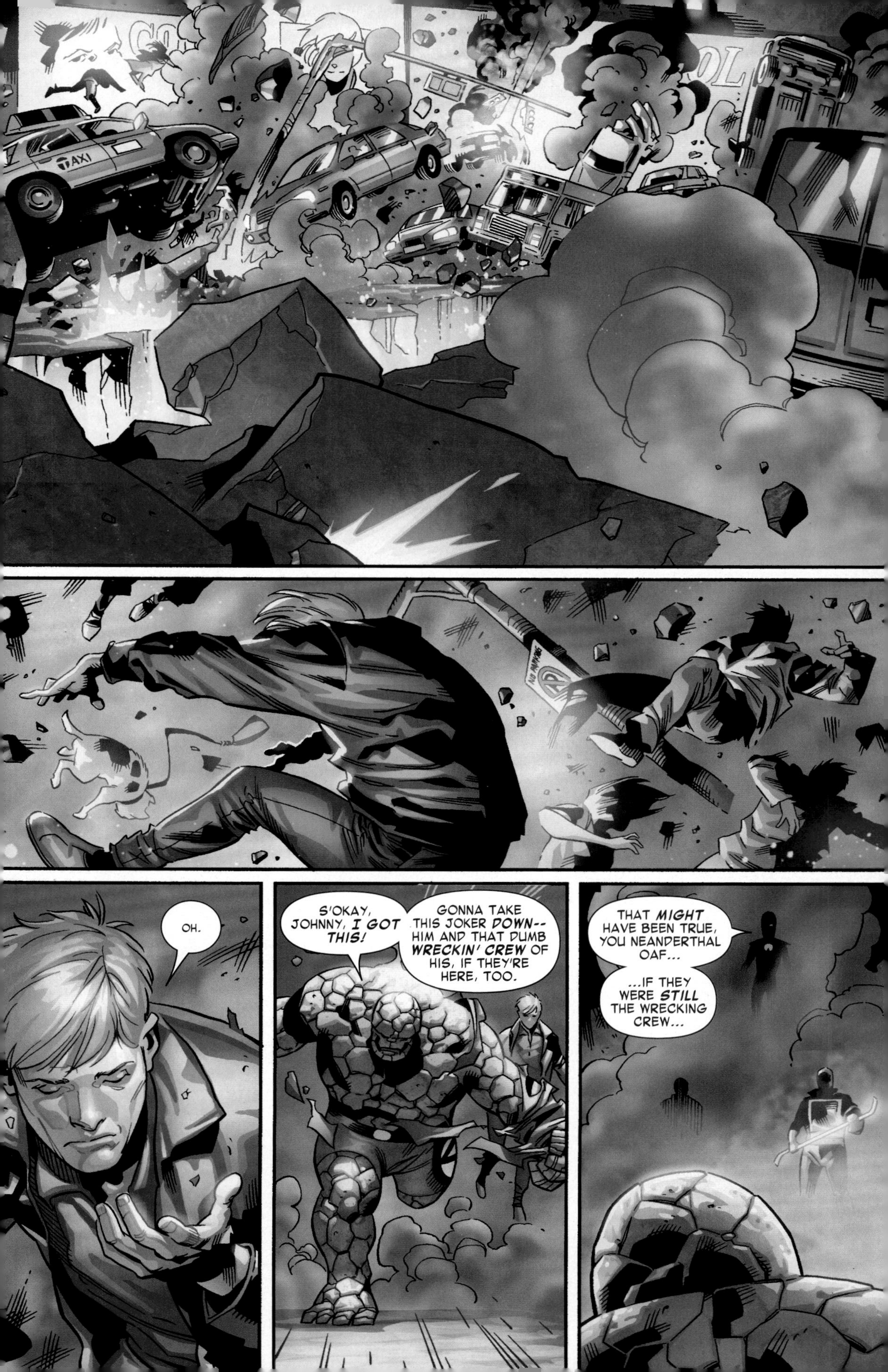

TAXI
NO PARKING
OH.
S'OKAY, JOHNNY, *I GOT THIS!*
GONNA TAKE THIS JOKER *DOWN*-- HIM AND THAT DUMB *WRECKIN' CREW* OF HIS, IF THEY'RE HERE, TOO.
THAT *MIGHT* HAVE BEEN TRUE, YOU NEANDERTHAL OAF...
...IF THEY WERE *STILL* THE WRECKING CREW...

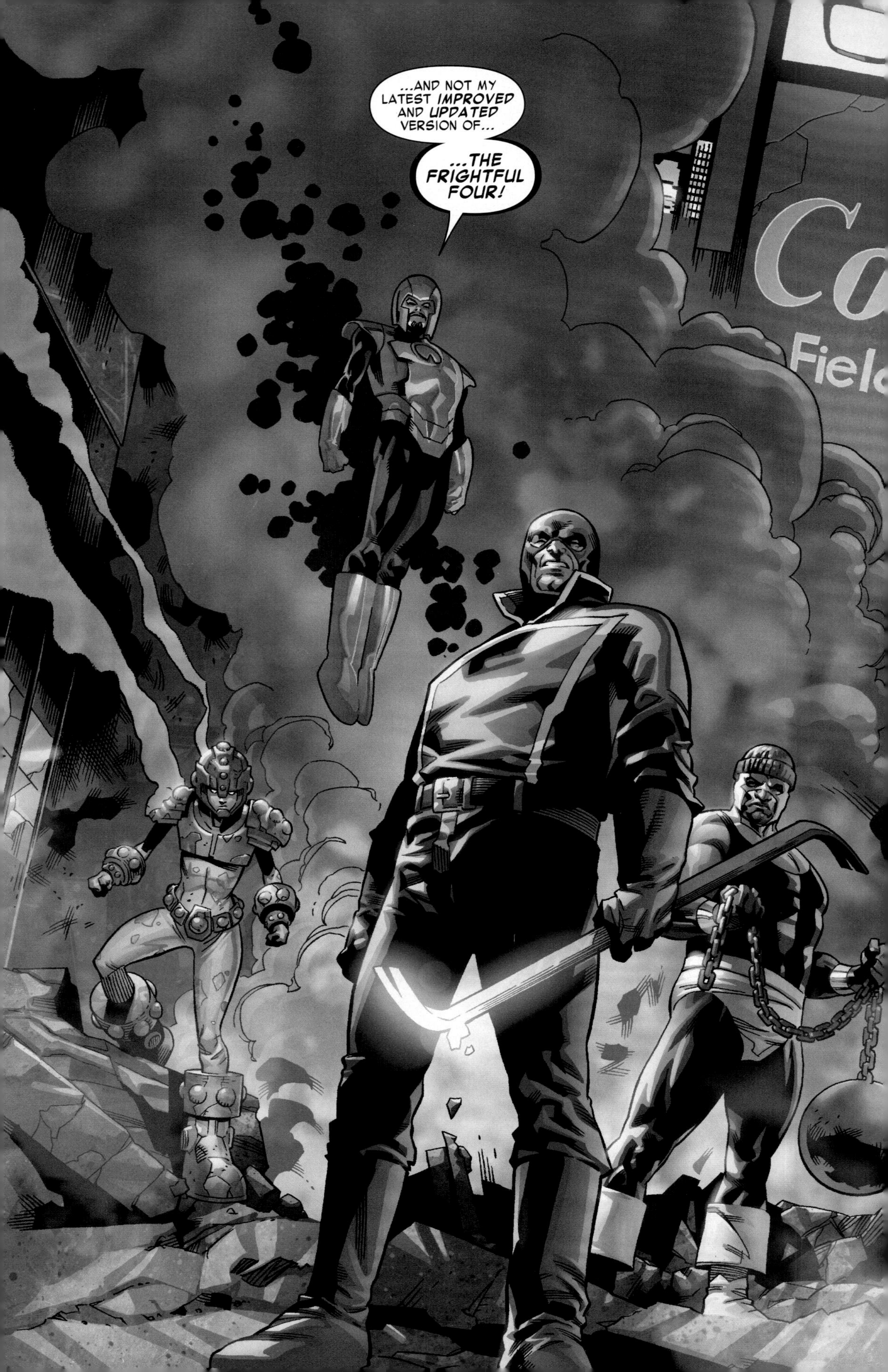
...AND NOT MY LATEST IMPROVED AND UPDATED VERSION OF...
...THE FRIGHTFUL FOUR!
Fiel

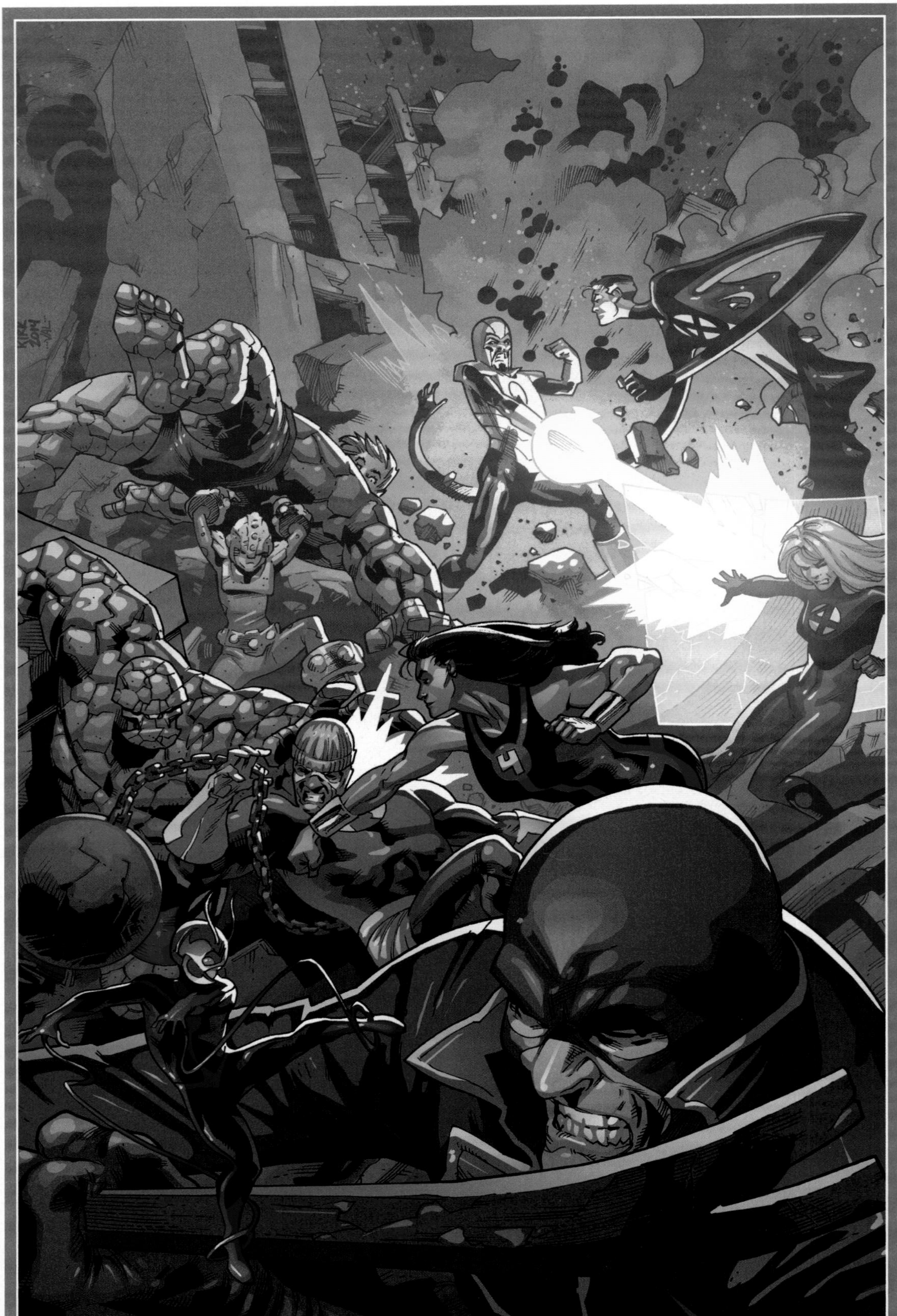

FOUR

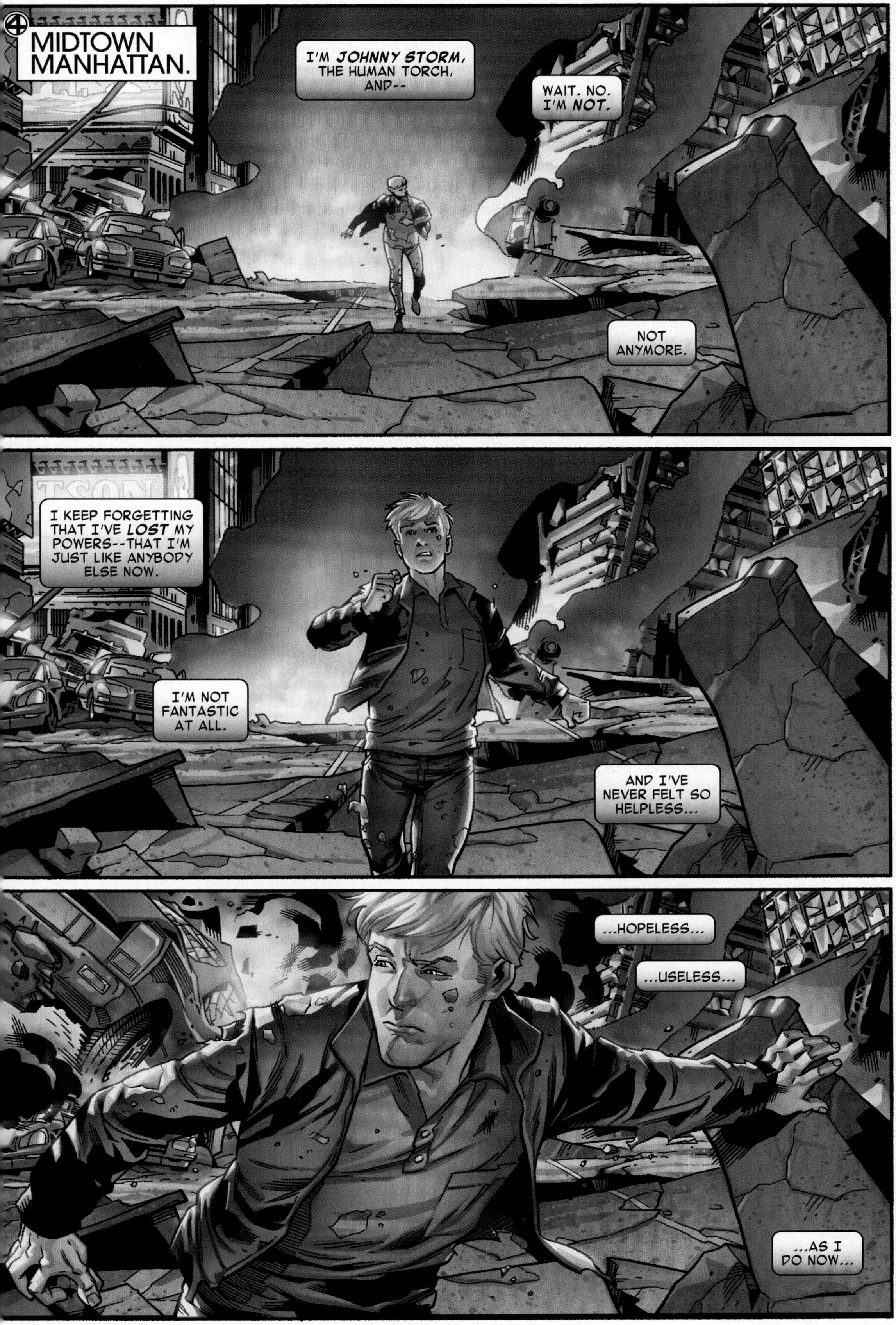
4
MIDTOWN MANHATTAN.
I'M JOHNNY STORM, THE HUMAN TORCH, AND--
WAIT. NO. I'M NOT.
NOT ANYMORE.
I KEEP FORGETTING THAT I'VE LOST MY POWERS--THAT I'M JUST LIKE ANYBODY ELSE NOW.
I'M NOT FANTASTIC AT ALL.
AND I'VE NEVER FELT SO HELPLESS...
...HOPELESS...
...USELESS...
...AS I DO NOW...

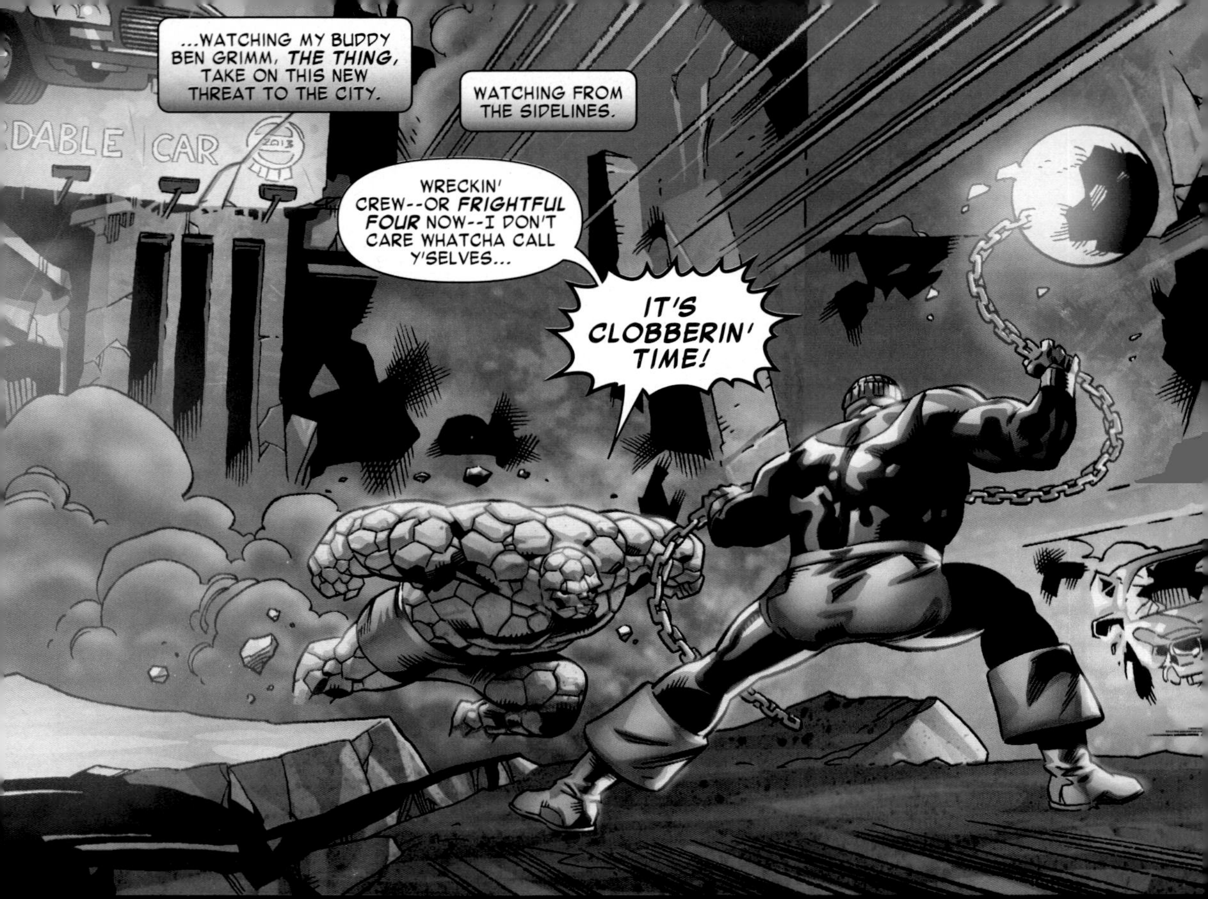

...WATCHING MY BUDDY BEN GRIMM, *THE THING,* TAKE ON THIS NEW THREAT TO THE CITY.
WATCHING FROM THE SIDELINES.
WRECKIN' CREW--OR *FRIGHTFUL FOUR* NOW--I DON'T CARE WHATCHA CALL Y'SELVES...
IT'S CLOBBERIN' TIME!

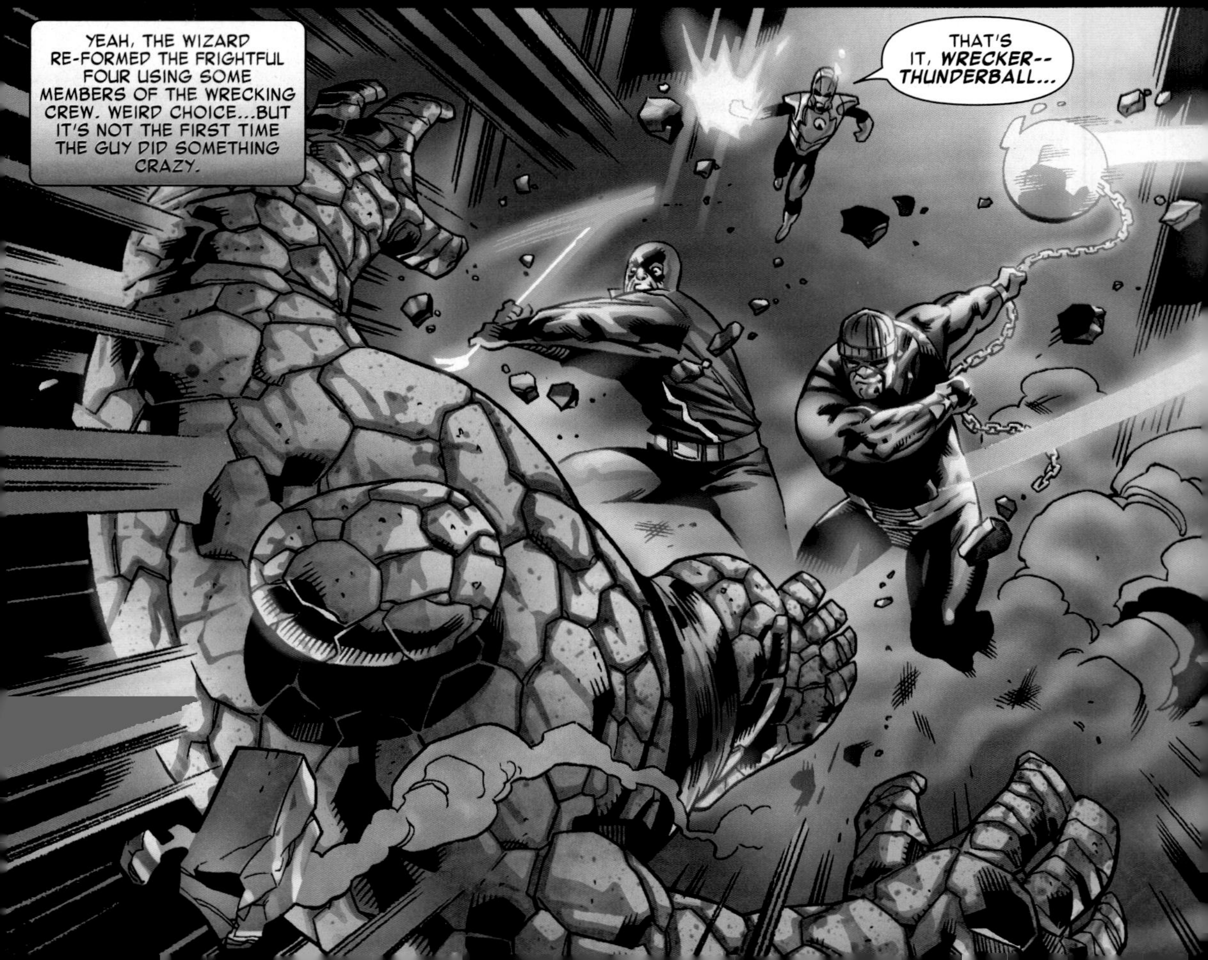

YEAH, THE WIZARD RE-FORMED THE FRIGHTFUL FOUR USING SOME MEMBERS OF THE WRECKING CREW. WEIRD CHOICE...BUT IT'S NOT THE FIRST TIME THE GUY DID SOMETHING CRAZY.
THAT'S IT, *WRECKER-- THUNDERBALL...*

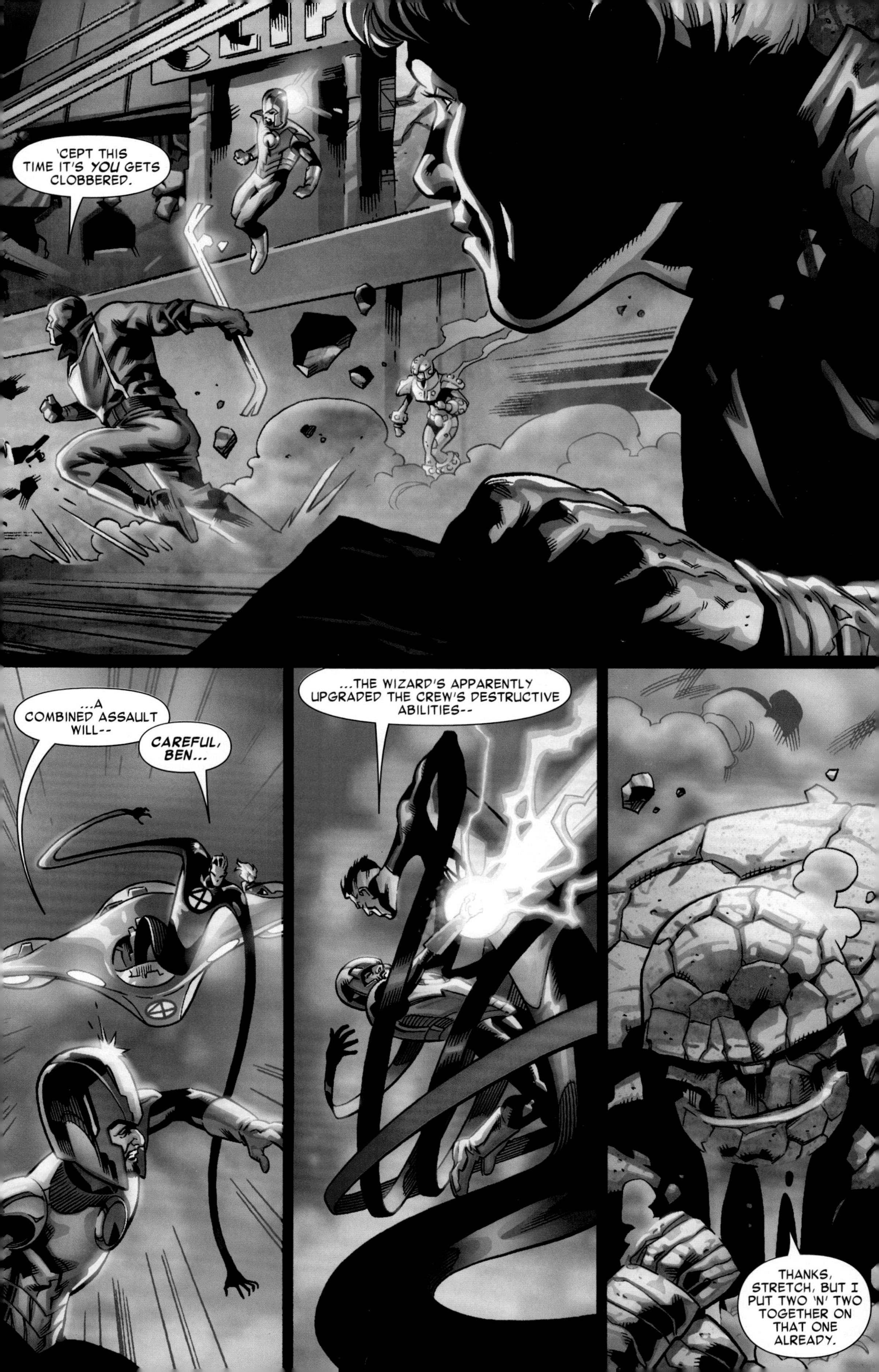
'CEPT THIS TIME IT'S *YOU* GETS CLOBBERED.
...A COMBINED ASSAULT WILL--
CAREFUL, BEN...
...THE WIZARD'S APPARENTLY UPGRADED THE CREW'S DESTRUCTIVE ABILITIES--
THANKS, STRETCH, BUT I PUT TWO 'N' TWO TOGETHER ON THAT ONE ALREADY.

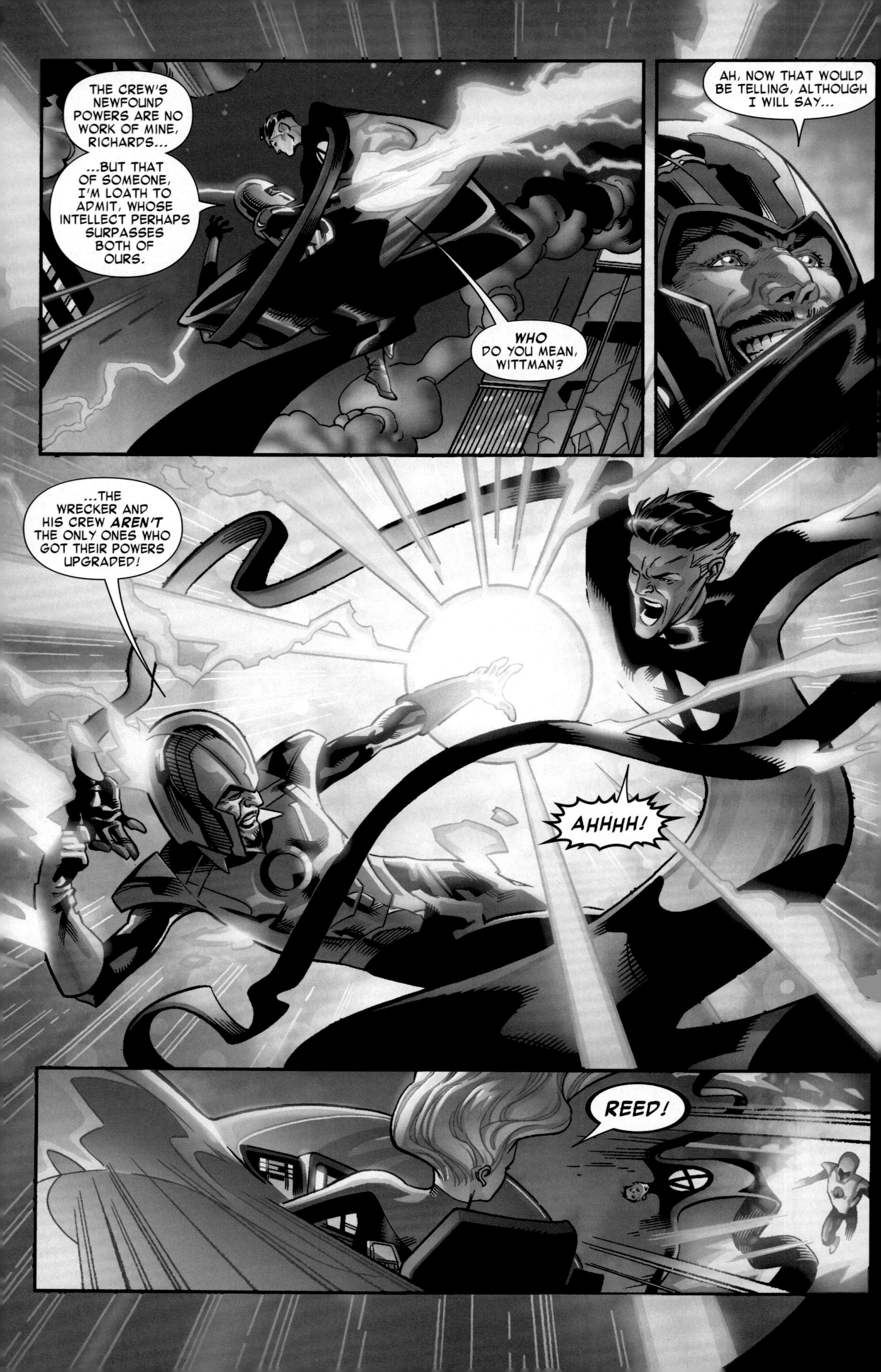
THE CREW'S NEWFOUND POWERS ARE NO WORK OF MINE, RICHARDS...
...BUT THAT OF SOMEONE, I'M LOATH TO ADMIT, WHOSE INTELLECT PERHAPS SURPASSES BOTH OF OURS.
WHO DO YOU MEAN, WITTMAN?
AH, NOW THAT WOULD BE TELLING, ALTHOUGH I WILL SAY...
...THE WRECKER AND HIS CREW AREN'T THE ONLY ONES WHO GOT THEIR POWERS UPGRADED!
AHHHH!
REED!

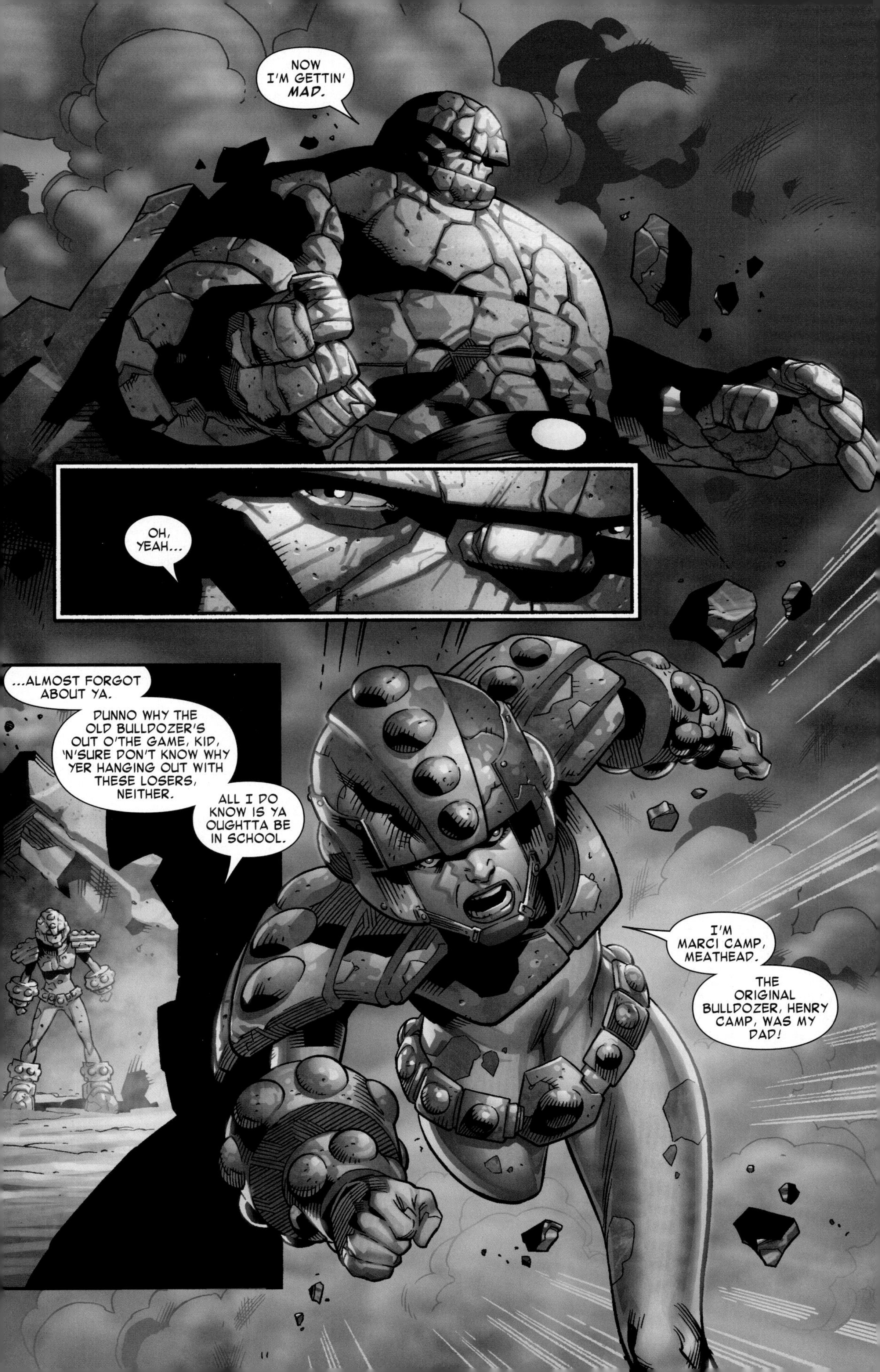
NOW I'M GETTIN' MAD.
OH, YEAH...
...ALMOST FORGOT ABOUT YA.
DUNNO WHY THE OLD BULLDOZER'S OUT O'THE GAME, KID, 'N'SURE DON'T KNOW WHY YER HANGING OUT WITH THESE LOSERS, NEITHER.
ALL I DO KNOW IS YA OUGHTTA BE IN SCHOOL.
I'M MARCI CAMP, MEATHEAD.
THE ORIGINAL BULLDOZER, HENRY CAMP, WAS MY DAD!

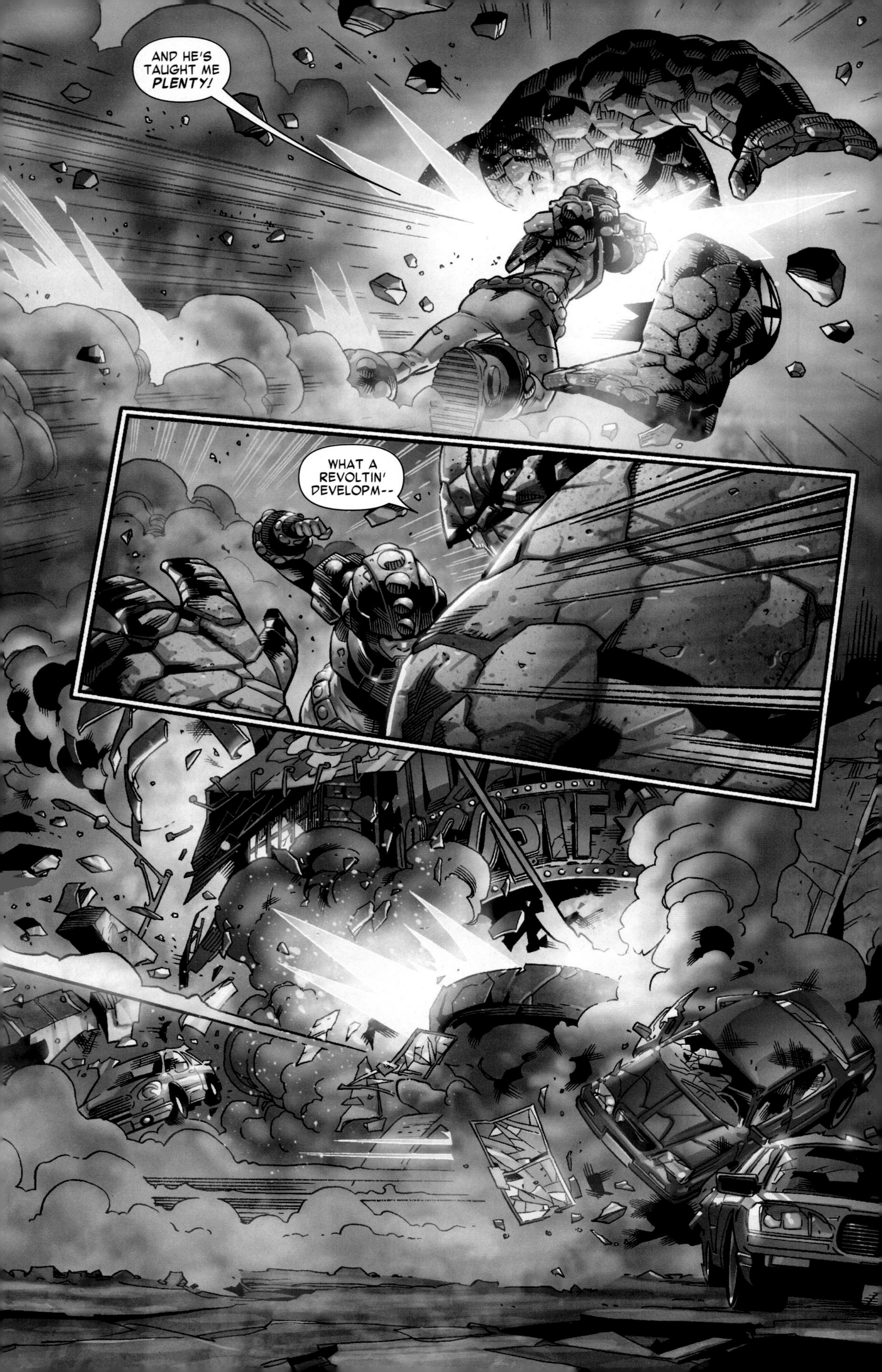
AND HE'S TAUGHT ME *PLENTY!*
WHAT A REVOLTIN' DEVELOPM--

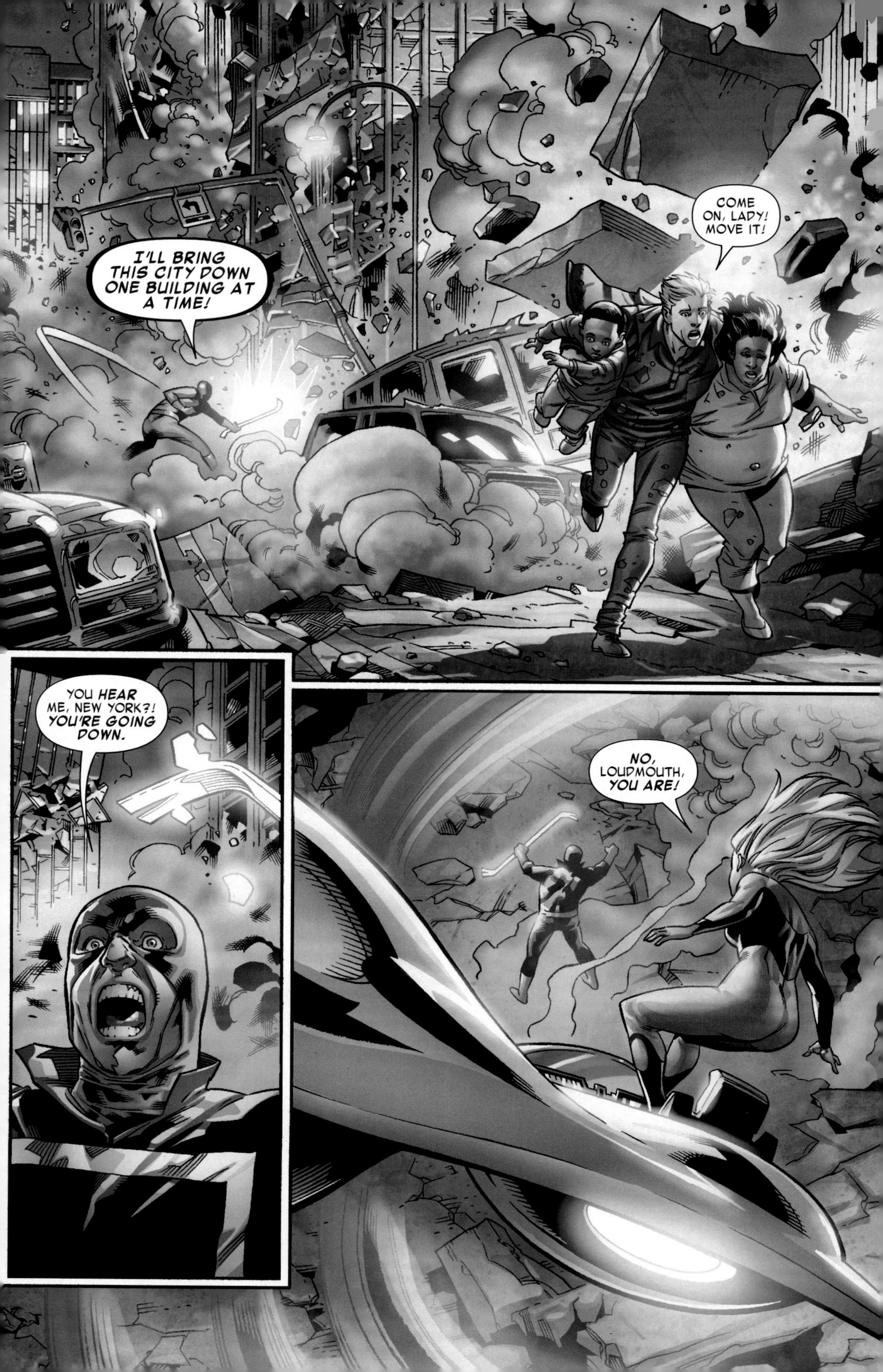
COME ON, LADY! MOVE IT!
I'LL BRING THIS CITY DOWN ONE BUILDING AT A TIME!
YOU HEAR ME, NEW YORK?! YOU'RE GOING DOWN.
NO, LOUDMOUTH, YOU ARE!

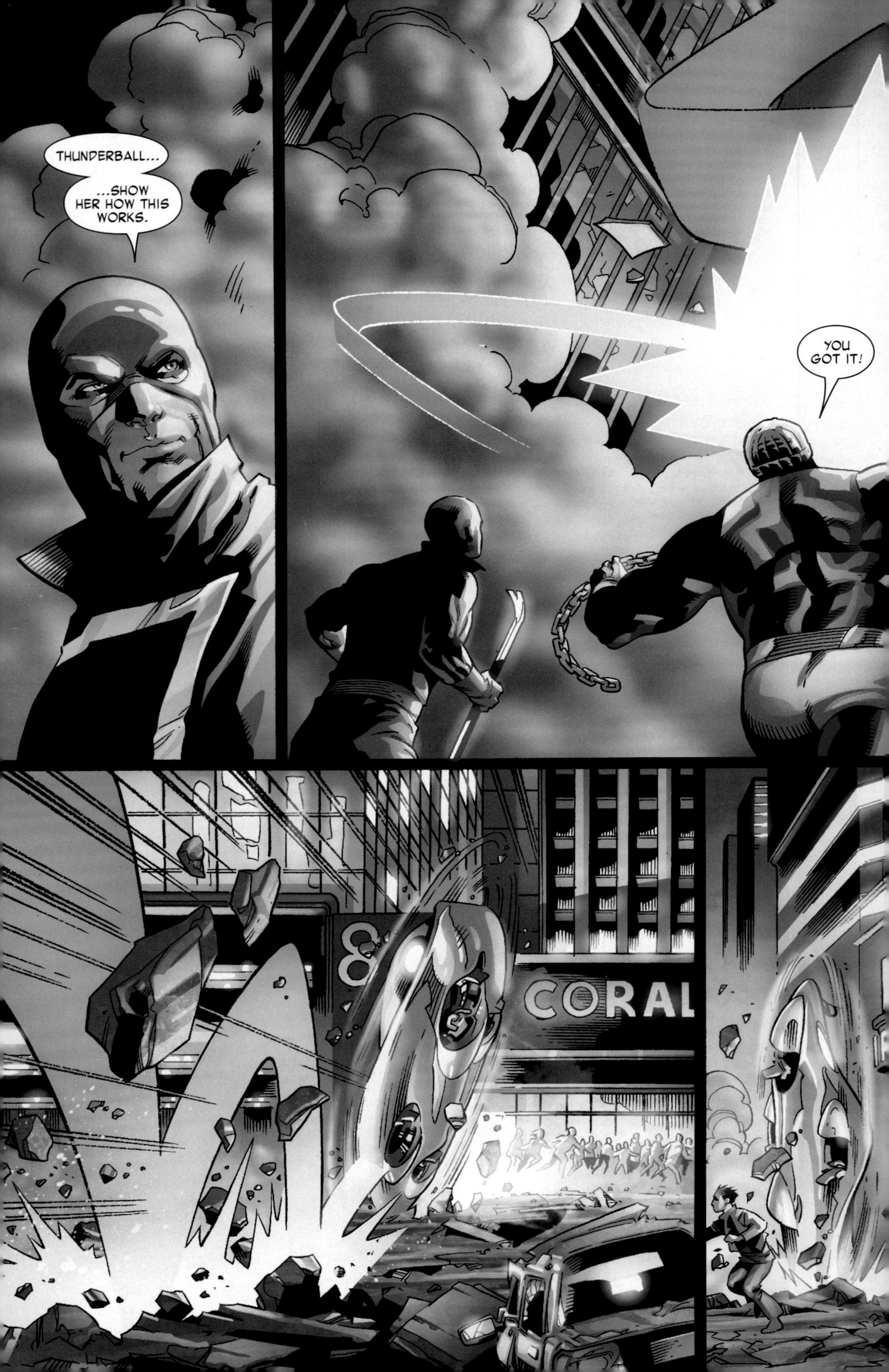
THUNDERBALL...
...SHOW HER HOW THIS WORKS.
YOU GOT IT!
CORAL

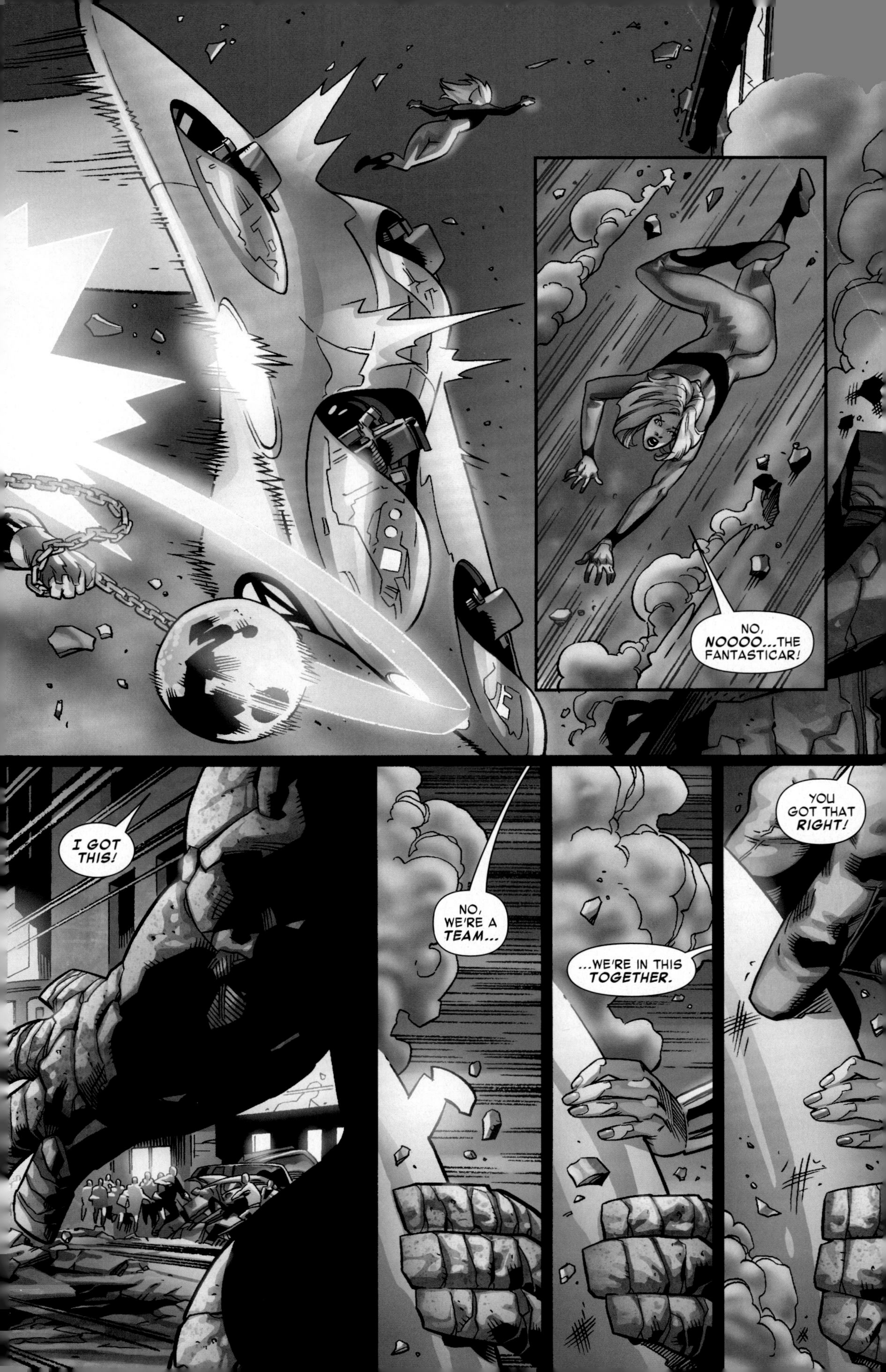
NO, NOOOO...THE FANTASTICAR!
I GOT THIS!
NO, WE'RE A TEAM...
...WE'RE IN THIS TOGETHER.
YOU GOT THAT RIGHT!

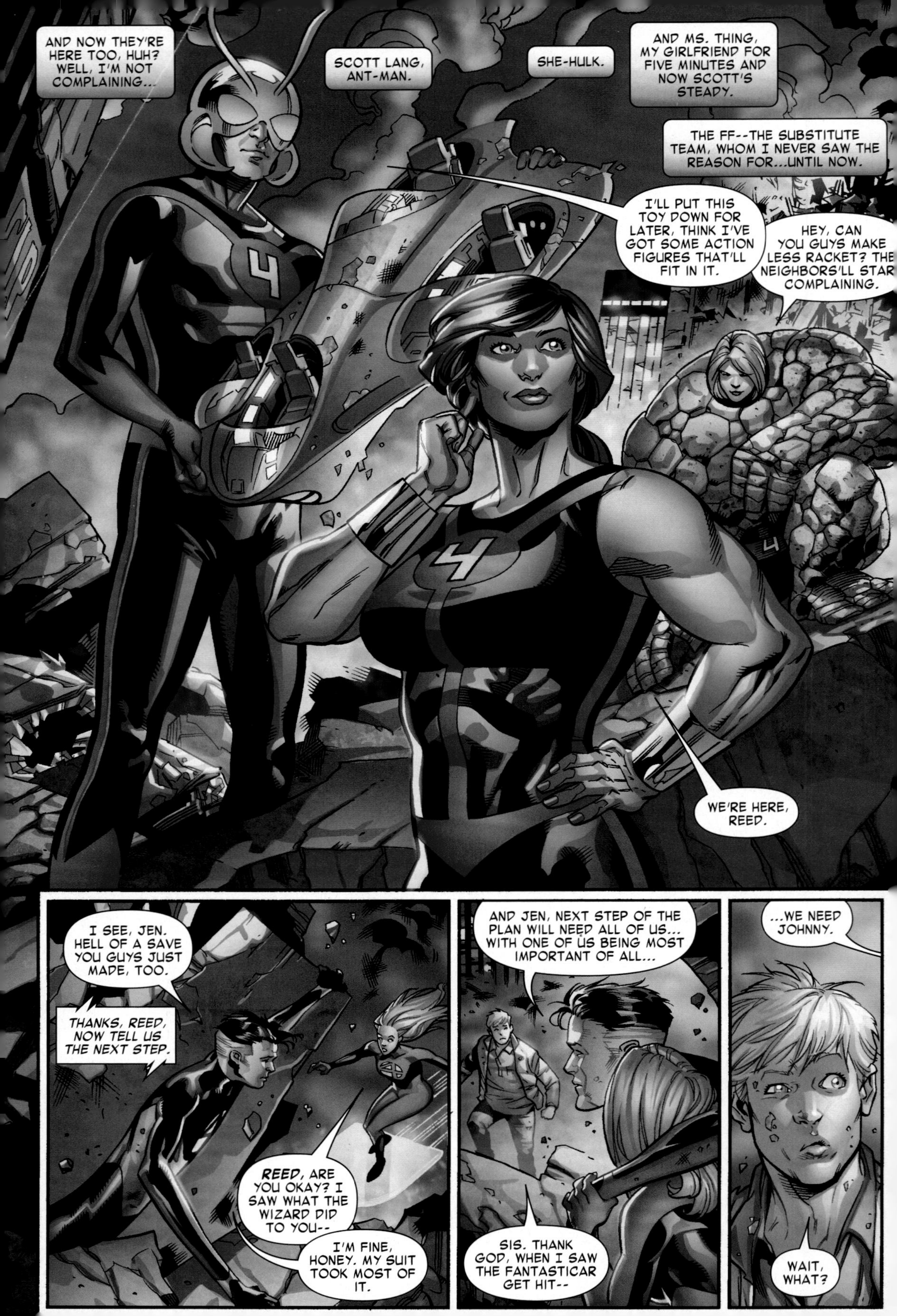
AND NOW THEY'RE HERE TOO, HUH? WELL, I'M NOT COMPLAINING...
SCOTT LANG, ANT-MAN.
SHE-HULK.
AND MS. THING, MY GIRLFRIEND FOR FIVE MINUTES AND NOW SCOTT'S STEADY.
THE FF--THE SUBSTITUTE TEAM, WHOM I NEVER SAW THE REASON FOR...UNTIL NOW.
I'LL PUT THIS TOY DOWN FOR LATER, THINK I'VE GOT SOME ACTION FIGURES THAT'LL FIT IN IT.
HEY, CAN YOU GUYS MAKE LESS RACKET? THE NEIGHBORS'LL STAR COMPLAINING.
WE'RE HERE, REED.
I SEE, JEN. HELL OF A SAVE YOU GUYS JUST MADE, TOO.
THANKS, REED, NOW TELL US THE NEXT STEP.
REED, ARE YOU OKAY? I SAW WHAT THE WIZARD DID TO YOU--
I'M FINE, HONEY. MY SUIT TOOK MOST OF IT.
AND JEN, NEXT STEP OF THE PLAN WILL NEED ALL OF US... WITH ONE OF US BEING MOST IMPORTANT OF ALL...
SIS. THANK GOD, WHEN I SAW THE FANTASTICAR GET HIT--
...WE NEED JOHNNY.
WAIT, WHAT?

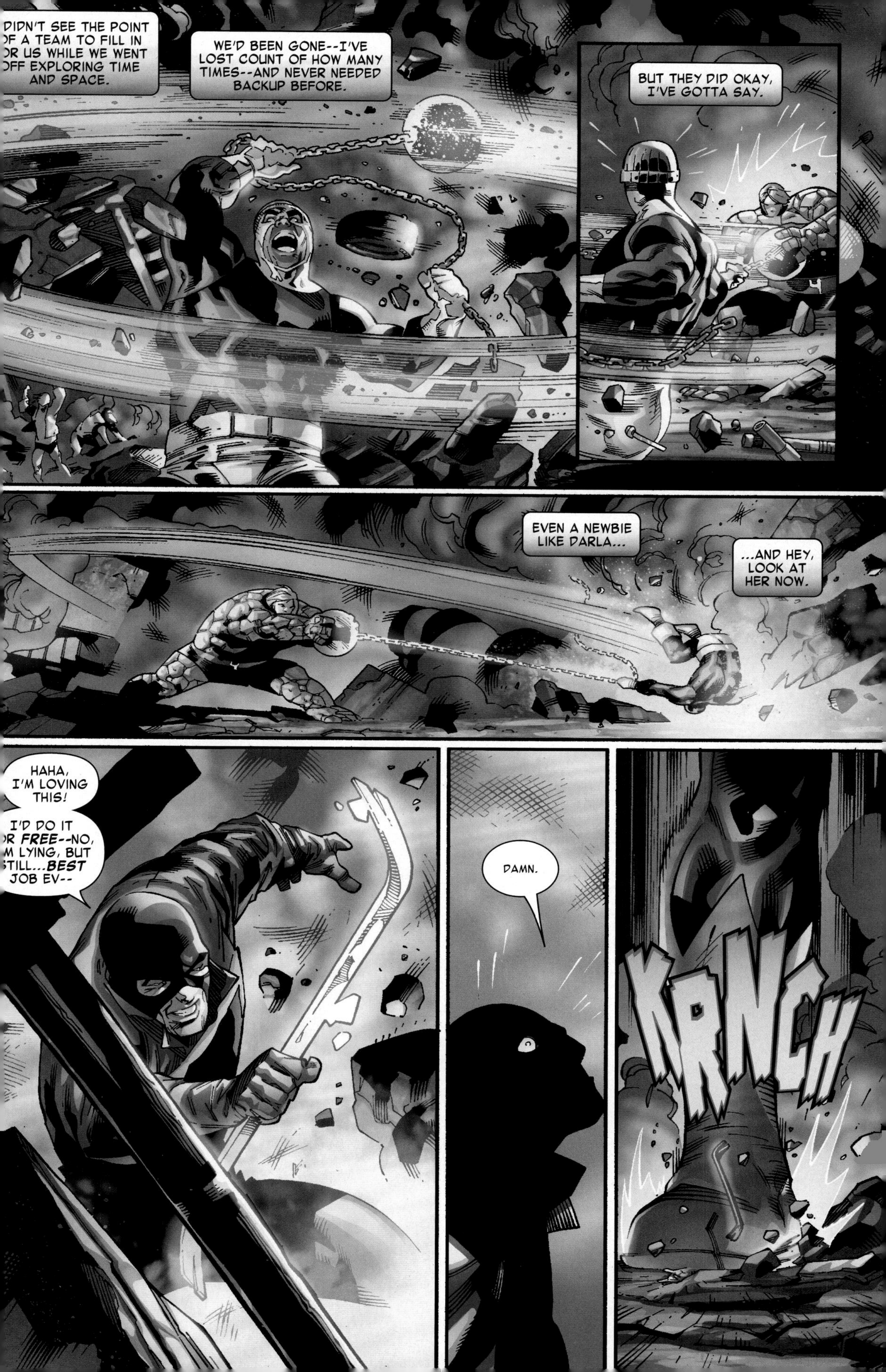
DIDN'T SEE THE POINT OF A TEAM TO FILL IN FOR US WHILE WE WENT OFF EXPLORING TIME AND SPACE.
WE'D BEEN GONE--I'VE LOST COUNT OF HOW MANY TIMES--AND NEVER NEEDED BACKUP BEFORE.
BUT THEY DID OKAY, I'VE GOTTA SAY.
EVEN A NEWBIE LIKE DARLA...
...AND HEY, LOOK AT HER NOW.
HAHA, I'M LOVING THIS!
I'D DO IT FOR *FREE*--NO, I'M LYING, BUT STILL...*BEST* JOB EV--
DAMN.
KRNCH

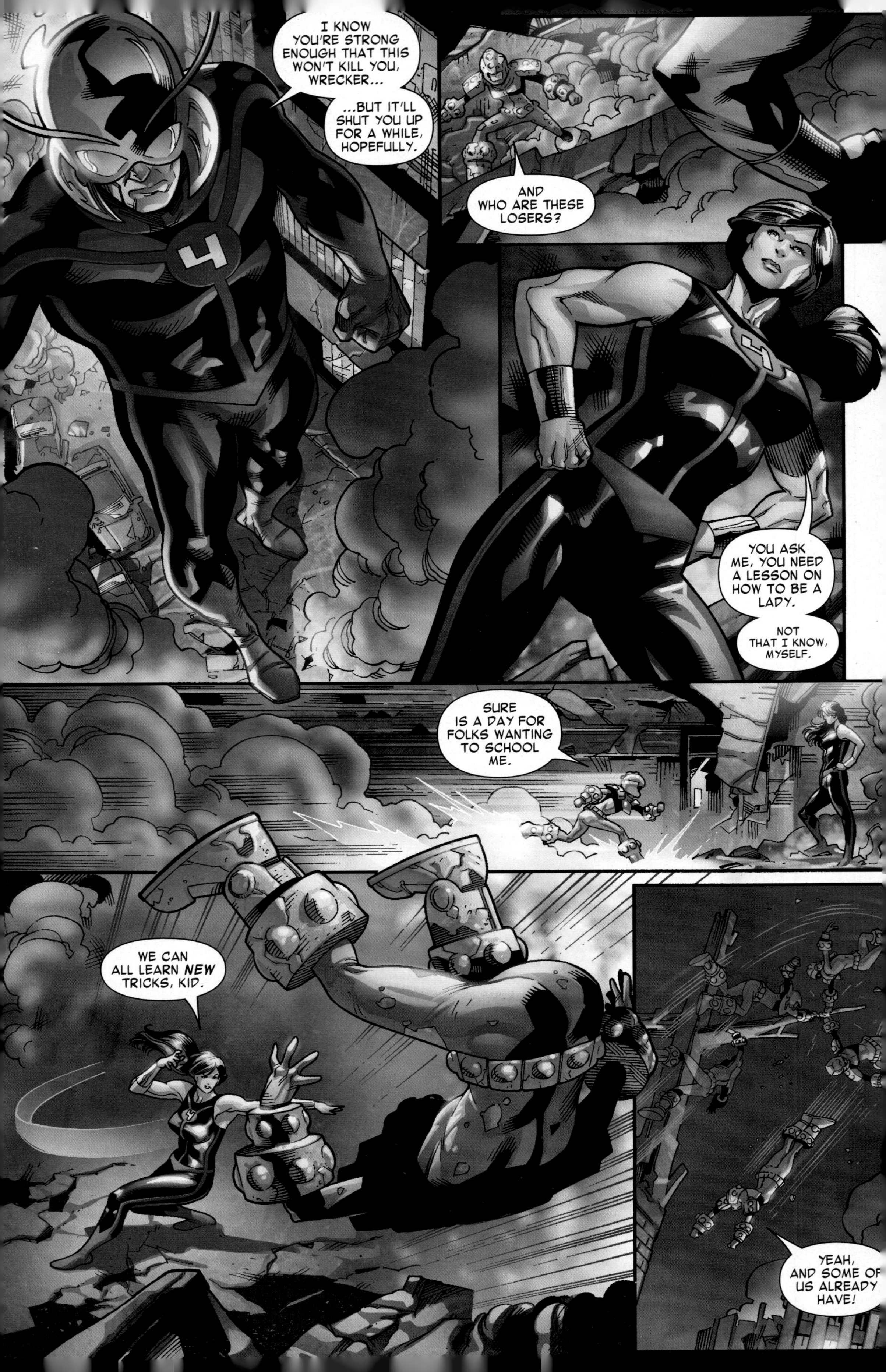
I KNOW YOU'RE STRONG ENOUGH THAT THIS WON'T KILL YOU, WRECKER...
...BUT IT'LL SHUT YOU UP FOR A WHILE, HOPEFULLY.
AND WHO ARE THESE LOSERS?
YOU ASK ME, YOU NEED A LESSON ON HOW TO BE A LADY.
NOT THAT I KNOW, MYSELF.
SURE IS A DAY FOR FOLKS WANTING TO SCHOOL ME.
WE CAN ALL LEARN NEW TRICKS, KID.
YEAH, AND SOME OF US ALREADY HAVE!

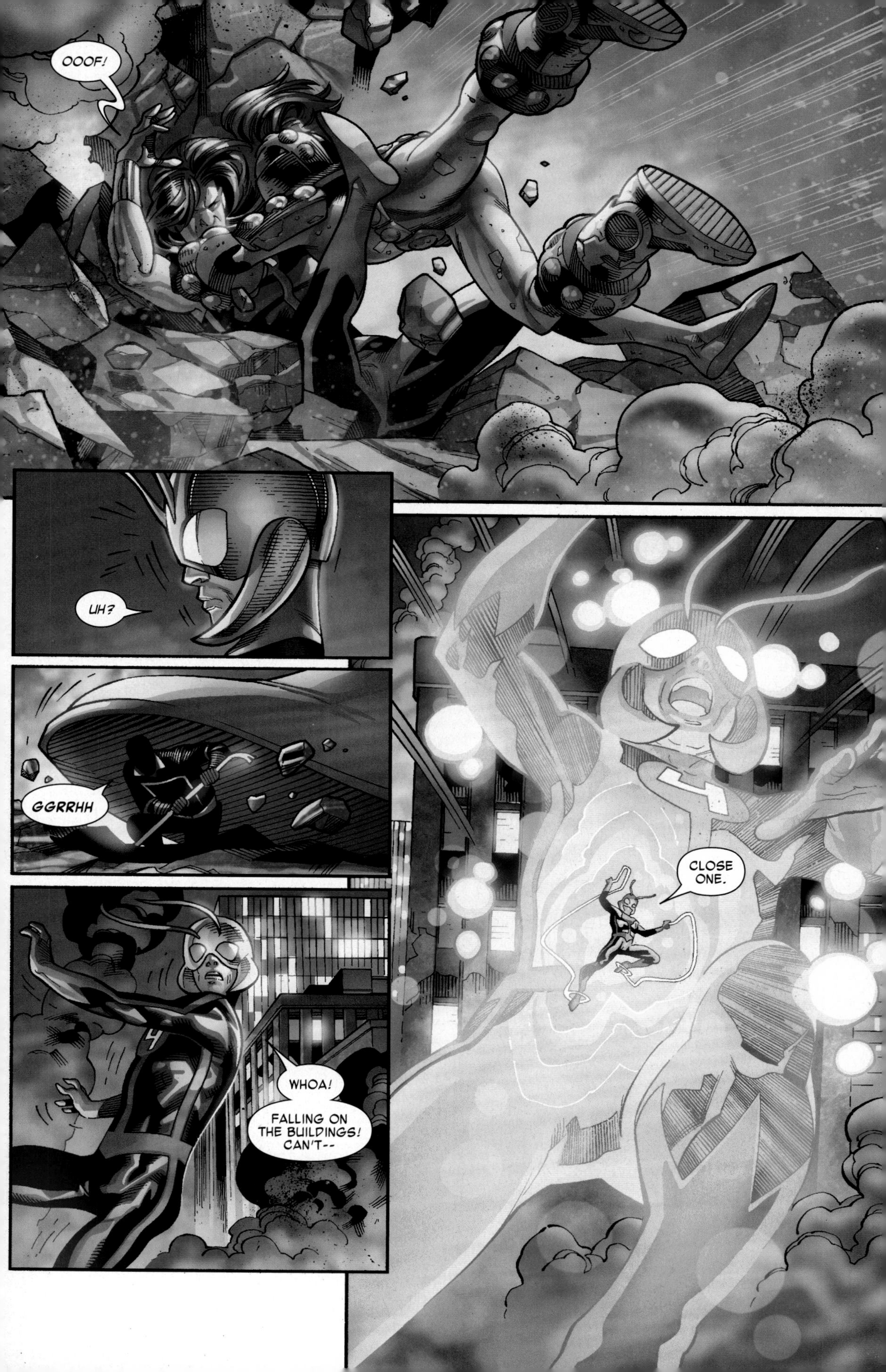
OOOF!
UH?
GGRRHH
WHOA!
FALLING ON THE BUILDINGS! CAN'T--
CLOSE ONE.

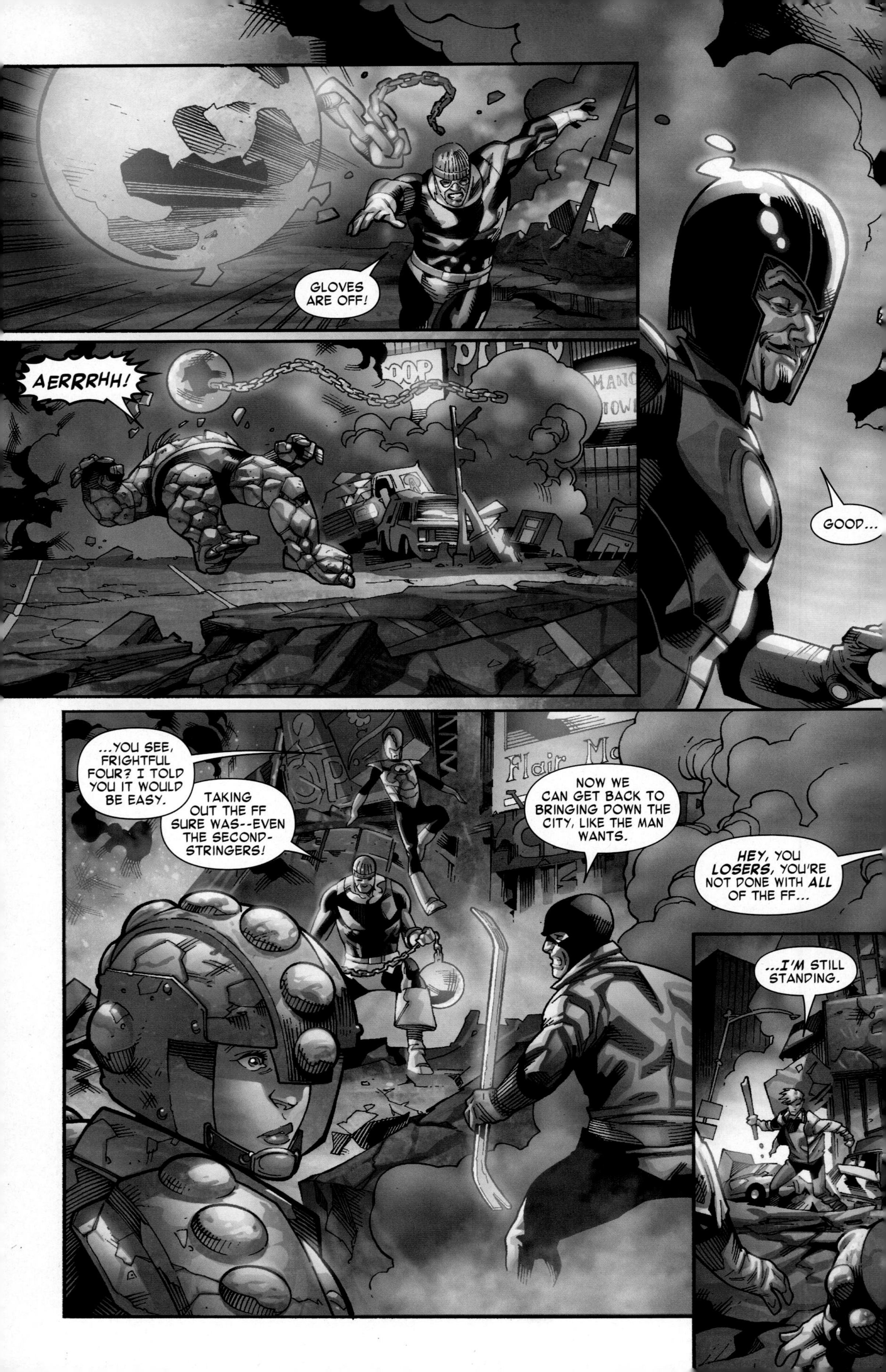
GLOVES ARE OFF!
AERRRHH!
GOOD...
...YOU SEE, FRIGHTFUL FOUR? I TOLD YOU IT WOULD BE EASY.
TAKING OUT THE FF SURE WAS--EVEN THE SECOND-STRINGERS!
NOW WE CAN GET BACK TO BRINGING DOWN THE CITY, LIKE THE MAN WANTS.
HEY, YOU LOSERS, YOU'RE NOT DONE WITH ALL OF THE FF...
...I'M STILL STANDING.

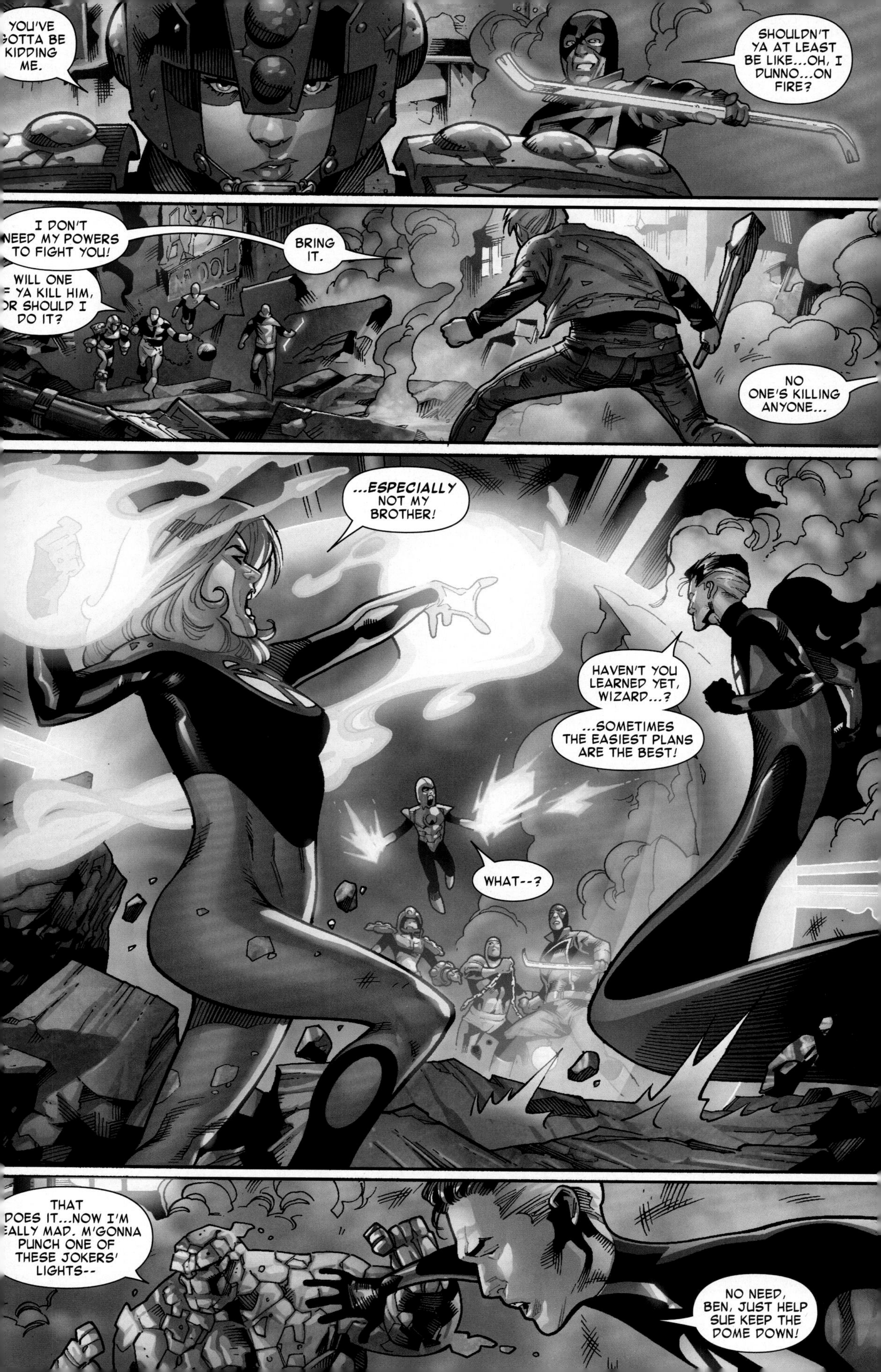
YOU'VE GOTTA BE KIDDING ME.
SHOULDN'T YA AT LEAST BE LIKE...OH, I DUNNO...ON FIRE?
I DON'T NEED MY POWERS TO FIGHT YOU!
BRING IT.
WILL ONE OF YA KILL HIM, OR SHOULD I DO IT?
NO ONE'S KILLING ANYONE...
...ESPECIALLY NOT MY BROTHER!
HAVEN'T YOU LEARNED YET, WIZARD...?
...SOMETIMES THE EASIEST PLANS ARE THE BEST!
WHAT--?
THAT DOES IT...NOW I'M REALLY MAD. M'GONNA PUNCH ONE OF THESE JOKERS' LIGHTS--
NO NEED, BEN, JUST HELP SUE KEEP THE DOME DOWN!

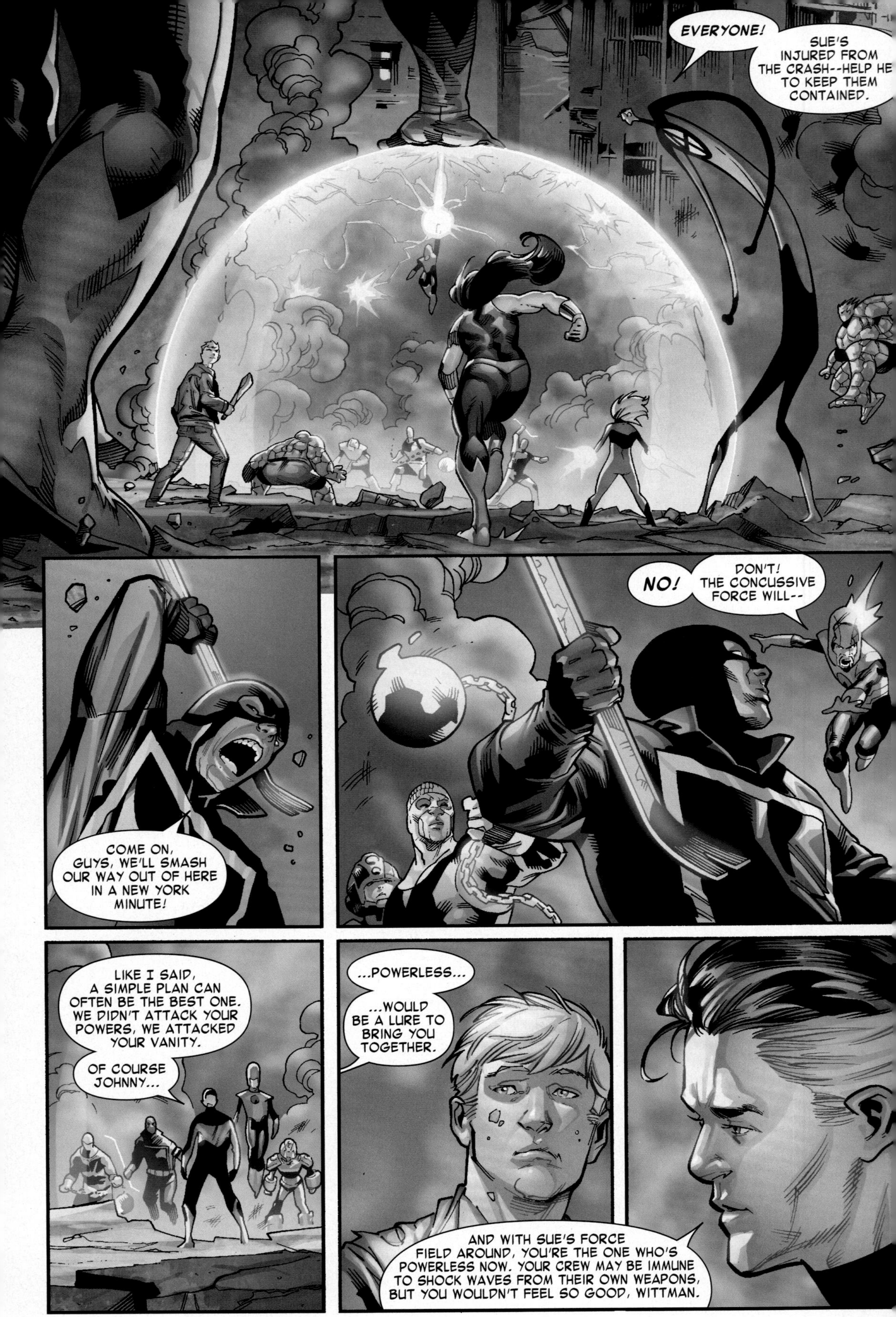
EVERYONE!
SUE'S INJURED FROM THE CRASH--HELP HE TO KEEP THEM CONTAINED.
COME ON, GUYS, WE'LL SMASH OUR WAY OUT OF HERE IN A NEW YORK MINUTE!
NO!
DON'T! THE CONCUSSIVE FORCE WILL--
LIKE I SAID, A SIMPLE PLAN CAN OFTEN BE THE BEST ONE. WE DIDN'T ATTACK YOUR POWERS, WE ATTACKED YOUR VANITY.
OF COURSE JOHNNY...
...POWERLESS...
...WOULD BE A LURE TO BRING YOU TOGETHER.
AND WITH SUE'S FORCE FIELD AROUND, YOU'RE THE ONE WHO'S POWERLESS NOW. YOUR CREW MAY BE IMMUNE TO SHOCK WAVES FROM THEIR OWN WEAPONS, BUT YOU WOULDN'T FEEL SO GOOD, WITTMAN.

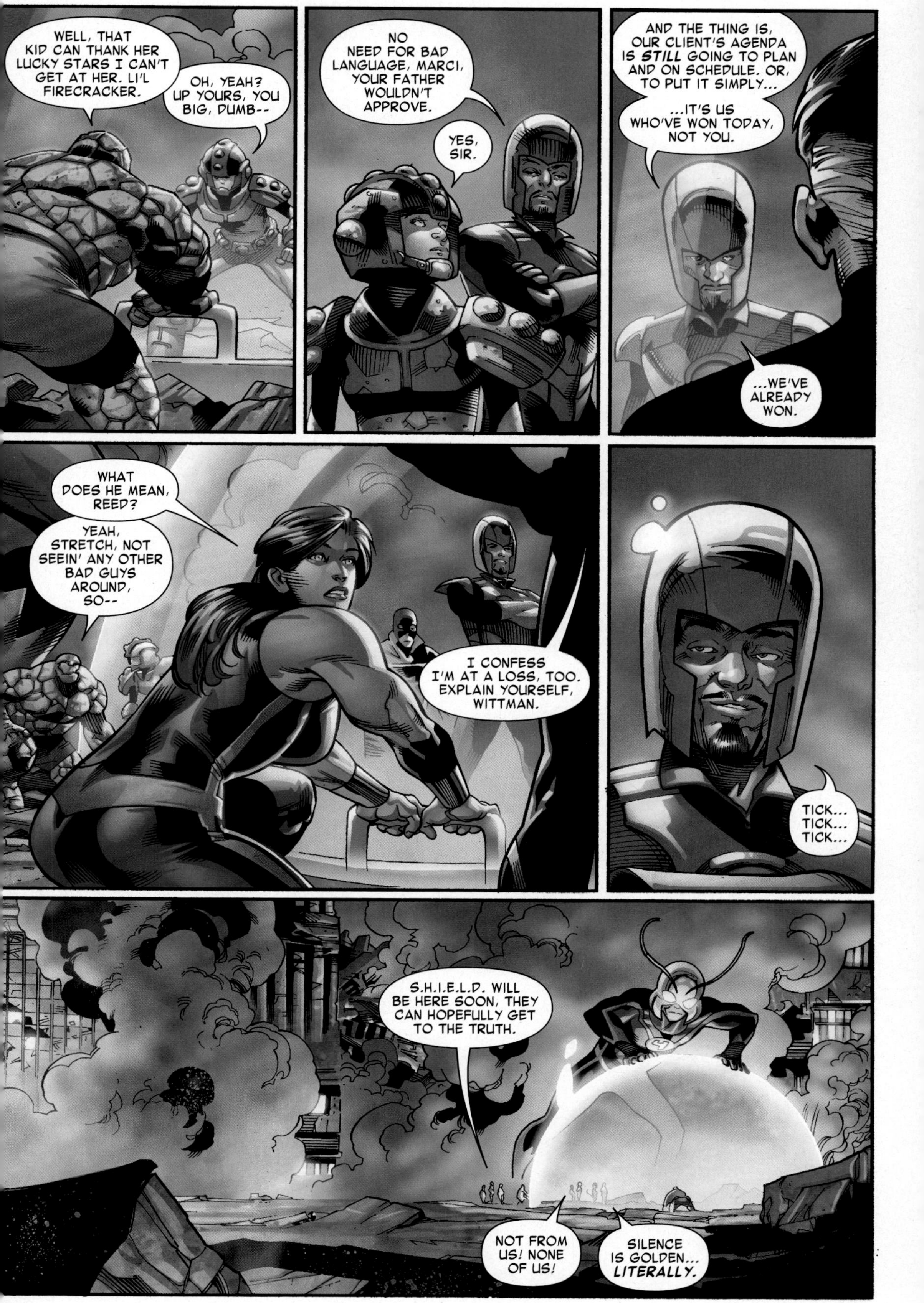
WELL, THAT KID CAN THANK HER LUCKY STARS I CAN'T GET AT HER. LI'L FIRECRACKER.
OH, YEAH? UP YOURS, YOU BIG, DUMB--
NO NEED FOR BAD LANGUAGE, MARCI, YOUR FATHER WOULDN'T APPROVE.
YES, SIR.
AND THE THING IS, OUR CLIENT'S AGENDA IS STILL GOING TO PLAN AND ON SCHEDULE. OR, TO PUT IT SIMPLY...
...IT'S US WHO'VE WON TODAY, NOT YOU.
...WE'VE ALREADY WON.
WHAT DOES HE MEAN, REED?
YEAH, STRETCH, NOT SEEIN' ANY OTHER BAD GUYS AROUND, SO--
I CONFESS I'M AT A LOSS, TOO. EXPLAIN YOURSELF, WITTMAN.
TICK... TICK... TICK...
S.H.I.E.L.D. WILL BE HERE SOON, THEY CAN HOPEFULLY GET TO THE TRUTH.
NOT FROM US! NONE OF US!
SILENCE IS GOLDEN... LITERALLY.

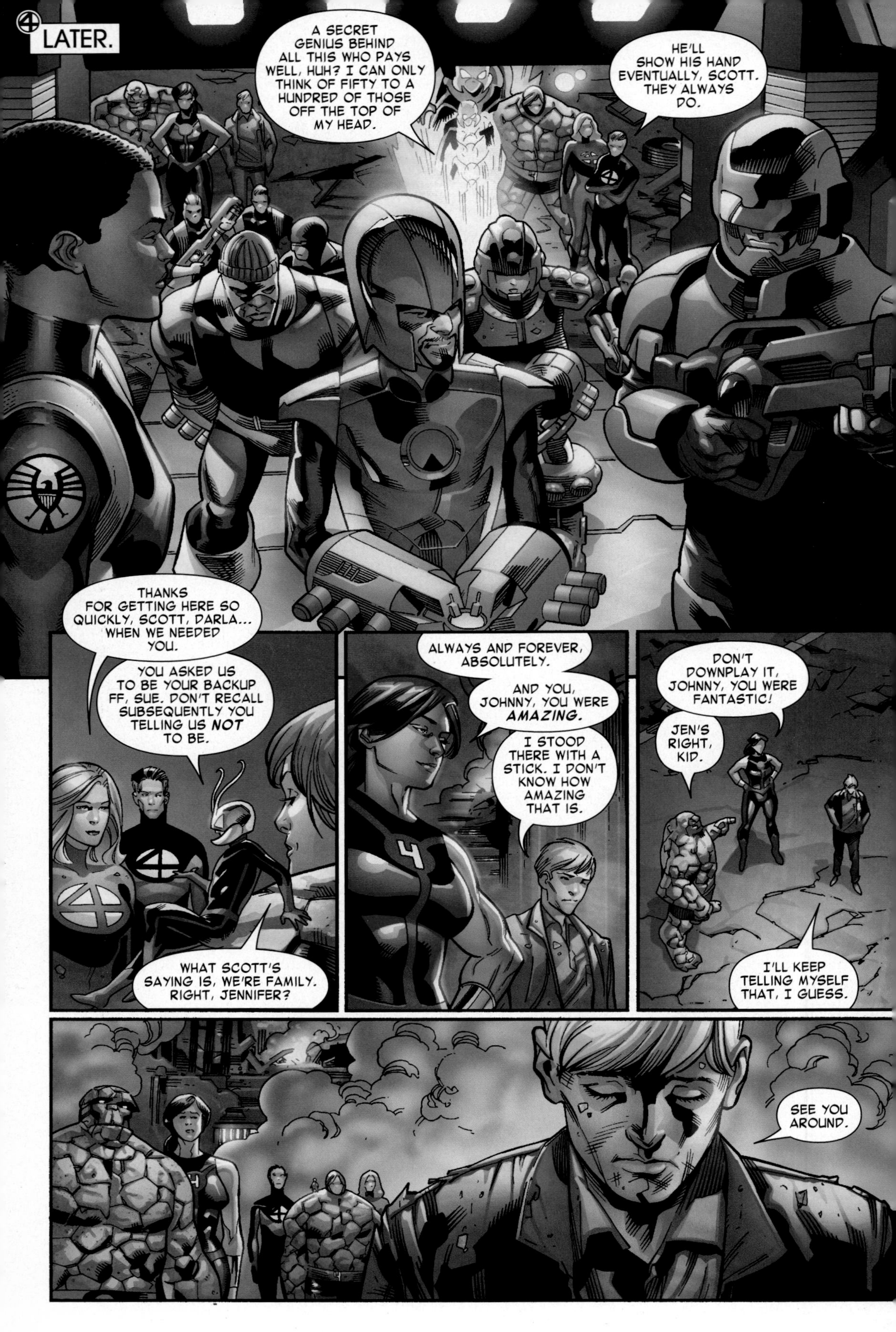
LATER.
A SECRET GENIUS BEHIND ALL THIS WHO PAYS WELL, HUH? I CAN ONLY THINK OF FIFTY TO A HUNDRED OF THOSE OFF THE TOP OF MY HEAD.
HE'LL SHOW HIS HAND EVENTUALLY, SCOTT. THEY ALWAYS DO.
THANKS FOR GETTING HERE SO QUICKLY, SCOTT, DARLA... WHEN WE NEEDED YOU.
YOU ASKED US TO BE YOUR BACKUP FF, SUE. DON'T RECALL SUBSEQUENTLY YOU TELLING US NOT TO BE.
WHAT SCOTT'S SAYING IS, WE'RE FAMILY. RIGHT, JENNIFER?
ALWAYS AND FOREVER, ABSOLUTELY.
AND YOU, JOHNNY, YOU WERE AMAZING.
I STOOD THERE WITH A STICK. I DON'T KNOW HOW AMAZING THAT IS.
DON'T DOWNPLAY IT, JOHNNY, YOU WERE FANTASTIC!
JEN'S RIGHT, KID.
I'LL KEEP TELLING MYSELF THAT, I GUESS.
SEE YOU AROUND.

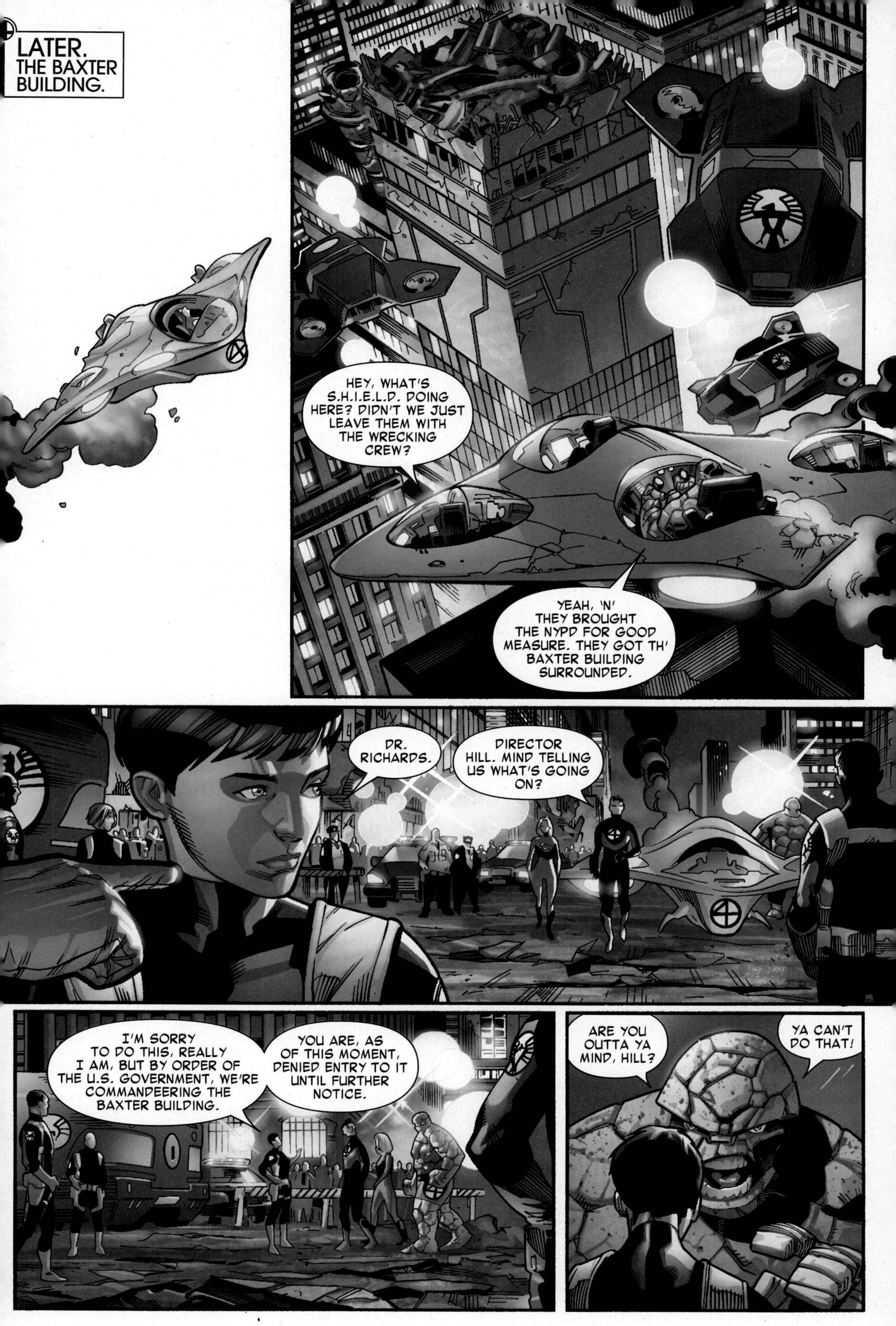
LATER. THE BAXTER BUILDING.
HEY, WHAT'S S.H.I.E.L.D. DOING HERE? DIDN'T WE JUST LEAVE THEM WITH THE WRECKING CREW?
YEAH, 'N' THEY BROUGHT THE NYPD FOR GOOD MEASURE. THEY GOT TH' BAXTER BUILDING SURROUNDED.
DR. RICHARDS.
DIRECTOR HILL. MIND TELLING US WHAT'S GOING ON?
I'M SORRY TO DO THIS, REALLY I AM, BUT BY ORDER OF THE U.S. GOVERNMENT, WE'RE COMMANDEERING THE BAXTER BUILDING.
YOU ARE, AS OF THIS MOMENT, DENIED ENTRY TO IT UNTIL FURTHER NOTICE.
ARE YOU OUTTA YA MIND, HILL?
YA CAN'T DO THAT!

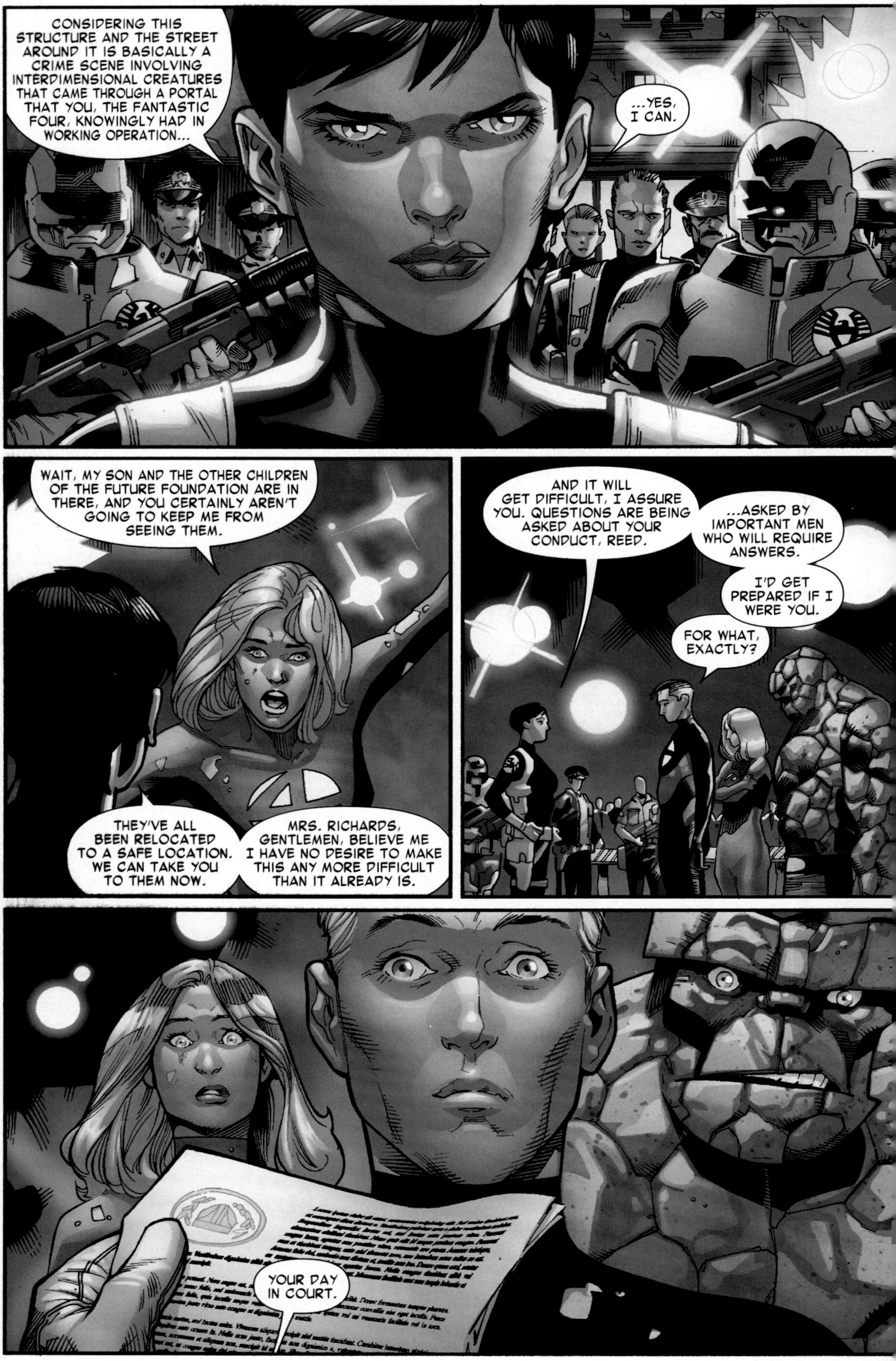
CONSIDERING THIS STRUCTURE AND THE STREET AROUND IT IS BASICALLY A CRIME SCENE INVOLVING INTERDIMENSIONAL CREATURES THAT CAME THROUGH A PORTAL THAT YOU, THE FANTASTIC FOUR, KNOWINGLY HAD IN WORKING OPERATION...
...YES, I CAN.
WAIT, MY SON AND THE OTHER CHILDREN OF THE FUTURE FOUNDATION ARE IN THERE, AND YOU CERTAINLY AREN'T GOING TO KEEP ME FROM SEEING THEM.
THEY'VE ALL BEEN RELOCATED TO A SAFE LOCATION. WE CAN TAKE YOU TO THEM NOW.
MRS. RICHARDS, GENTLEMEN, BELIEVE ME I HAVE NO DESIRE TO MAKE THIS ANY MORE DIFFICULT THAN IT ALREADY IS.
AND IT WILL GET DIFFICULT, I ASSURE YOU. QUESTIONS ARE BEING ASKED ABOUT YOUR CONDUCT, REED.
...ASKED BY IMPORTANT MEN WHO WILL REQUIRE ANSWERS.
I'D GET PREPARED IF I WERE YOU.
FOR WHAT, EXACTLY?
YOUR DAY IN COURT.

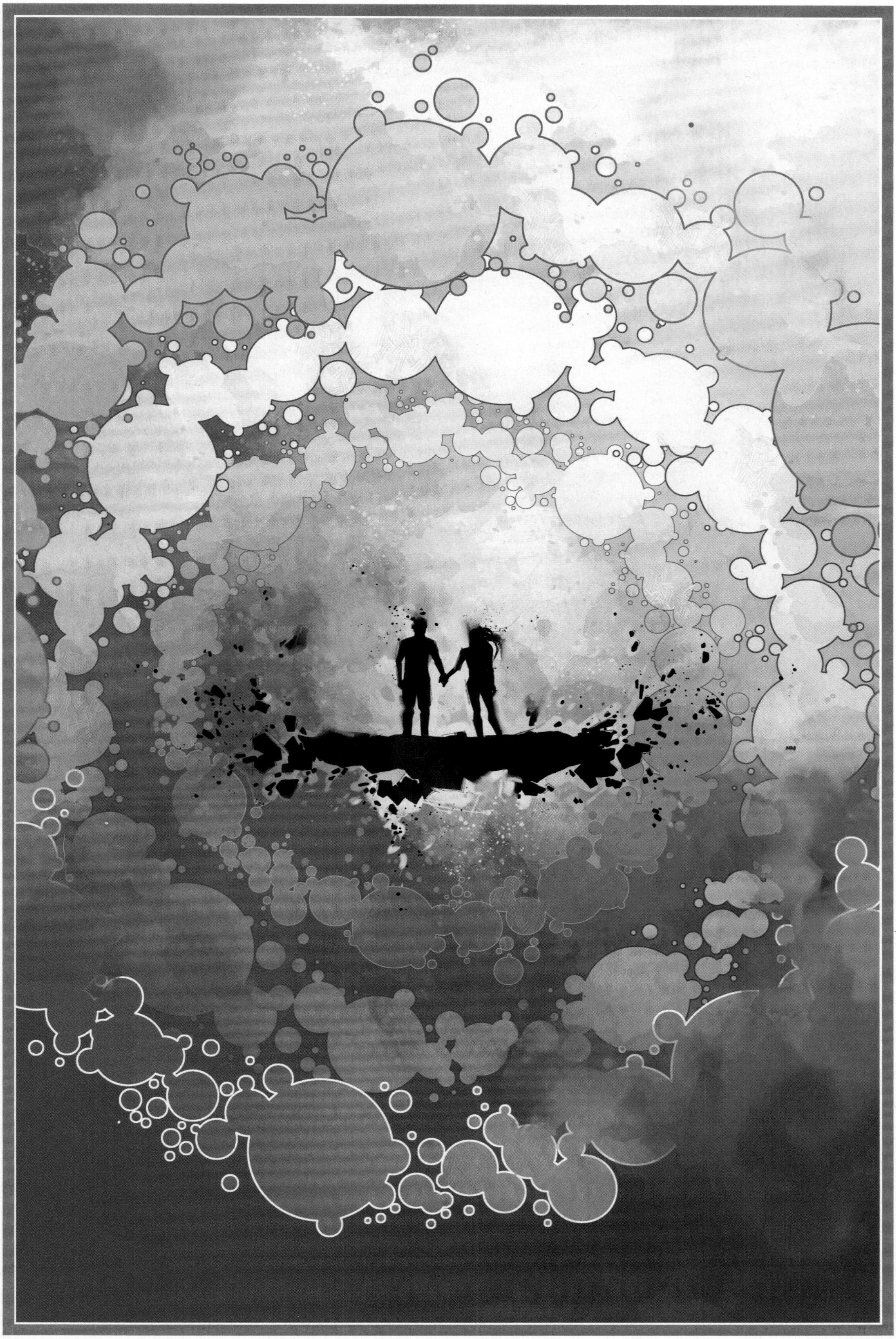

FIVE • variant by Jonathan Hickman

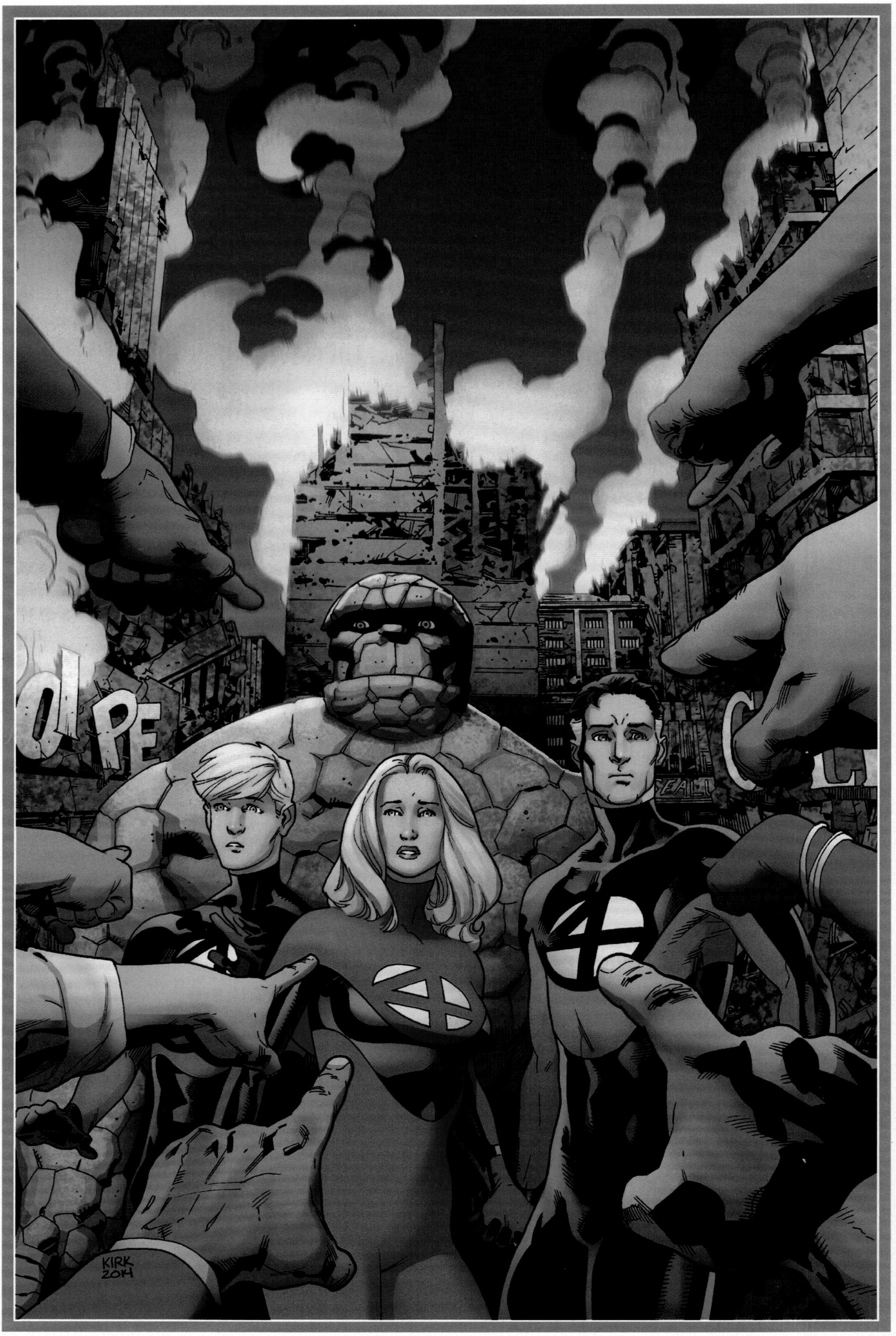
KIRK
2014

FIVE

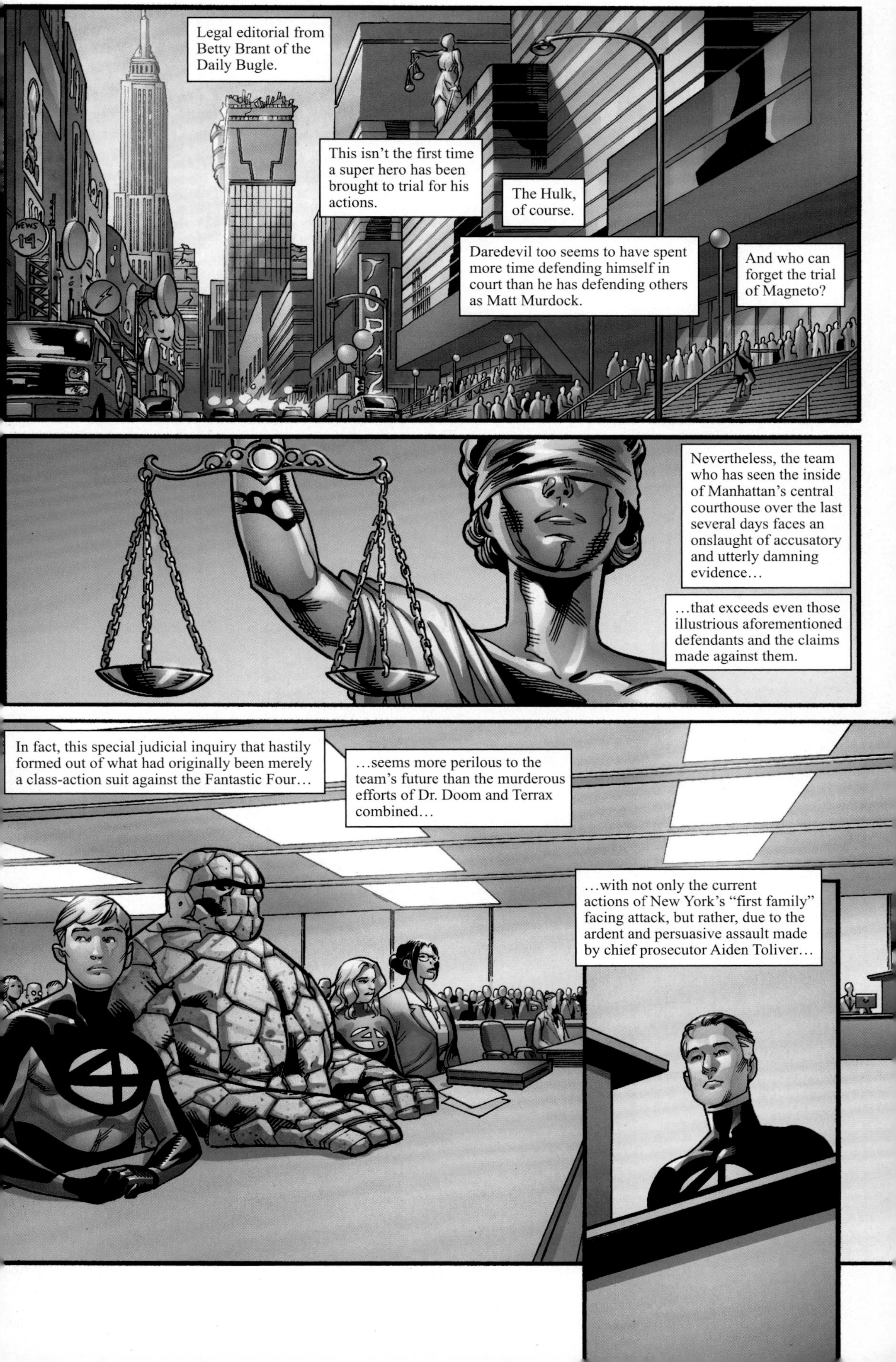
Legal editorial from Betty Brant of the Daily Bugle.
This isn't the first time a super hero has been brought to trial for his actions.
The Hulk, of course.
Daredevil too seems to have spent more time defending himself in court than he has defending others as Matt Murdock.
And who can forget the trial of Magneto?
Nevertheless, the team who has seen the inside of Manhattan's central courthouse over the last several days faces an onslaught of accusatory and utterly damning evidence…
…that exceeds even those illustrious aforementioned defendants and the claims made against them.
In fact, this special judicial inquiry that hastily formed out of what had originally been merely a class-action suit against the Fantastic Four…
…seems more perilous to the team's future than the murderous efforts of Dr. Doom and Terrax combined…
…with not only the current actions of New York's "first family" facing attack, but rather, due to the ardent and persuasive assault made by chief prosecutor Aiden Toliver…

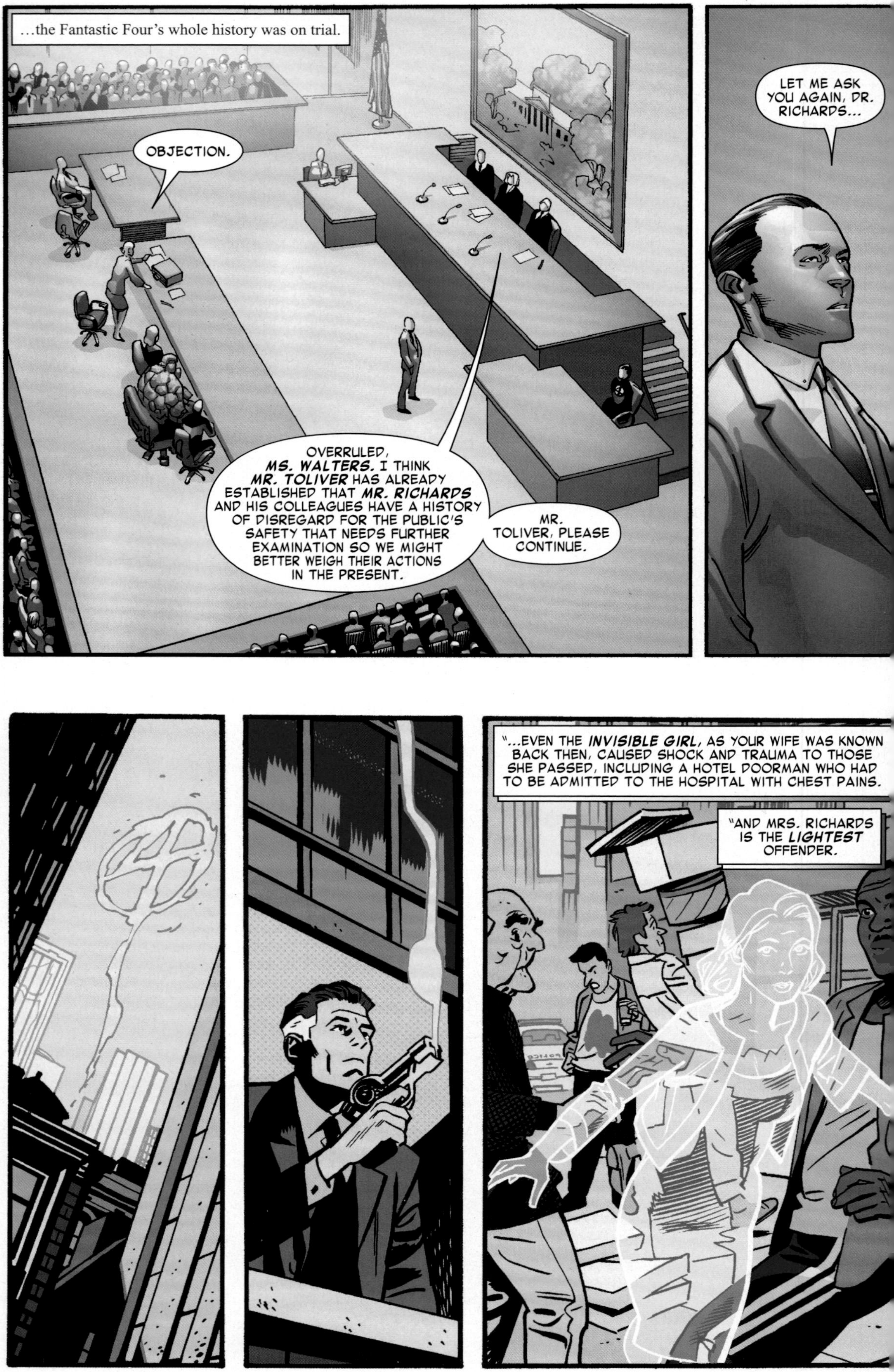
…the Fantastic Four's whole history was on trial.
OBJECTION.
OVERRULED, MS. WALTERS. I THINK MR. TOLIVER HAS ALREADY ESTABLISHED THAT MR. RICHARDS AND HIS COLLEAGUES HAVE A HISTORY OF DISREGARD FOR THE PUBLIC'S SAFETY THAT NEEDS FURTHER EXAMINATION SO WE MIGHT BETTER WEIGH THEIR ACTIONS IN THE PRESENT.
MR. TOLIVER, PLEASE CONTINUE.
LET ME ASK YOU AGAIN, DR. RICHARDS...
"...EVEN THE INVISIBLE GIRL, AS YOUR WIFE WAS KNOWN BACK THEN, CAUSED SHOCK AND TRAUMA TO THOSE SHE PASSED, INCLUDING A HOTEL DOORMAN WHO HAD TO BE ADMITTED TO THE HOSPITAL WITH CHEST PAINS.
"AND MRS. RICHARDS IS THE LIGHTEST OFFENDER.

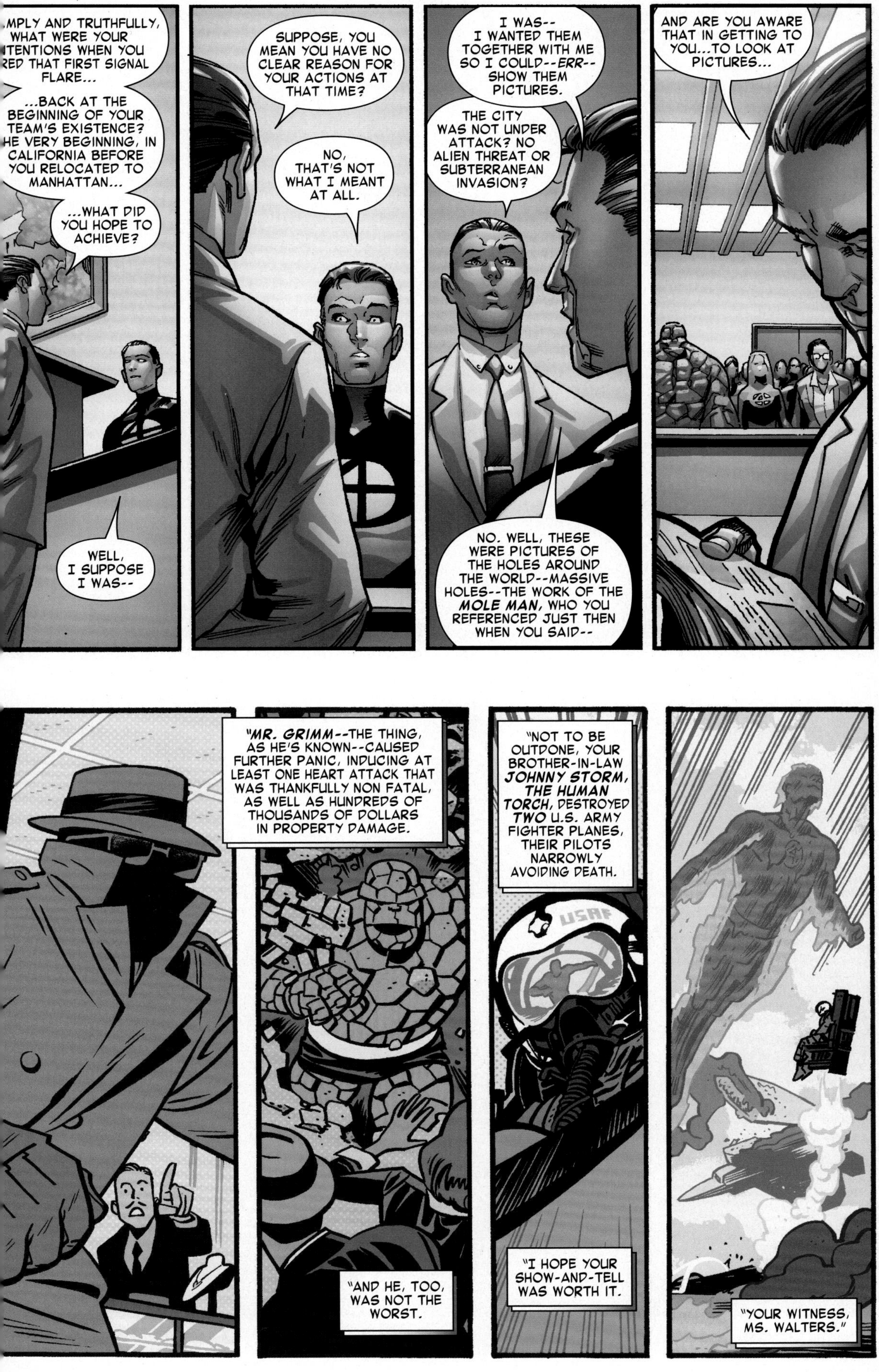

...MPLY AND TRUTHFULLY, WHAT WERE YOUR ...NTENTIONS WHEN YOU ...RED THAT FIRST SIGNAL FLARE...
...BACK AT THE BEGINNING OF YOUR TEAM'S EXISTENCE? ...HE VERY BEGINNING, IN CALIFORNIA BEFORE YOU RELOCATED TO MANHATTAN...
...WHAT DID YOU HOPE TO ACHIEVE?
WELL, I SUPPOSE I WAS--
SUPPOSE, YOU MEAN YOU HAVE NO CLEAR REASON FOR YOUR ACTIONS AT THAT TIME?
NO, THAT'S NOT WHAT I MEANT AT ALL.
I WAS-- I WANTED THEM TOGETHER WITH ME SO I COULD--ERR-- SHOW THEM PICTURES.
THE CITY WAS NOT UNDER ATTACK? NO ALIEN THREAT OR SUBTERRANEAN INVASION?
NO. WELL, THESE WERE PICTURES OF THE HOLES AROUND THE WORLD--MASSIVE HOLES--THE WORK OF THE MOLE MAN, WHO YOU REFERENCED JUST THEN WHEN YOU SAID--
AND ARE YOU AWARE THAT IN GETTING TO YOU...TO LOOK AT PICTURES...
"MR. GRIMM--THE THING, AS HE'S KNOWN--CAUSED FURTHER PANIC, INDUCING AT LEAST ONE HEART ATTACK THAT WAS THANKFULLY NON FATAL, AS WELL AS HUNDREDS OF THOUSANDS OF DOLLARS IN PROPERTY DAMAGE.
"AND HE, TOO, WAS NOT THE WORST.
"NOT TO BE OUTDONE, YOUR BROTHER-IN-LAW JOHNNY STORM, THE HUMAN TORCH, DESTROYED TWO U.S. ARMY FIGHTER PLANES, THEIR PILOTS NARROWLY AVOIDING DEATH.
USAF
"I HOPE YOUR SHOW-AND-TELL WAS WORTH IT.
"YOUR WITNESS, MS. WALTERS."

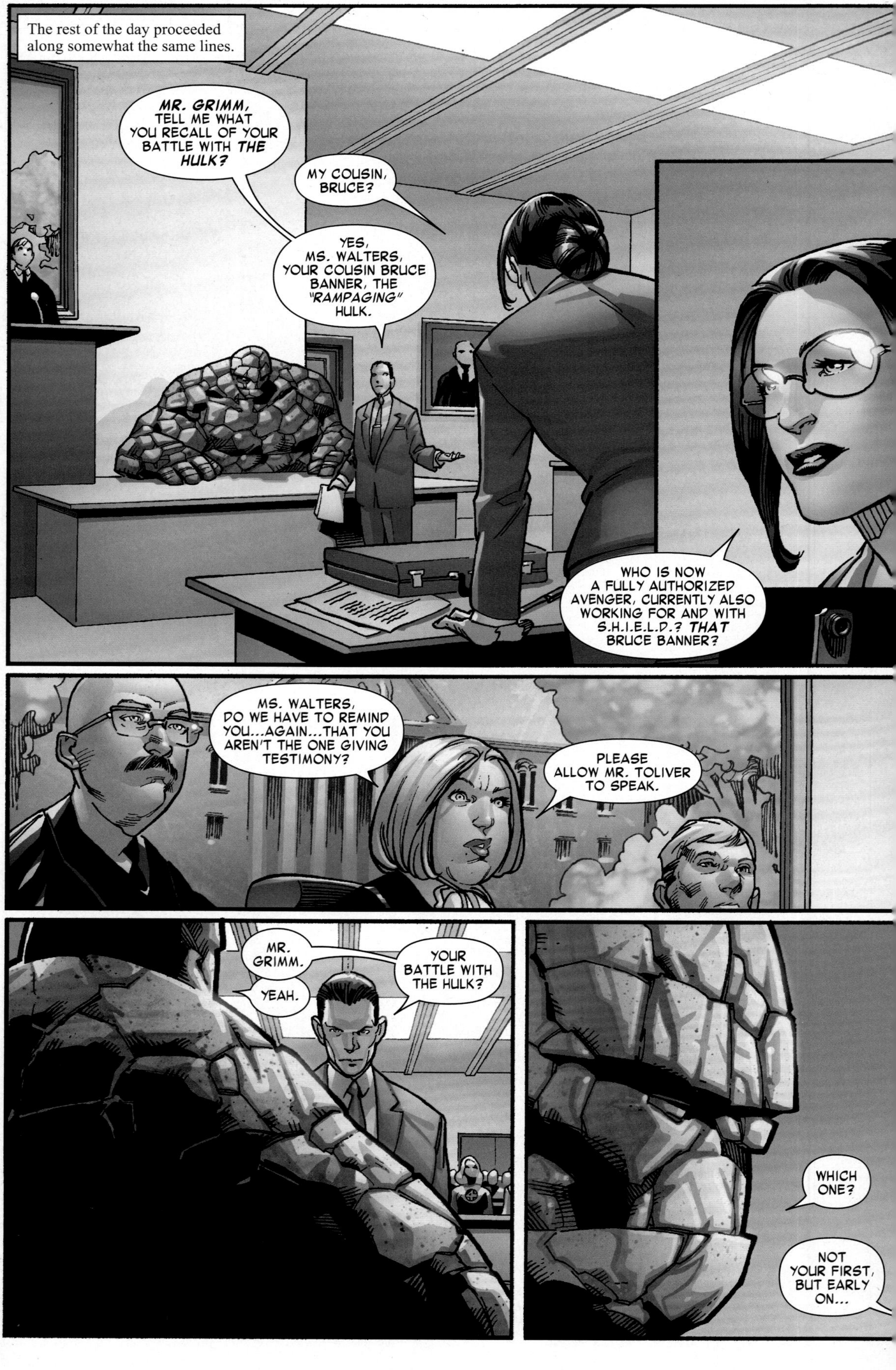
The rest of the day proceeded along somewhat the same lines.
MR. GRIMM, TELL ME WHAT YOU RECALL OF YOUR BATTLE WITH THE HULK?
MY COUSIN, BRUCE?
YES, MS. WALTERS, YOUR COUSIN BRUCE BANNER, THE "RAMPAGING" HULK.
WHO IS NOW A FULLY AUTHORIZED AVENGER, CURRENTLY ALSO WORKING FOR AND WITH S.H.I.E.L.D.? THAT BRUCE BANNER?
MS. WALTERS, DO WE HAVE TO REMIND YOU...AGAIN...THAT YOU AREN'T THE ONE GIVING TESTIMONY?
PLEASE ALLOW MR. TOLIVER TO SPEAK.
MR. GRIMM.
YEAH.
YOUR BATTLE WITH THE HULK?
WHICH ONE?
NOT YOUR FIRST, BUT EARLY ON...

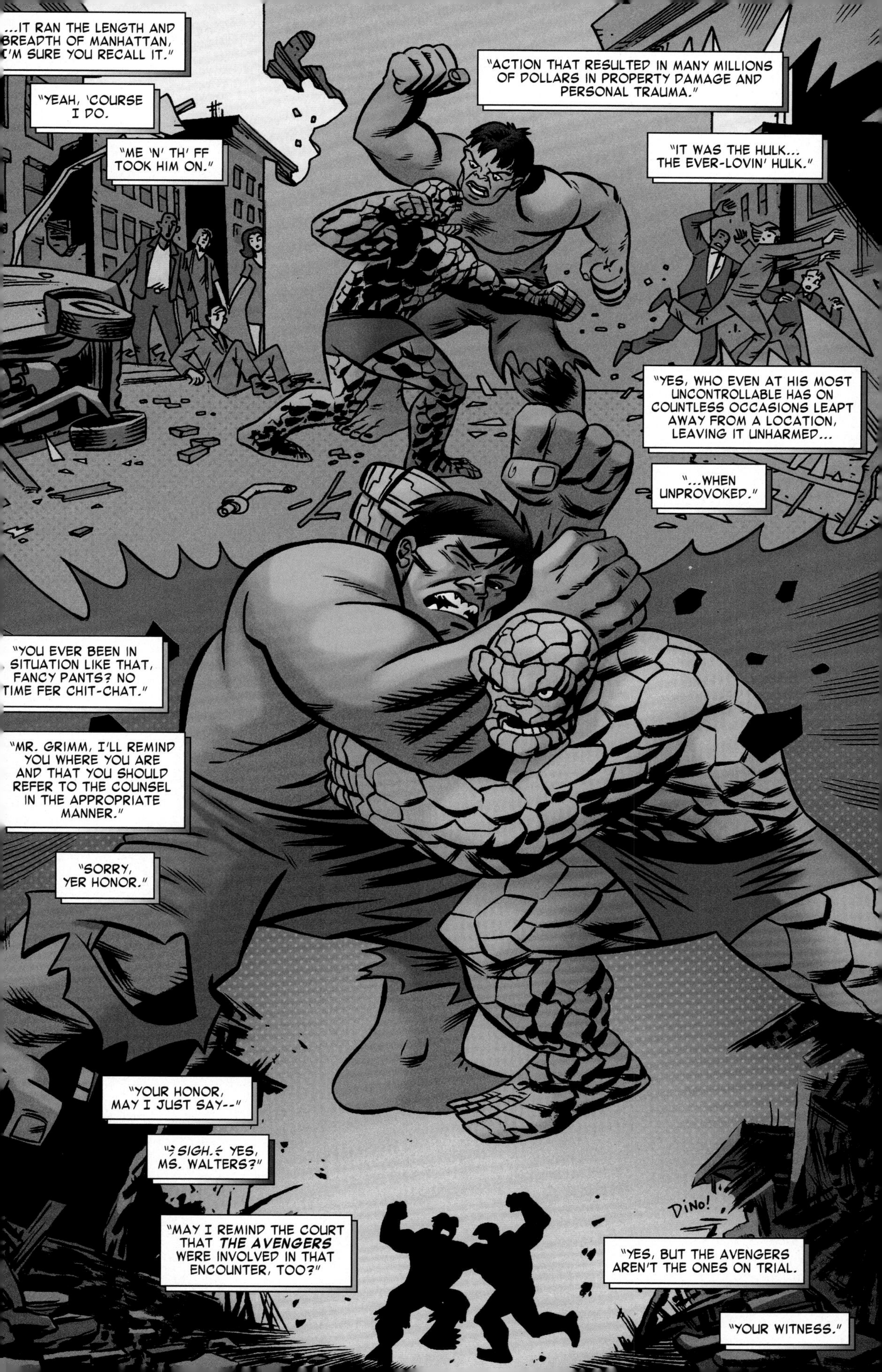

...IT RAN THE LENGTH AND BREADTH OF MANHATTAN, I'M SURE YOU RECALL IT."
"YEAH, 'COURSE I DO.
"ME 'N' TH' FF TOOK HIM ON."
"ACTION THAT RESULTED IN MANY MILLIONS OF DOLLARS IN PROPERTY DAMAGE AND PERSONAL TRAUMA."
"IT WAS THE HULK... THE EVER-LOVIN' HULK."
"YES, WHO EVEN AT HIS MOST UNCONTROLLABLE HAS ON COUNTLESS OCCASIONS LEAPT AWAY FROM A LOCATION, LEAVING IT UNHARMED...
"...WHEN UNPROVOKED."
"YOU EVER BEEN IN SITUATION LIKE THAT, FANCY PANTS? NO TIME FER CHIT-CHAT."
"MR. GRIMM, I'LL REMIND YOU WHERE YOU ARE AND THAT YOU SHOULD REFER TO THE COUNSEL IN THE APPROPRIATE MANNER."
"SORRY, YER HONOR."
"YOUR HONOR, MAY I JUST SAY--"
"SIGH. YES, MS. WALTERS?"
"MAY I REMIND THE COURT THAT *THE AVENGERS* WERE INVOLVED IN THAT ENCOUNTER, TOO?"
DINO!
"YES, BUT THE AVENGERS AREN'T THE ONES ON TRIAL.
"YOUR WITNESS."

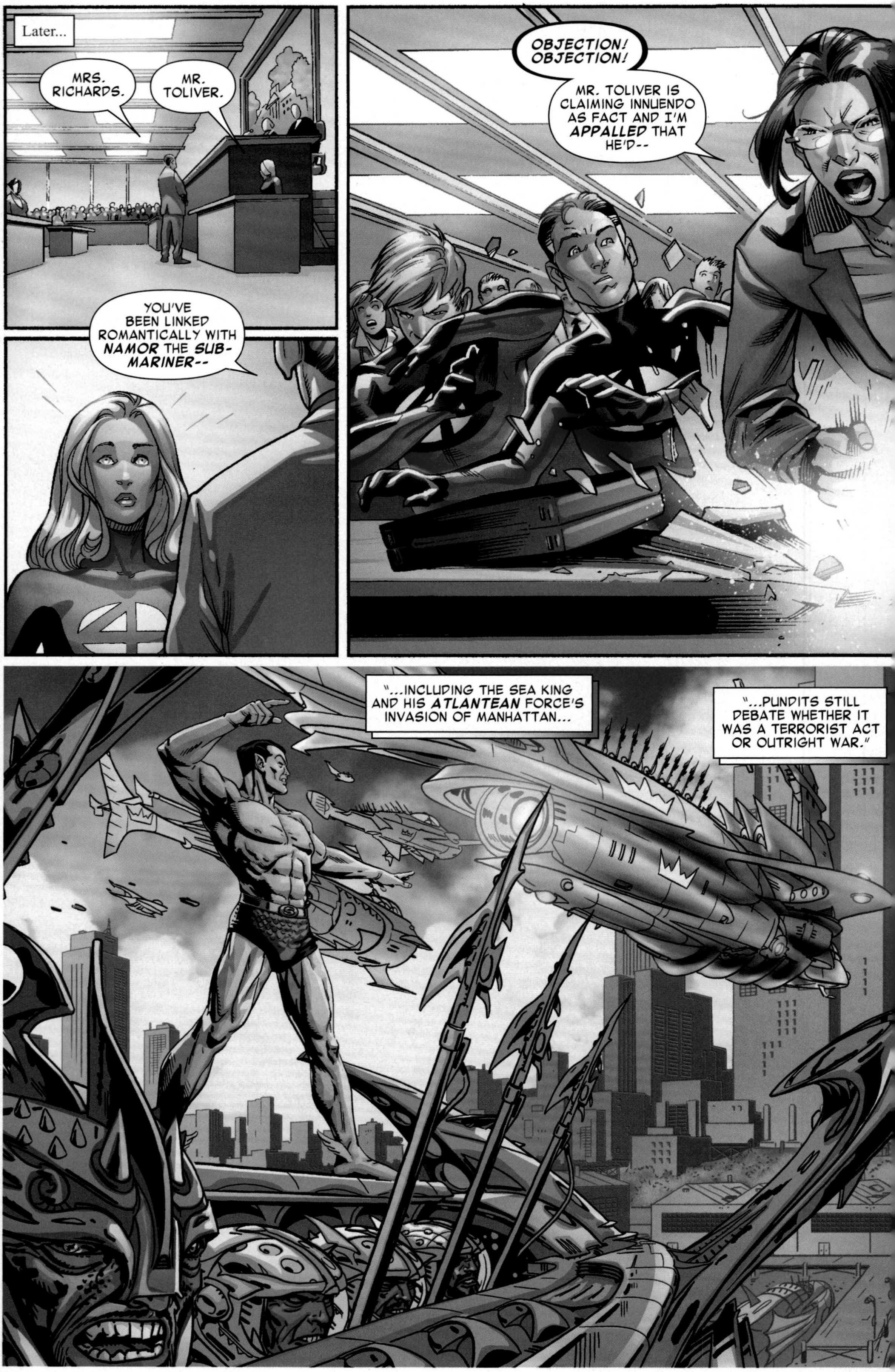

Later...
MRS. RICHARDS.
MR. TOLIVER.
YOU'VE BEEN LINKED ROMANTICALLY WITH NAMOR THE SUB-MARINER--
OBJECTION! OBJECTION!
MR. TOLIVER IS CLAIMING INNUENDO AS FACT AND I'M APPALLED THAT HE'D--
"...INCLUDING THE SEA KING AND HIS ATLANTEAN FORCE'S INVASION OF MANHATTAN...
"...PUNDITS STILL DEBATE WHETHER IT WAS A TERRORIST ACT OR OUTRIGHT WAR."

I WITHDRAW THE QUESTION.

OH, REALLY, MR. TOLIVER? I DIDN'T REALIZE YOU'D ASKED ONE...

YOU MERELY CITED SOME GOSSIP FROM THE TABLOIDS OF A FEW YEARS BACK.

NONE IF WHICH IS TRUE, BY THE WAY.

NAMOR AND I--HE AND THE WHOLE FANTASTIC FOUR, I SHOULD SAY--HAVE ENJOYED A MUTUAL REGARD WHICH STEMS FROM OUR MANY ENCOUNTERS OVER THE YEARS.

YES, YOU HAVE QUITE A LIST OF THEM BY NOW, I IMAGINE...

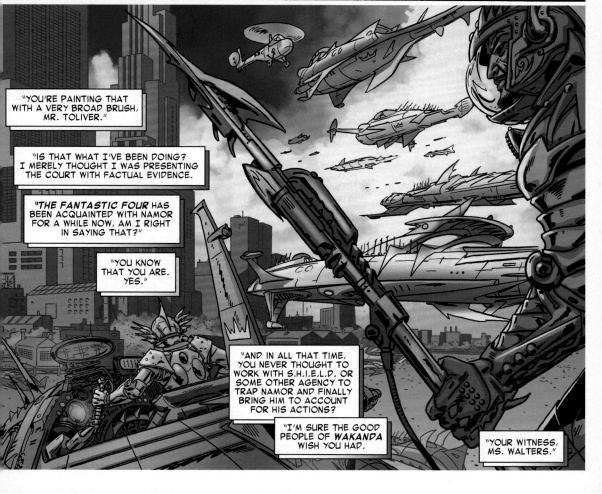

"YOU'RE PAINTING THAT WITH A VERY BROAD BRUSH, MR. TOLIVER."

"IS THAT WHAT I'VE BEEN DOING? I MERELY THOUGHT I WAS PRESENTING THE COURT WITH FACTUAL EVIDENCE.

"*THE FANTASTIC FOUR* HAS BEEN ACQUAINTED WITH NAMOR FOR A WHILE NOW, AM I RIGHT IN SAYING THAT?"

"YOU KNOW THAT YOU ARE. YES."

"AND IN ALL THAT TIME, YOU NEVER THOUGHT TO WORK WITH S.H.I.E.L.D. OR SOME OTHER AGENCY TO TRAP NAMOR AND FINALLY BRING HIM TO ACCOUNT FOR HIS ACTIONS?

"I'M SURE THE GOOD PEOPLE OF *WAKANDA* WISH YOU HAD.

"YOUR WITNESS, MS. WALTERS."

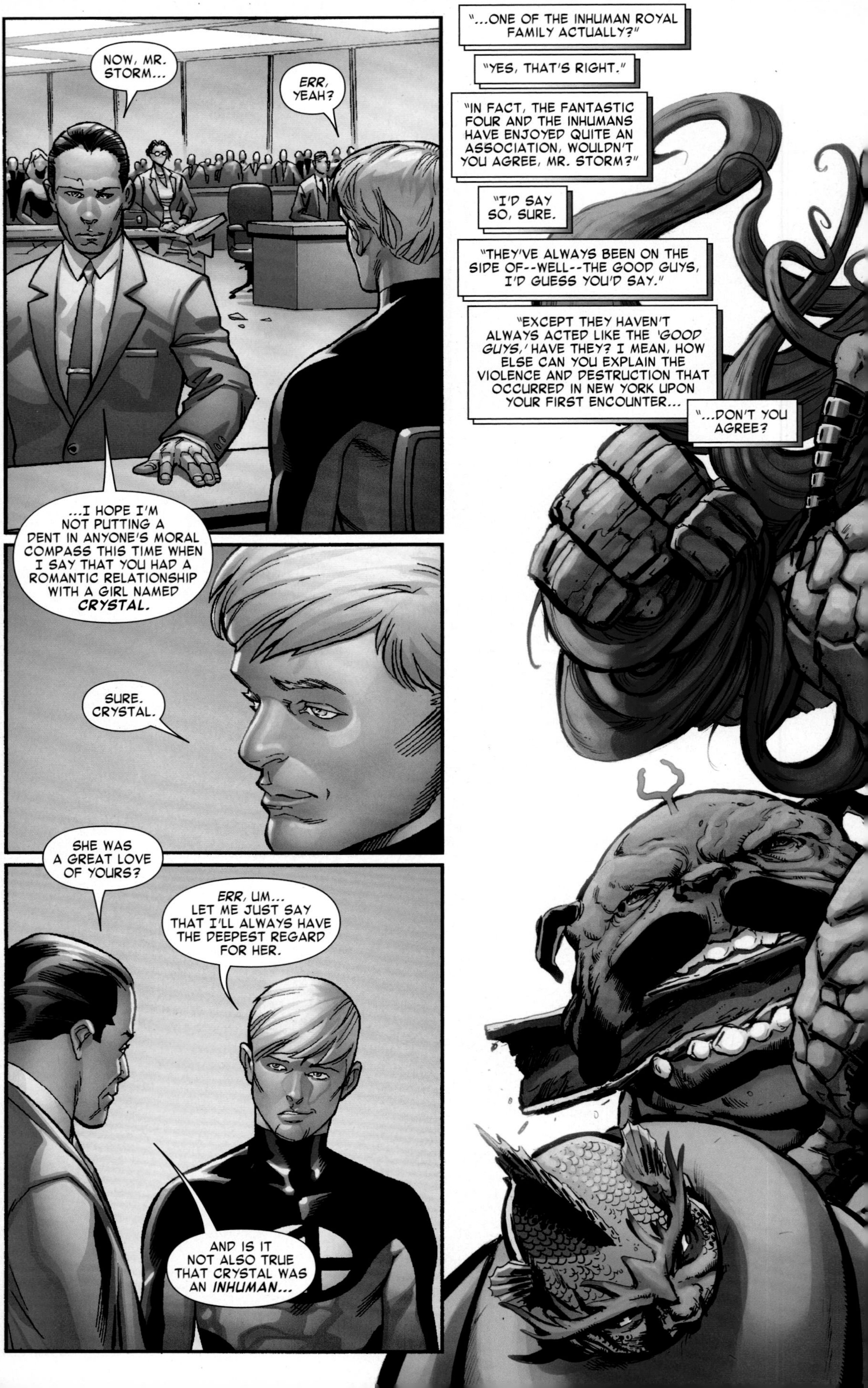
NOW, MR. STORM...
ERR, YEAH?
...I HOPE I'M NOT PUTTING A DENT IN ANYONE'S MORAL COMPASS THIS TIME WHEN I SAY THAT YOU HAD A ROMANTIC RELATIONSHIP WITH A GIRL NAMED CRYSTAL.
SURE. CRYSTAL.
SHE WAS A GREAT LOVE OF YOURS?
ERR, UM... LET ME JUST SAY THAT I'LL ALWAYS HAVE THE DEEPEST REGARD FOR HER.
AND IS IT NOT ALSO TRUE THAT CRYSTAL WAS AN INHUMAN...
"...ONE OF THE INHUMAN ROYAL FAMILY ACTUALLY?"
"YES, THAT'S RIGHT."
"IN FACT, THE FANTASTIC FOUR AND THE INHUMANS HAVE ENJOYED QUITE AN ASSOCIATION, WOULDN'T YOU AGREE, MR. STORM?"
"I'D SAY SO, SURE.
"THEY'VE ALWAYS BEEN ON THE SIDE OF--WELL--THE GOOD GUYS, I'D GUESS YOU'D SAY."
"EXCEPT THEY HAVEN'T ALWAYS ACTED LIKE THE 'GOOD GUYS,' HAVE THEY? I MEAN, HOW ELSE CAN YOU EXPLAIN THE VIOLENCE AND DESTRUCTION THAT OCCURRED IN NEW YORK UPON YOUR FIRST ENCOUNTER...
"...DON'T YOU AGREE?

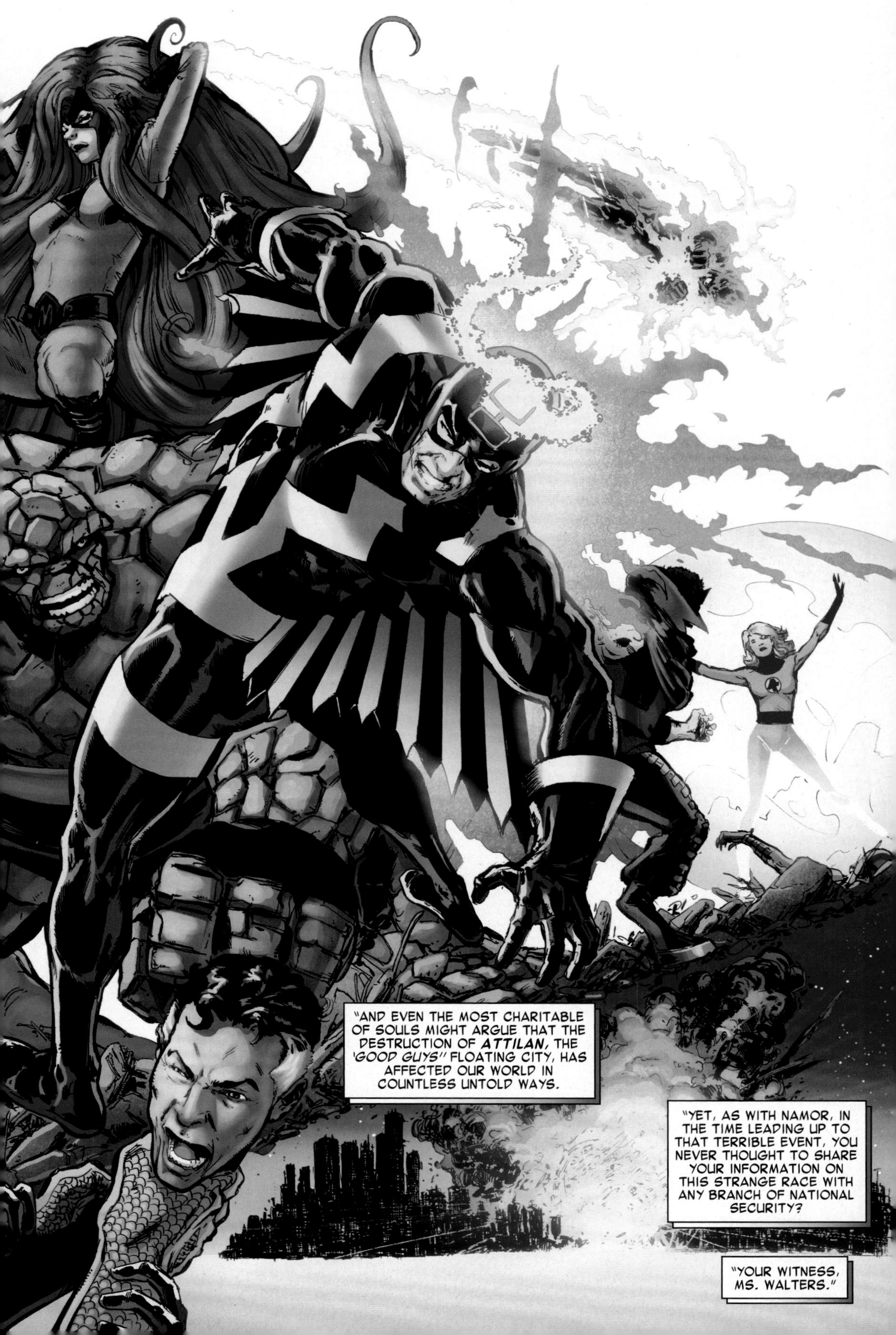
"AND EVEN THE MOST CHARITABLE OF SOULS MIGHT ARGUE THAT THE DESTRUCTION OF ATTILAN, THE 'GOOD GUYS'' FLOATING CITY, HAS AFFECTED OUR WORLD IN COUNTLESS UNTOLD WAYS.
"YET, AS WITH NAMOR, IN THE TIME LEADING UP TO THAT TERRIBLE EVENT, YOU NEVER THOUGHT TO SHARE YOUR INFORMATION ON THIS STRANGE RACE WITH ANY BRANCH OF NATIONAL SECURITY?
"YOUR WITNESS, MS. WALTERS."

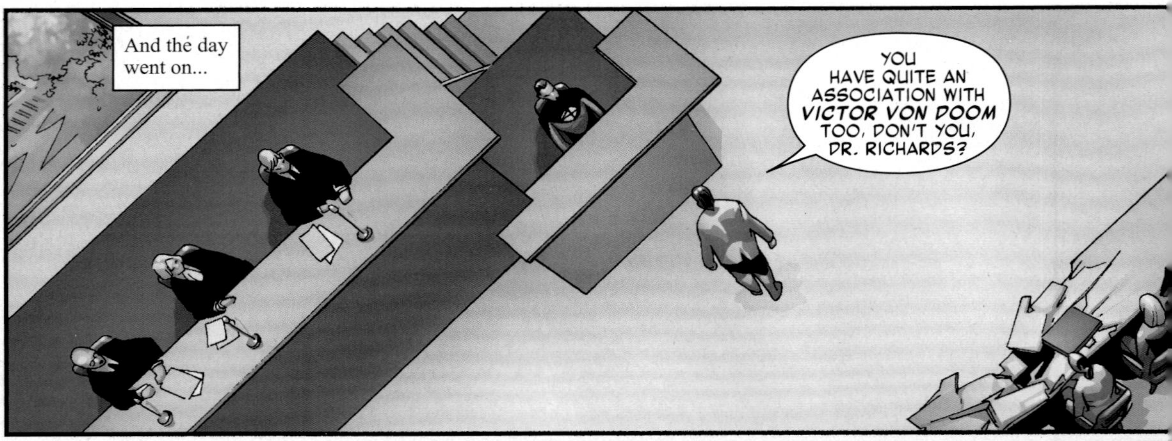
And thé day went on...
YOU HAVE QUITE AN ASSOCIATION WITH VICTOR VON DOOM TOO, DON'T YOU, DR. RICHARDS?

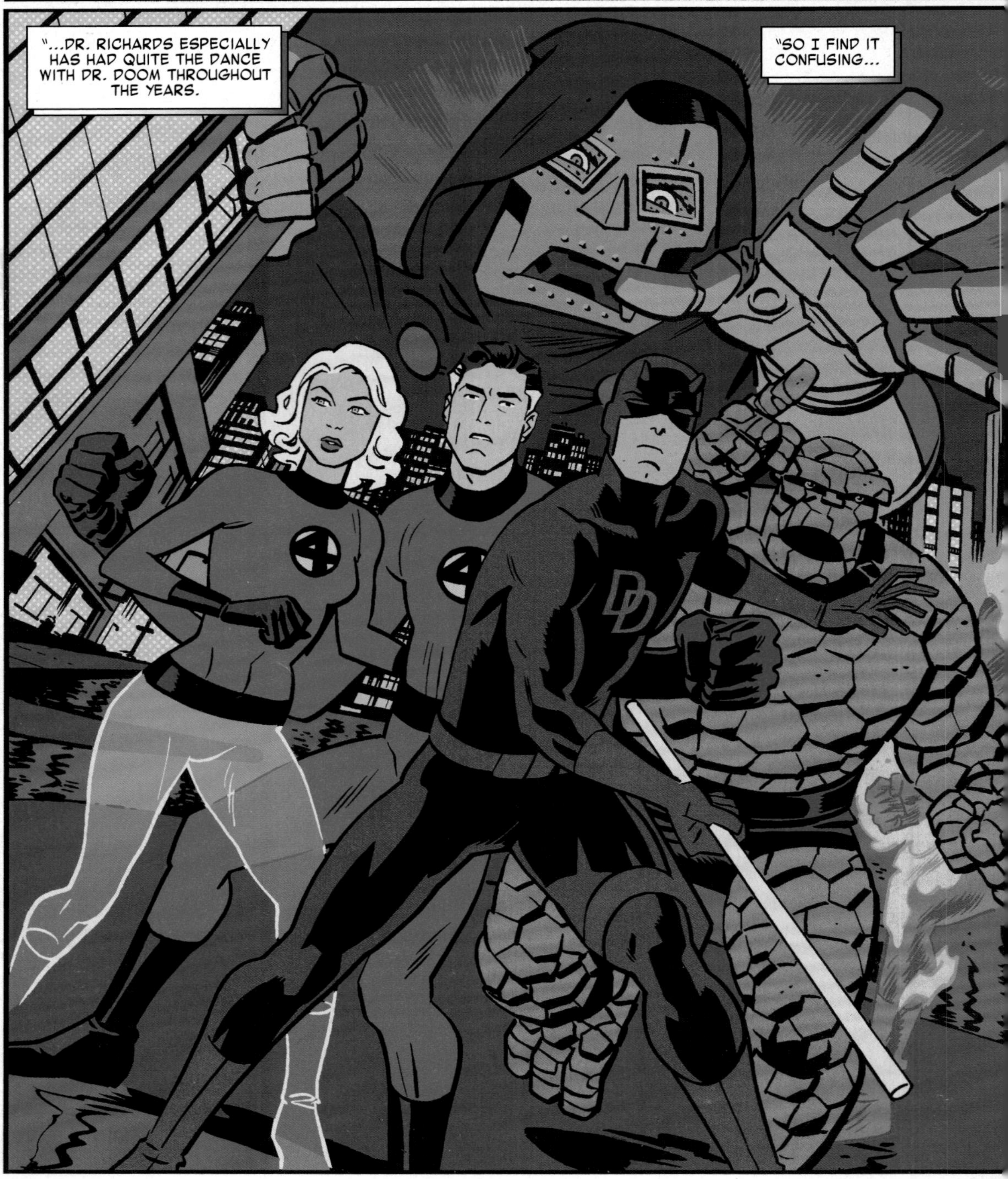
"...DR. RICHARDS ESPECIALLY HAS HAD QUITE THE DANCE WITH DR. DOOM THROUGHOUT THE YEARS.
"SO I FIND IT CONFUSING...

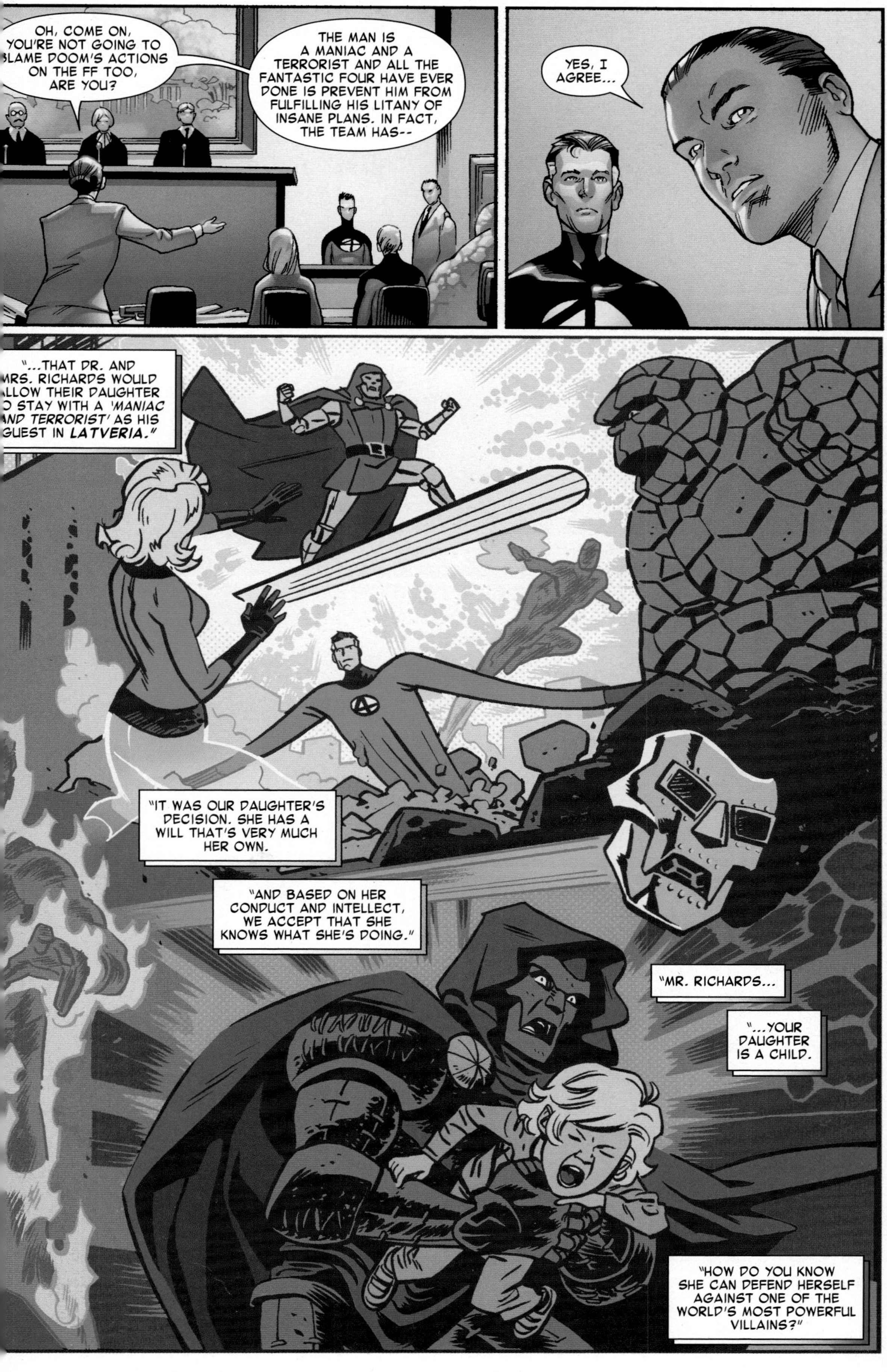
OH, COME ON, YOU'RE NOT GOING TO LAME DOOM'S ACTIONS ON THE FF TOO, ARE YOU?
THE MAN IS A MANIAC AND A TERRORIST AND ALL THE FANTASTIC FOUR HAVE EVER DONE IS PREVENT HIM FROM FULFILLING HIS LITANY OF INSANE PLANS. IN FACT, THE TEAM HAS--
YES, I AGREE...
"...THAT DR. AND RS. RICHARDS WOULD LLOW THEIR DAUGHTER O STAY WITH A 'MANIAC ND TERRORIST' AS HIS GUEST IN LATVERIA."
"IT WAS OUR DAUGHTER'S DECISION. SHE HAS A WILL THAT'S VERY MUCH HER OWN.
"AND BASED ON HER CONDUCT AND INTELLECT, WE ACCEPT THAT SHE KNOWS WHAT SHE'S DOING."
"MR. RICHARDS...
"...YOUR DAUGHTER IS A CHILD.
"HOW DO YOU KNOW SHE CAN DEFEND HERSELF AGAINST ONE OF THE WORLD'S MOST POWERFUL VILLAINS?"

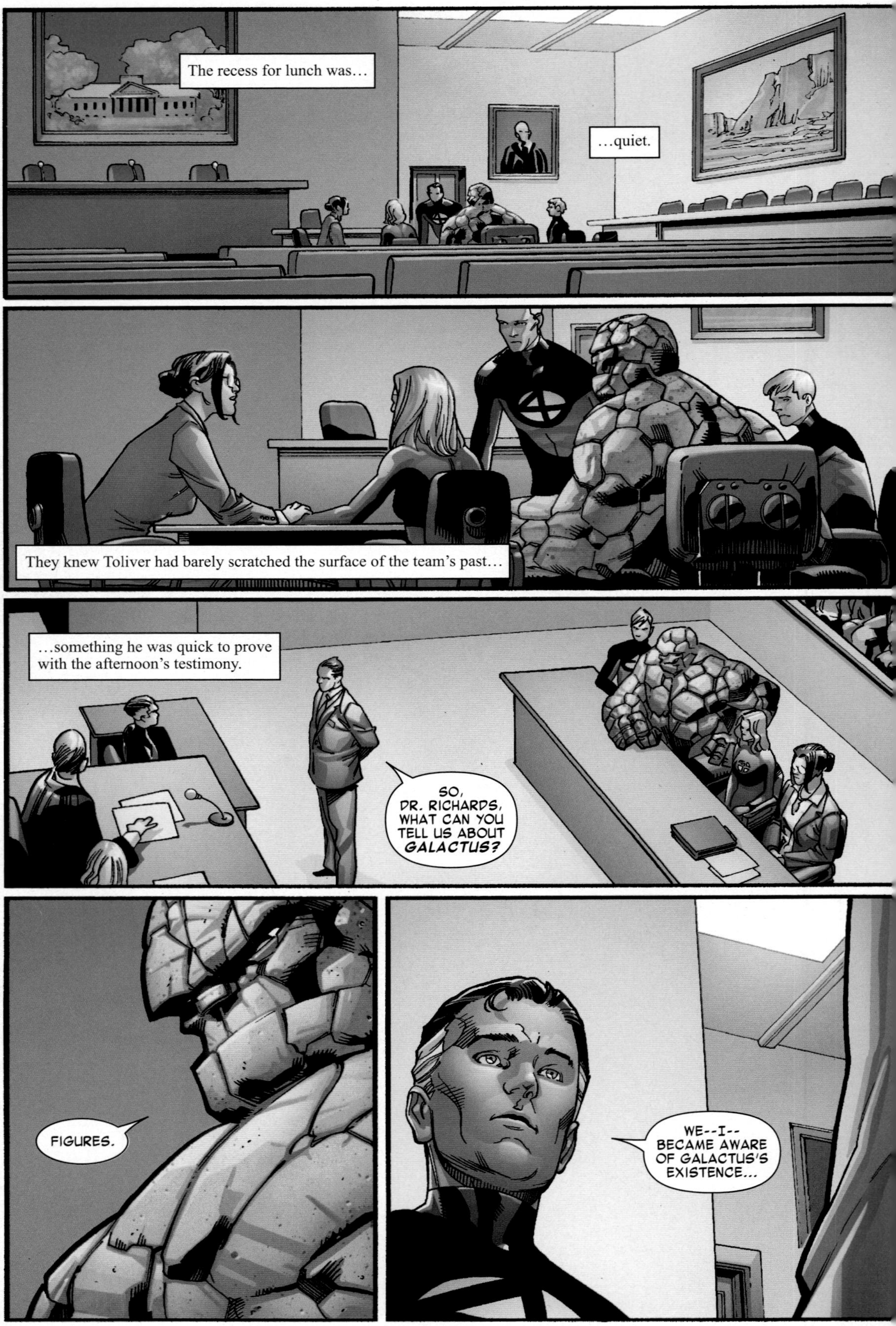

The recess for lunch was...
...quiet.
They knew Toliver had barely scratched the surface of the team's past...
...something he was quick to prove with the afternoon's testimony.
SO, DR. RICHARDS, WHAT CAN YOU TELL US ABOUT GALACTUS?
FIGURES.
WE--I-- BECAME AWARE OF GALACTUS'S EXISTENCE...

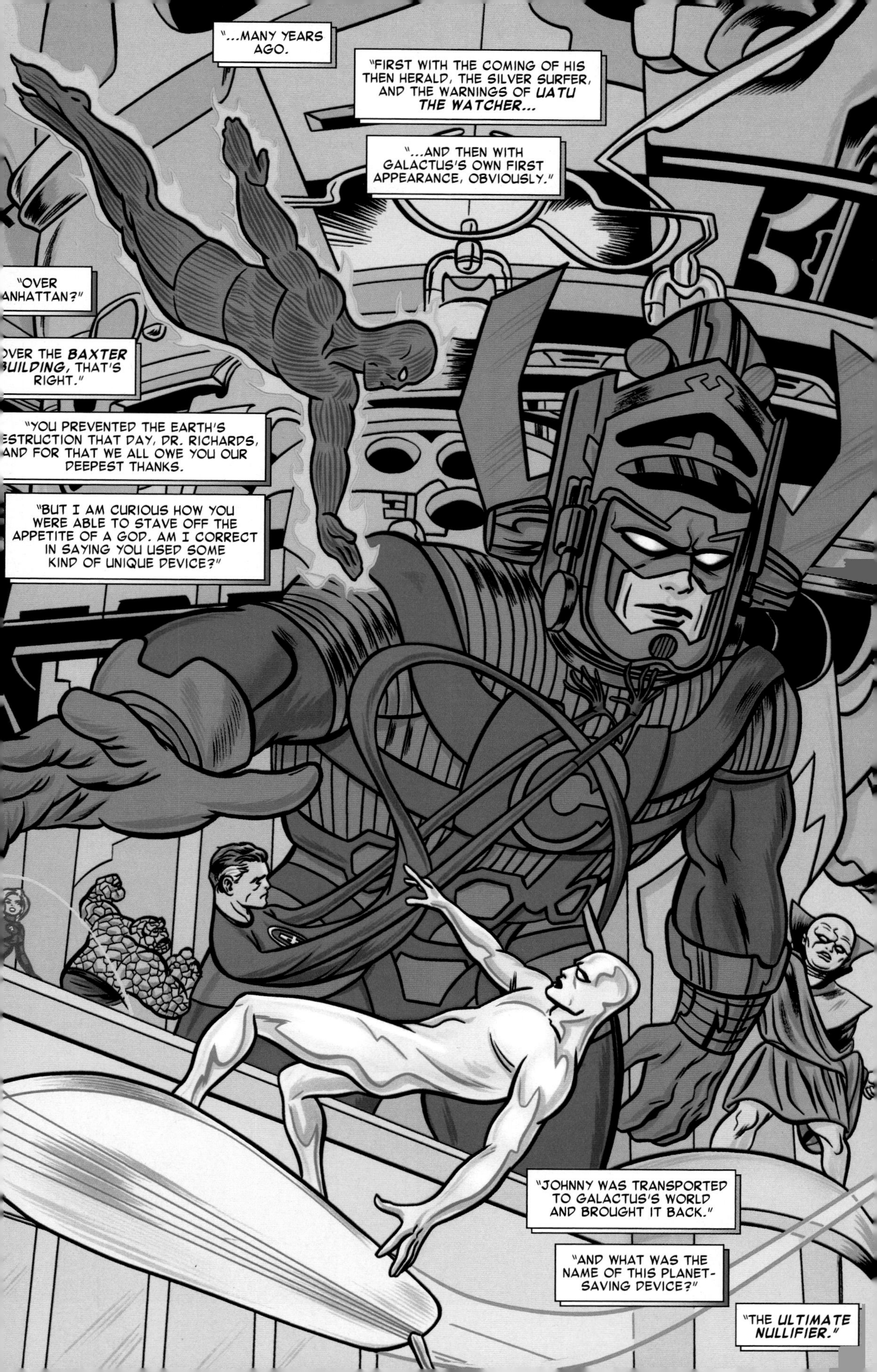
"...MANY YEARS AGO.
"FIRST WITH THE COMING OF HIS THEN HERALD, THE SILVER SURFER, AND THE WARNINGS OF *UATU THE WATCHER...*
"...AND THEN WITH GALACTUS'S OWN FIRST APPEARANCE, OBVIOUSLY."
"OVER ANHATTAN?"
OVER THE *BAXTER UILDING,* THAT'S RIGHT."
"YOU PREVENTED THE EARTH'S ESTRUCTION THAT DAY, DR. RICHARDS, AND FOR THAT WE ALL OWE YOU OUR DEEPEST THANKS.
"BUT I AM CURIOUS HOW YOU WERE ABLE TO STAVE OFF THE APPETITE OF A GOD. AM I CORRECT IN SAYING YOU USED SOME KIND OF UNIQUE DEVICE?"
"JOHNNY WAS TRANSPORTED TO GALACTUS'S WORLD AND BROUGHT IT BACK."
"AND WHAT WAS THE NAME OF THIS PLANET-SAVING DEVICE?"
"THE *ULTIMATE NULLIFIER.*"

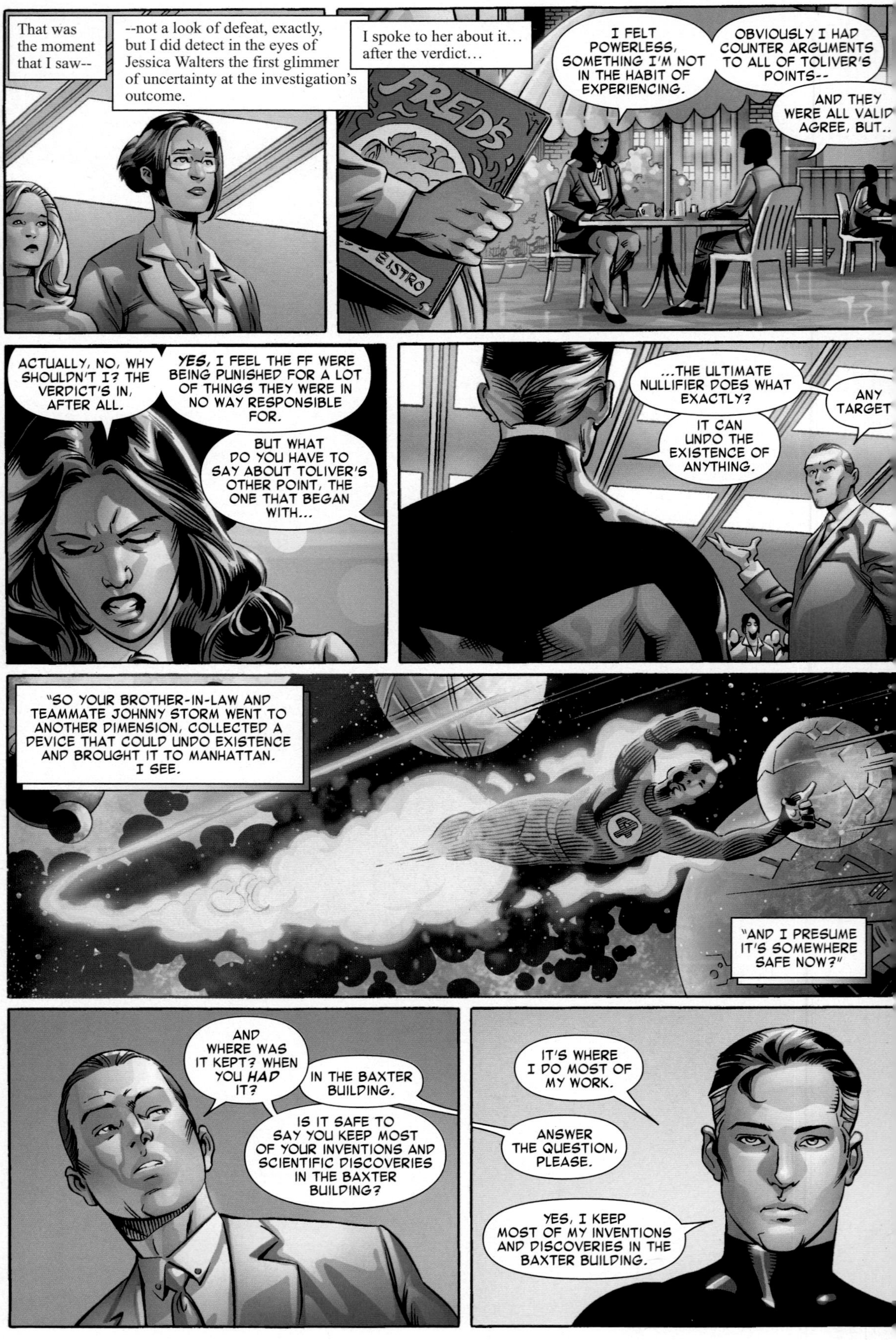
That was the moment that I saw--
--not a look of defeat, exactly, but I did detect in the eyes of Jessica Walters the first glimmer of uncertainty at the investigation's outcome.
I spoke to her about it… after the verdict…
FRED'S
I FELT POWERLESS, SOMETHING I'M NOT IN THE HABIT OF EXPERIENCING.
OBVIOUSLY I HAD COUNTER ARGUMENTS TO ALL OF TOLIVER'S POINTS--
AND THEY WERE ALL VALID AGREE, BUT…
ACTUALLY, NO, WHY SHOULDN'T I? THE VERDICT'S IN, AFTER ALL.
YES, I FEEL THE FF WERE BEING PUNISHED FOR A LOT OF THINGS THEY WERE IN NO WAY RESPONSIBLE FOR.
BUT WHAT DO YOU HAVE TO SAY ABOUT TOLIVER'S OTHER POINT, THE ONE THAT BEGAN WITH…
…THE ULTIMATE NULLIFIER DOES WHAT EXACTLY?
IT CAN UNDO THE EXISTENCE OF ANYTHING.
ANY TARGET
"SO YOUR BROTHER-IN-LAW AND TEAMMATE JOHNNY STORM WENT TO ANOTHER DIMENSION, COLLECTED A DEVICE THAT COULD UNDO EXISTENCE AND BROUGHT IT TO MANHATTAN. I SEE.
"AND I PRESUME IT'S SOMEWHERE SAFE NOW?"
AND WHERE WAS IT KEPT? WHEN YOU HAD IT?
IN THE BAXTER BUILDING.
IS IT SAFE TO SAY YOU KEEP MOST OF YOUR INVENTIONS AND SCIENTIFIC DISCOVERIES IN THE BAXTER BUILDING?
IT'S WHERE I DO MOST OF MY WORK.
ANSWER THE QUESTION, PLEASE.
YES, I KEEP MOST OF MY INVENTIONS AND DISCOVERIES IN THE BAXTER BUILDING.

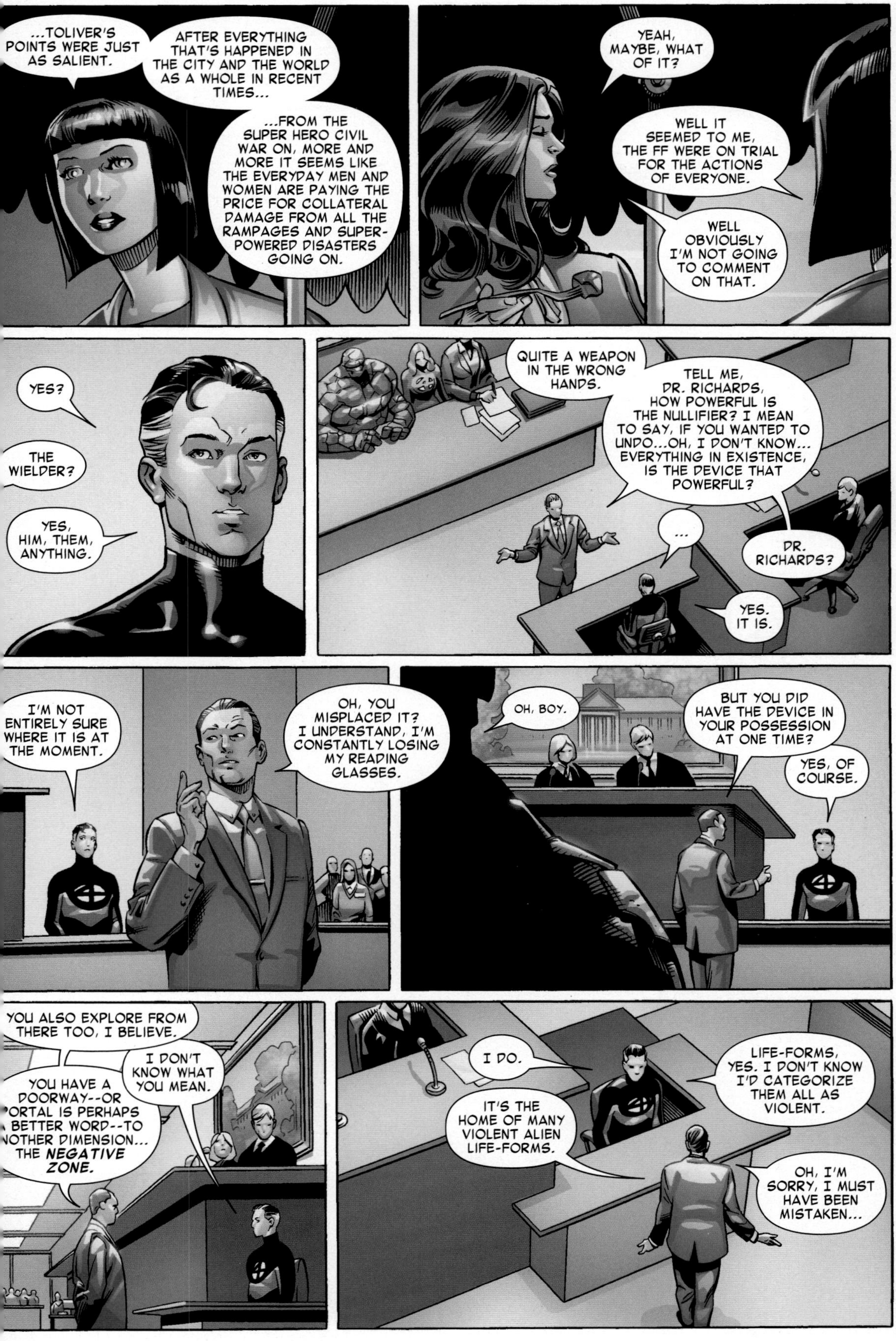
...TOLIVER'S POINTS WERE JUST AS SALIENT.
AFTER EVERYTHING THAT'S HAPPENED IN THE CITY AND THE WORLD AS A WHOLE IN RECENT TIMES...
...FROM THE SUPER HERO CIVIL WAR ON, MORE AND MORE IT SEEMS LIKE THE EVERYDAY MEN AND WOMEN ARE PAYING THE PRICE FOR COLLATERAL DAMAGE FROM ALL THE RAMPAGES AND SUPER-POWERED DISASTERS GOING ON.
YEAH, MAYBE, WHAT OF IT?
WELL IT SEEMED TO ME, THE FF WERE ON TRIAL FOR THE ACTIONS OF EVERYONE.
WELL OBVIOUSLY I'M NOT GOING TO COMMENT ON THAT.
YES?
THE WIELDER?
YES, HIM, THEM, ANYTHING.
QUITE A WEAPON IN THE WRONG HANDS.
TELL ME, DR. RICHARDS, HOW POWERFUL IS THE NULLIFIER? I MEAN TO SAY, IF YOU WANTED TO UNDO...OH, I DON'T KNOW... EVERYTHING IN EXISTENCE, IS THE DEVICE THAT POWERFUL?
...
DR. RICHARDS?
YES. IT IS.
I'M NOT ENTIRELY SURE WHERE IT IS AT THE MOMENT.
OH, YOU MISPLACED IT? I UNDERSTAND, I'M CONSTANTLY LOSING MY READING GLASSES.
OH, BOY.
BUT YOU DID HAVE THE DEVICE IN YOUR POSSESSION AT ONE TIME?
YES, OF COURSE.
YOU ALSO EXPLORE FROM THERE TOO, I BELIEVE.
YOU HAVE A DOORWAY--OR PORTAL IS PERHAPS A BETTER WORD--TO ANOTHER DIMENSION... THE NEGATIVE ZONE.
I DON'T KNOW WHAT YOU MEAN.
I DO.
IT'S THE HOME OF MANY VIOLENT ALIEN LIFE-FORMS.
LIFE-FORMS, YES. I DON'T KNOW I'D CATEGORIZE THEM ALL AS VIOLENT.
OH, I'M SORRY, I MUST HAVE BEEN MISTAKEN...

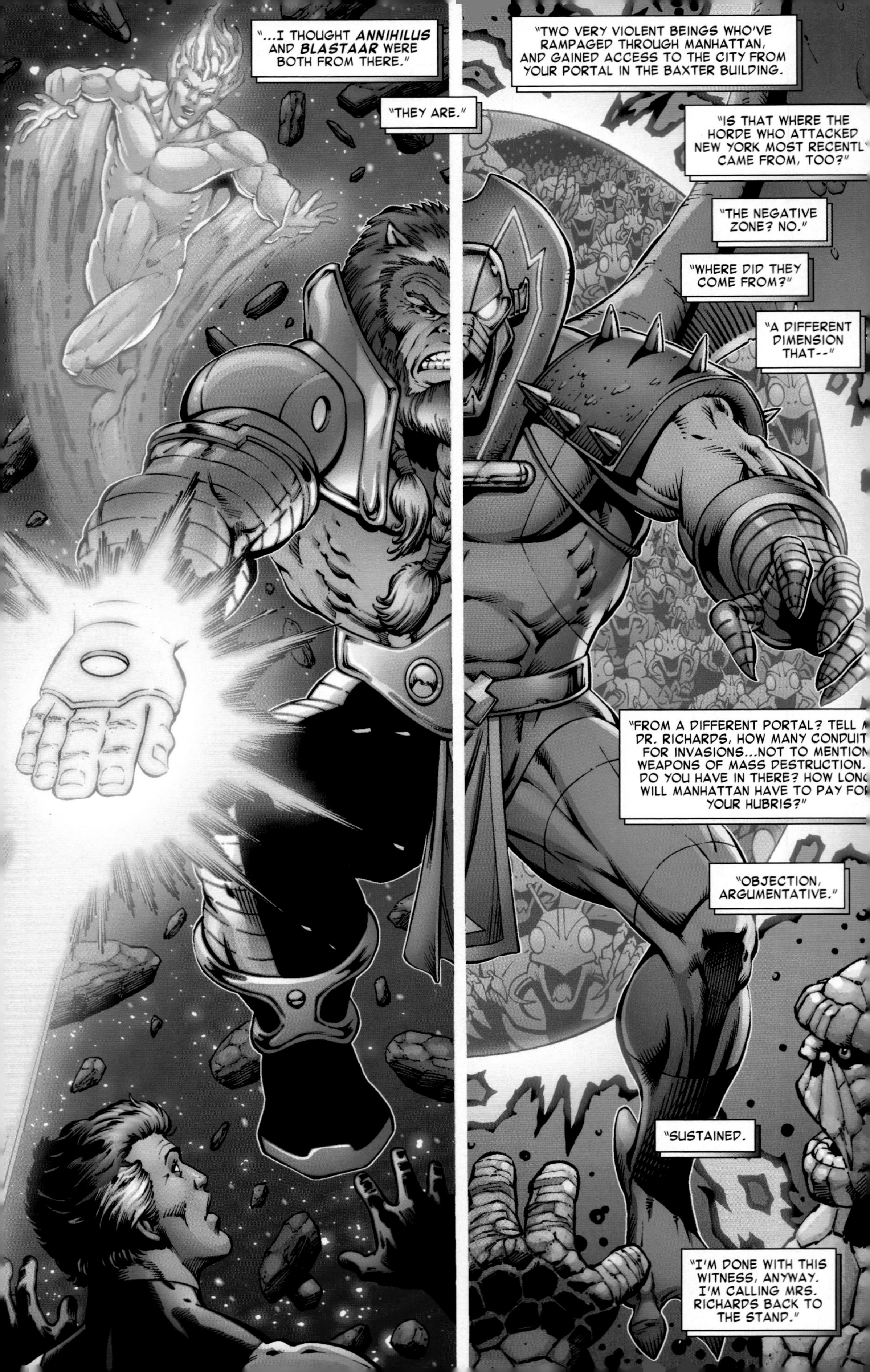
"...I THOUGHT ANNIHILUS AND BLASTAAR WERE BOTH FROM THERE."
"THEY ARE."
"TWO VERY VIOLENT BEINGS WHO'VE RAMPAGED THROUGH MANHATTAN, AND GAINED ACCESS TO THE CITY FROM YOUR PORTAL IN THE BAXTER BUILDING.
"IS THAT WHERE THE HORDE WHO ATTACKED NEW YORK MOST RECENTL CAME FROM, TOO?"
"THE NEGATIVE ZONE? NO."
"WHERE DID THEY COME FROM?"
"A DIFFERENT DIMENSION THAT--"
"FROM A DIFFERENT PORTAL? TELL DR. RICHARDS, HOW MANY CONDUIT FOR INVASIONS...NOT TO MENTION WEAPONS OF MASS DESTRUCTION. DO YOU HAVE IN THERE? HOW LON WILL MANHATTAN HAVE TO PAY FO YOUR HUBRIS?"
"OBJECTION, ARGUMENTATIVE."
"SUSTAINED.
"I'M DONE WITH THIS WITNESS, ANYWAY. I'M CALLING MRS. RICHARDS BACK TO THE STAND."

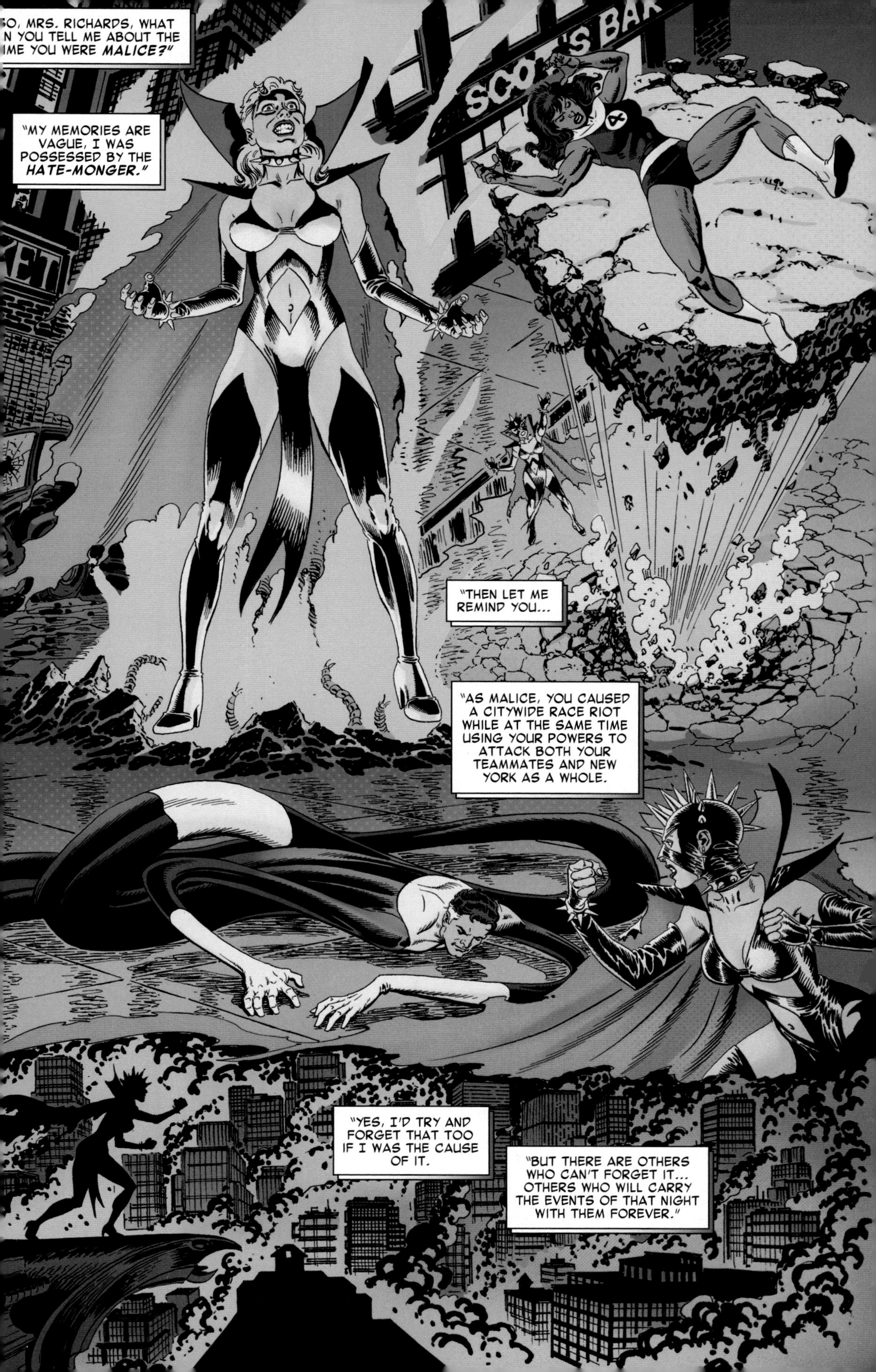

"SO, MRS. RICHARDS, WHAT
N YOU TELL ME ABOUT THE
IME YOU WERE *MALICE?*"
SCO S BA
"MY MEMORIES ARE VAGUE, I WAS POSSESSED BY THE *HATE-MONGER.*"
"THEN LET ME REMIND YOU...
"AS MALICE, YOU CAUSED A CITYWIDE RACE RIOT WHILE AT THE SAME TIME USING YOUR POWERS TO ATTACK BOTH YOUR TEAMMATES AND NEW YORK AS A WHOLE.
"YES, I'D TRY AND FORGET THAT TOO IF I WAS THE CAUSE OF IT.
"BUT THERE ARE OTHERS WHO CAN'T FORGET IT... OTHERS WHO WILL CARRY THE EVENTS OF THAT NIGHT WITH THEM FOREVER."

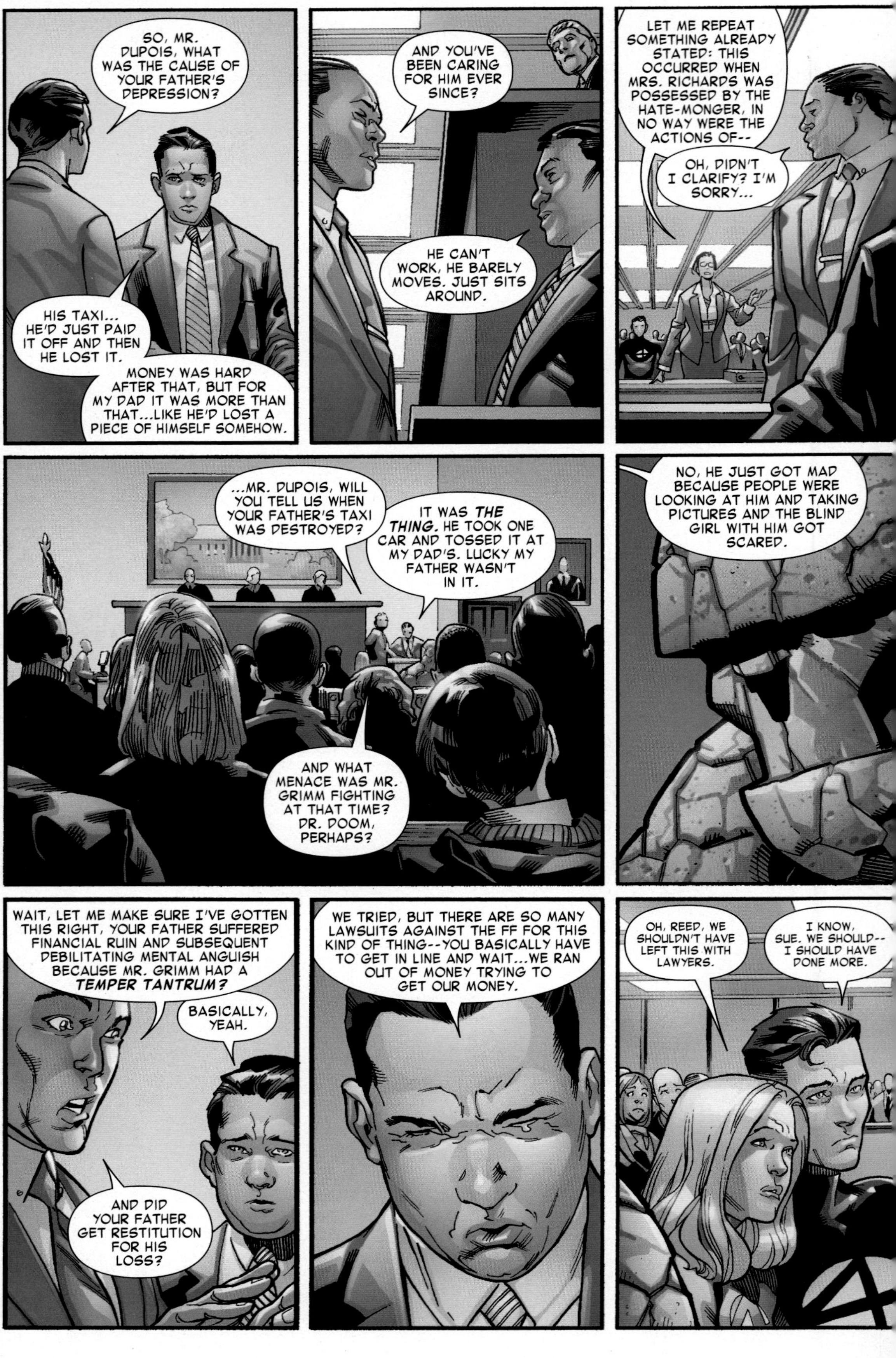
SO, MR. DUPOIS, WHAT WAS THE CAUSE OF YOUR FATHER'S DEPRESSION?
HIS TAXI... HE'D JUST PAID IT OFF AND THEN HE LOST IT.
MONEY WAS HARD AFTER THAT, BUT FOR MY DAD IT WAS MORE THAN THAT...LIKE HE'D LOST A PIECE OF HIMSELF SOMEHOW.
AND YOU'VE BEEN CARING FOR HIM EVER SINCE?
HE CAN'T WORK, HE BARELY MOVES. JUST SITS AROUND.
LET ME REPEAT SOMETHING ALREADY STATED: THIS OCCURRED WHEN MRS. RICHARDS WAS POSSESSED BY THE HATE-MONGER, IN NO WAY WERE THE ACTIONS OF--
OH, DIDN'T I CLARIFY? I'M SORRY...
...MR. DUPOIS, WILL YOU TELL US WHEN YOUR FATHER'S TAXI WAS DESTROYED?
IT WAS THE THING. HE TOOK ONE CAR AND TOSSED IT AT MY DAD'S. LUCKY MY FATHER WASN'T IN IT.
AND WHAT MENACE WAS MR. GRIMM FIGHTING AT THAT TIME? DR. DOOM, PERHAPS?
NO, HE JUST GOT MAD BECAUSE PEOPLE WERE LOOKING AT HIM AND TAKING PICTURES AND THE BLIND GIRL WITH HIM GOT SCARED.
WAIT, LET ME MAKE SURE I'VE GOTTEN THIS RIGHT, YOUR FATHER SUFFERED FINANCIAL RUIN AND SUBSEQUENT DEBILITATING MENTAL ANGUISH BECAUSE MR. GRIMM HAD A TEMPER TANTRUM?
BASICALLY, YEAH.
AND DID YOUR FATHER GET RESTITUTION FOR HIS LOSS?
WE TRIED, BUT THERE ARE SO MANY LAWSUITS AGAINST THE FF FOR THIS KIND OF THING--YOU BASICALLY HAVE TO GET IN LINE AND WAIT...WE RAN OUT OF MONEY TRYING TO GET OUR MONEY.
OH, REED, WE SHOULDN'T HAVE LEFT THIS WITH LAWYERS.
I KNOW, SUE. WE SHOULD--I SHOULD HAVE DONE MORE.

Toliver's closing argument was no less damning...

I COULD PRODUCE HUNDREDS--NO, THOUSANDS OF WITNESSES WHO'VE SUFFERED THE SAME PLIGHT--

--PHYSICAL OR FINANCIAL HARM CAUSED BY THE ACTIONS OF THE FANTASTIC FOUR...

...WHO ALSO AWAIT RESTITUTION-- NO, NO, THAT'S WRONG TOO--WHO STILL AWAIT JUSTICE.

AND YES, SOME OF THOSE ACTIONS ARE FROM THE FANTASTIC FOUR DEFENDING THE CITY. THAT'S TRUE.

BUT OTHERS, LIKE MR. GRIMM'S TANTRUM, WERE FOR REASONS AS RANDOM AND AS EASILY PREVENTABLE...

...IF THE FANTASTIC FOUR TRULY HAD CONCERN FOR THE CITY THEY CLAIMED TO PROTECT.

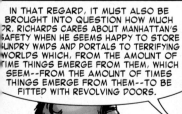

IN THAT REGARD, IT MUST ALSO BE BROUGHT INTO QUESTION HOW MUCH DR. RICHARDS CARES ABOUT MANHATTAN'S SAFETY WHEN HE SEEMS HAPPY TO STORE SUNDRY WMDS AND PORTALS TO TERRIFYING WORLDS WHICH, FROM THE AMOUNT OF TIME THINGS EMERGE FROM THEM, WHICH SEEM--FROM THE AMOUNT OF TIMES THINGS EMERGE FROM THEM--TO BE FITTED WITH REVOLVING DOORS.

I REFERRED TO DR. RICHARDS' HUBRIS EARLIER, BUT IT REALLY MUST BE NOTED HOW HE APPARENTLY FEELS ABOVE THE NORMAL RULES OF SOCIETY. HOW HE FEELS HE'S ENTITLED TO OPERATE WITH SUCH FLAGRANT DISREGARD FOR THE SAFETY OF THE CITY AROUND HIM...

...NOT TO MENTION HIS FAMILY, HIS TEAMMATES...

...AND THE SO-CALLED FUTURE FOUNDATION-- THE CHILDREN WHO LIVE WITH HIM.

IN CLOSING, LET ME SAY THAT...

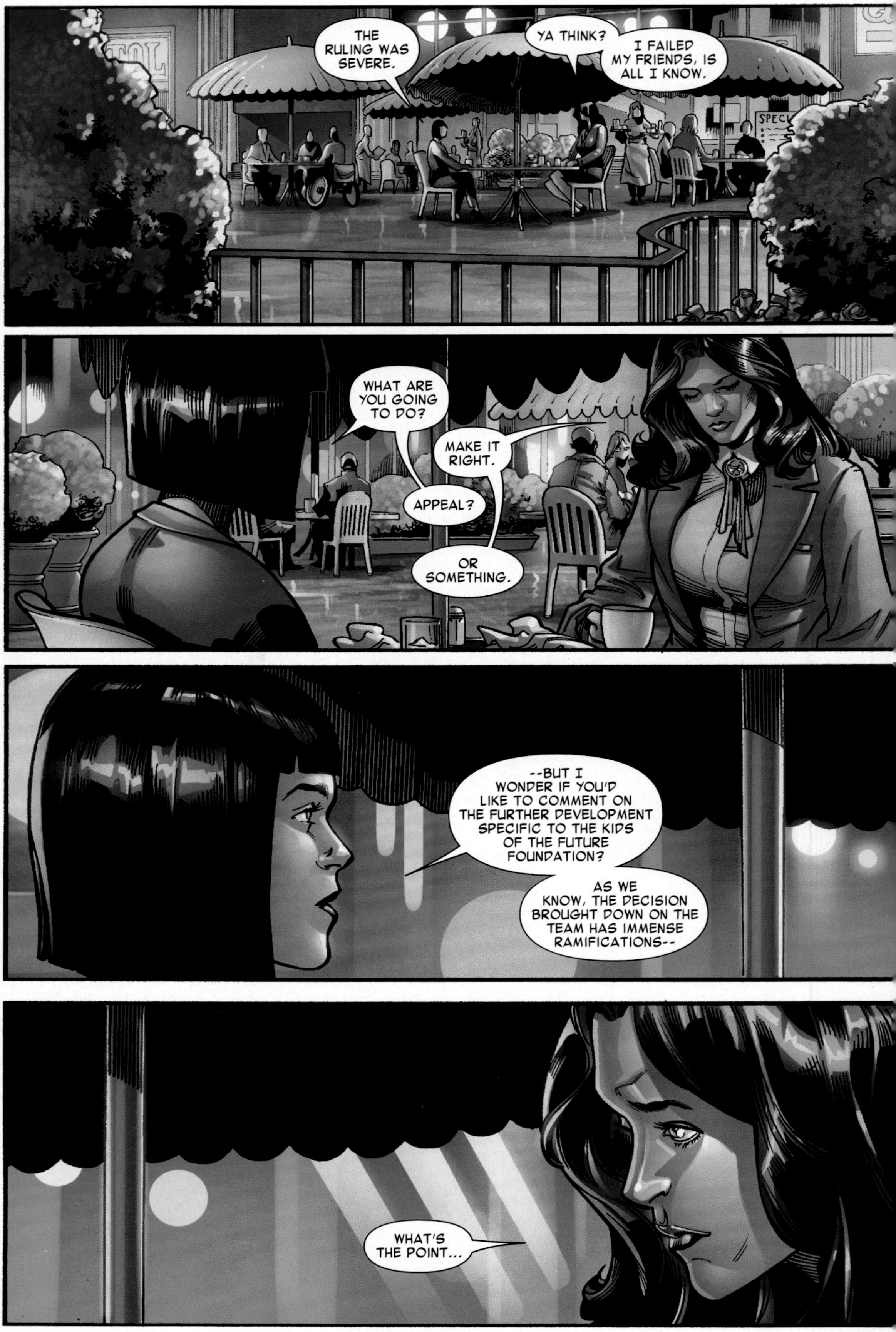
THE RULING WAS SEVERE.
YA THINK?
I FAILED MY FRIENDS, IS ALL I KNOW.
WHAT ARE YOU GOING TO DO?
MAKE IT RIGHT.
APPEAL?
OR SOMETHING.
--BUT I WONDER IF YOU'D LIKE TO COMMENT ON THE FURTHER DEVELOPMENT SPECIFIC TO THE KIDS OF THE FUTURE FOUNDATION?
AS WE KNOW, THE DECISION BROUGHT DOWN ON THE TEAM HAS IMMENSE RAMIFICATIONS--
WHAT'S THE POINT...

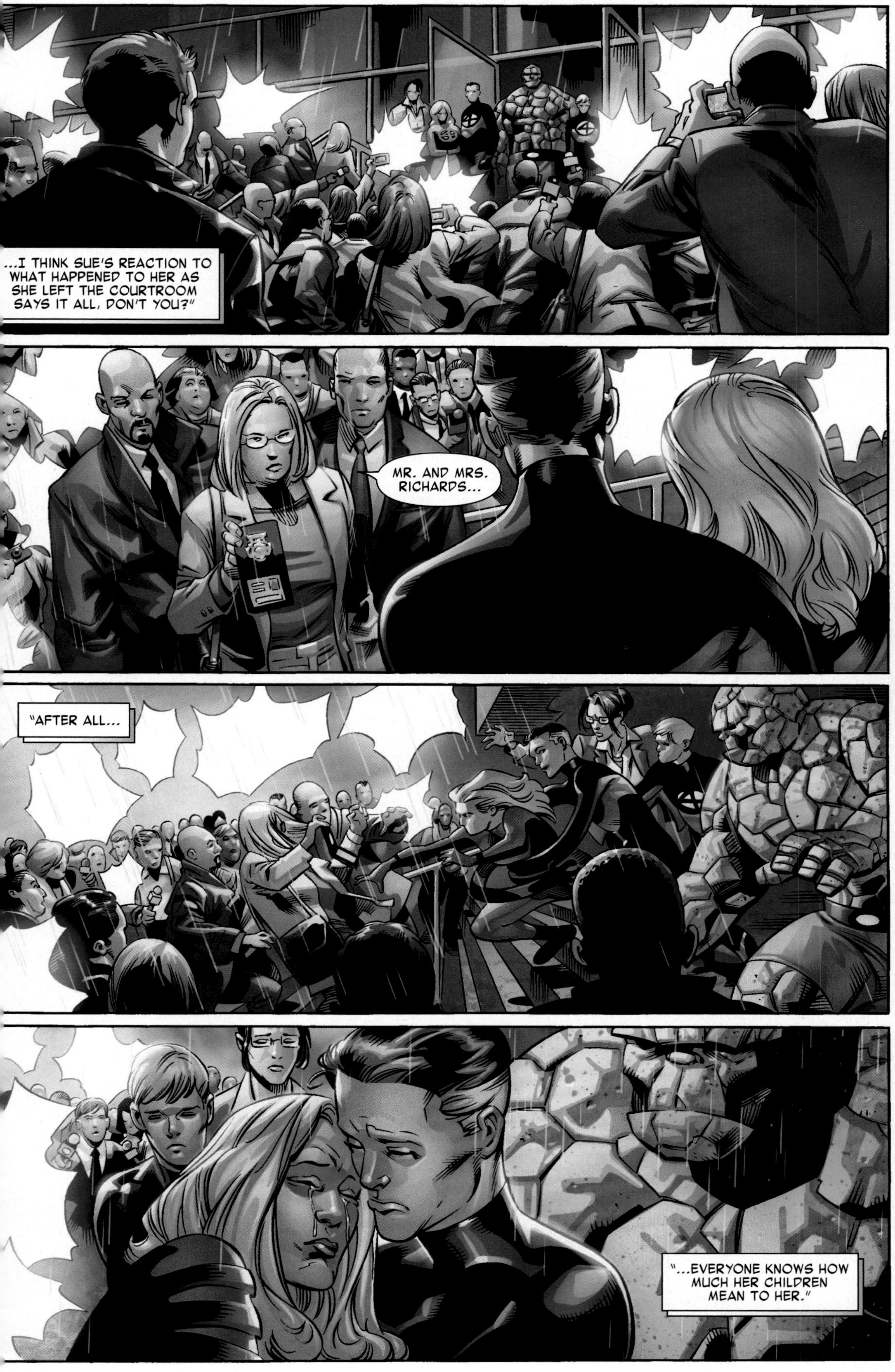

...I THINK SUE'S REACTION TO WHAT HAPPENED TO HER AS SHE LEFT THE COURTROOM SAYS IT ALL, DON'T YOU?"
MR. AND MRS. RICHARDS...
"AFTER ALL...
"...EVERYONE KNOWS HOW MUCH HER CHILDREN MEAN TO HER."

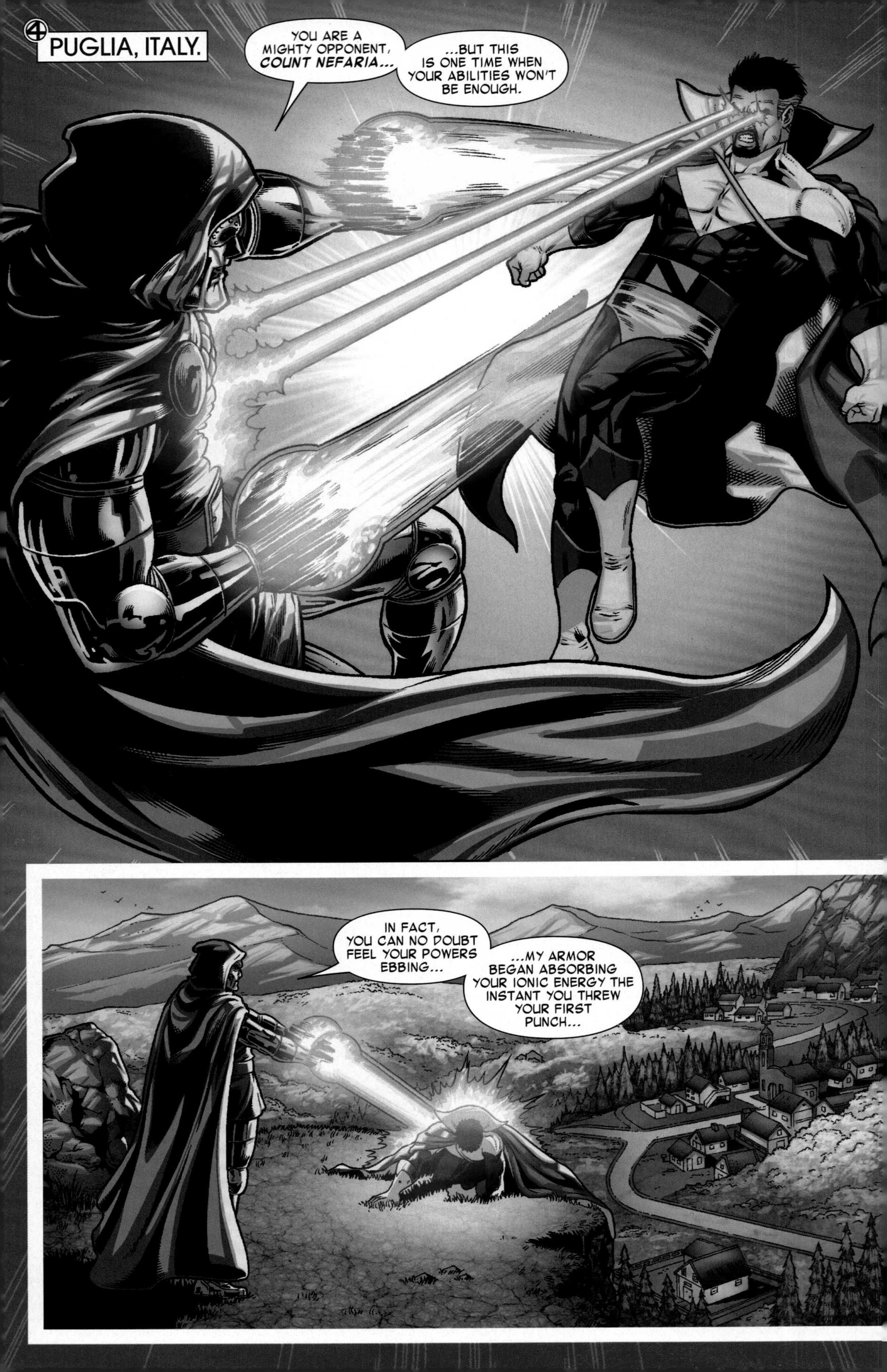
PUGLIA, ITALY.
YOU ARE A MIGHTY OPPONENT, COUNT NEFARIA...
...BUT THIS IS ONE TIME WHEN YOUR ABILITIES WON'T BE ENOUGH.
IN FACT, YOU CAN NO DOUBT FEEL YOUR POWERS EBBING...
...MY ARMOR BEGAN ABSORBING YOUR IONIC ENERGY THE INSTANT YOU THREW YOUR FIRST PUNCH...

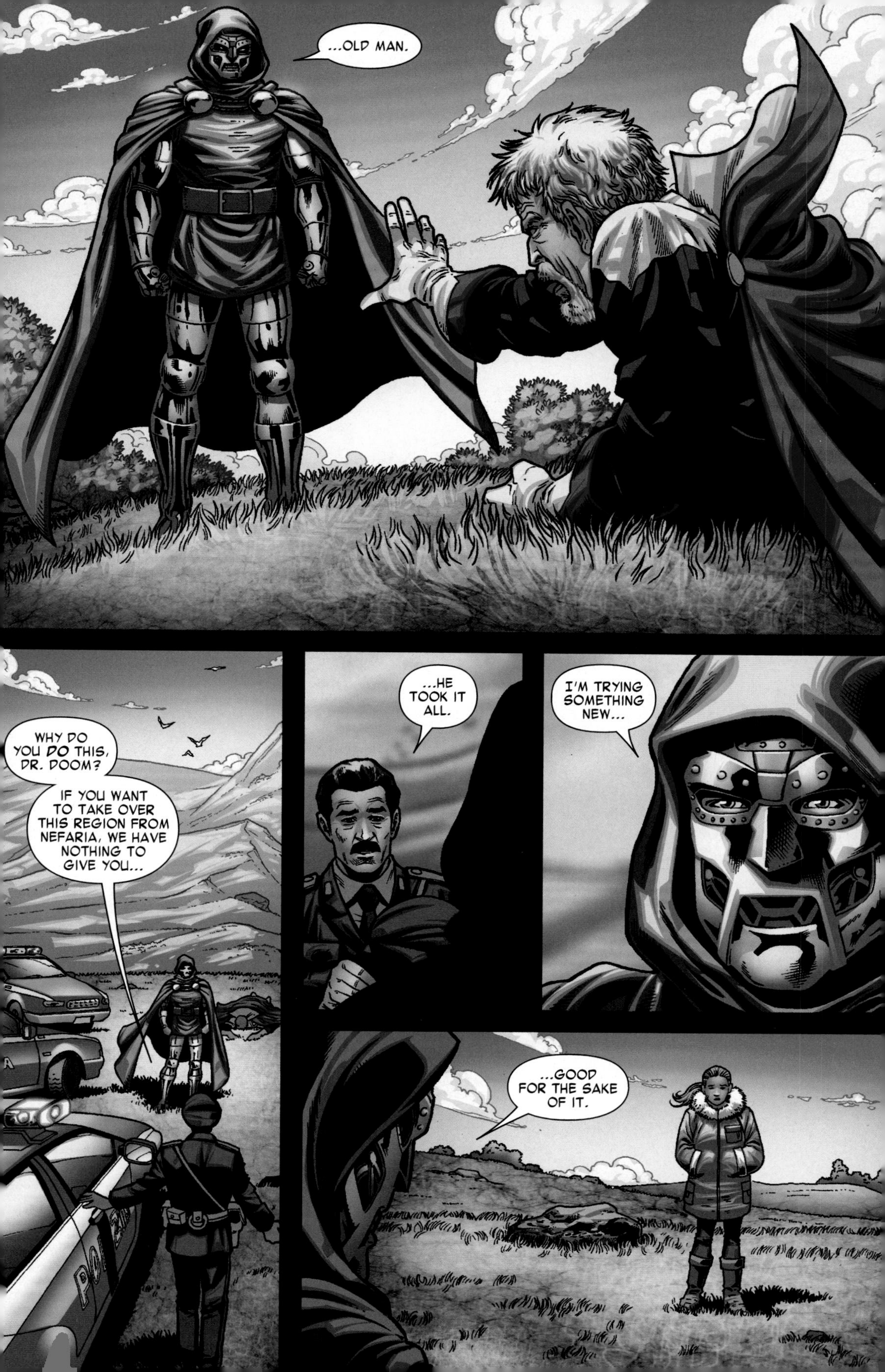
...OLD MAN.
WHY DO YOU DO THIS, DR. DOOM?
IF YOU WANT TO TAKE OVER THIS REGION FROM NEFARIA, WE HAVE NOTHING TO GIVE YOU...
...HE TOOK IT ALL.
I'M TRYING SOMETHING NEW...
...GOOD FOR THE SAKE OF IT.

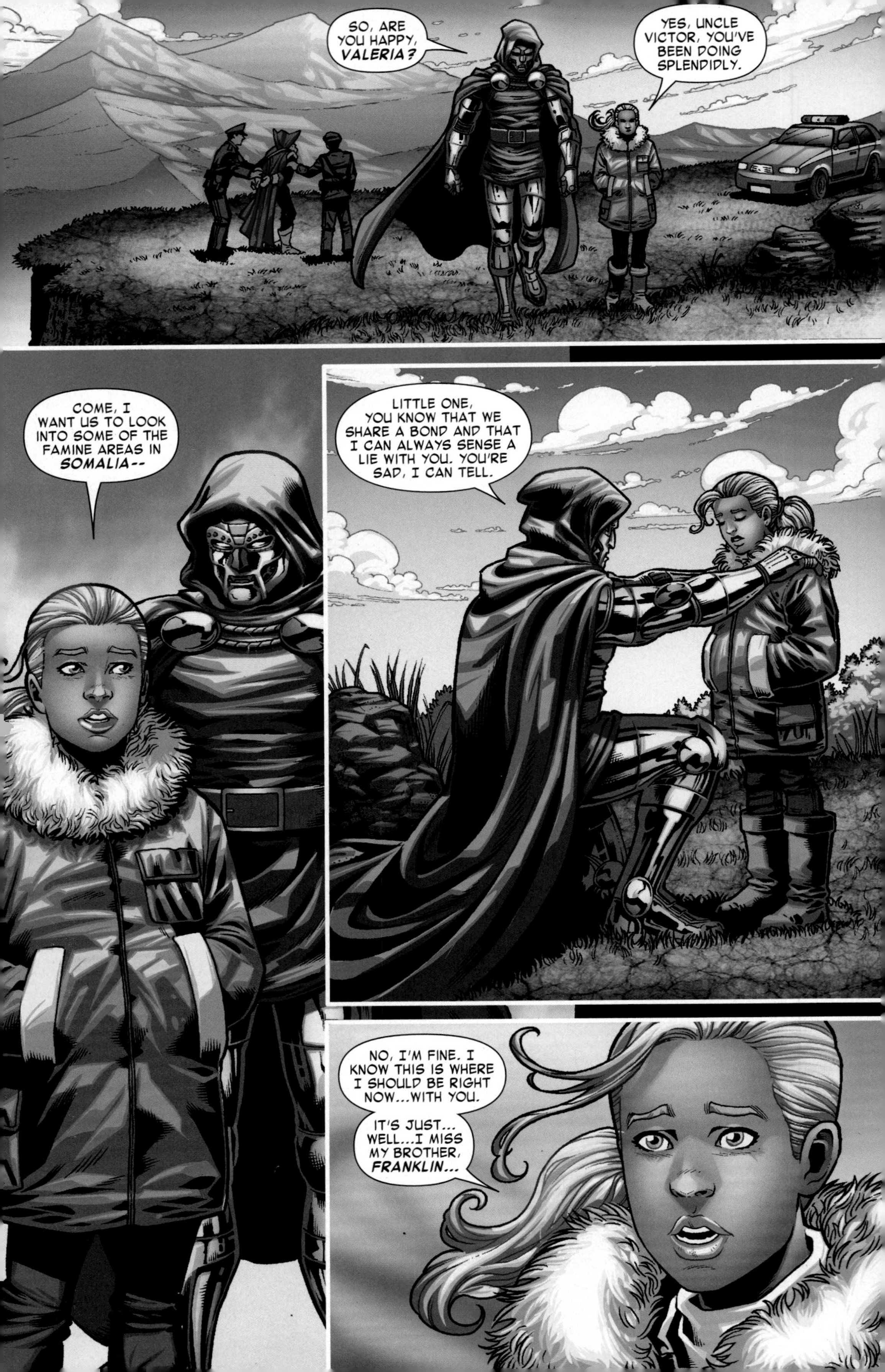
SO, ARE YOU HAPPY, *VALERIA?*
YES, UNCLE VICTOR, YOU'VE BEEN DOING SPLENDIDLY.
COME, I WANT US TO LOOK INTO SOME OF THE FAMINE AREAS IN *SOMALIA--*
LITTLE ONE, YOU KNOW THAT WE SHARE A BOND AND THAT I CAN ALWAYS SENSE A LIE WITH YOU. YOU'RE SAD, I CAN TELL.
NO, I'M FINE. I KNOW THIS IS WHERE I SHOULD BE RIGHT NOW...WITH YOU.
IT'S JUST... WELL...I MISS MY BROTHER, *FRANKLIN...*

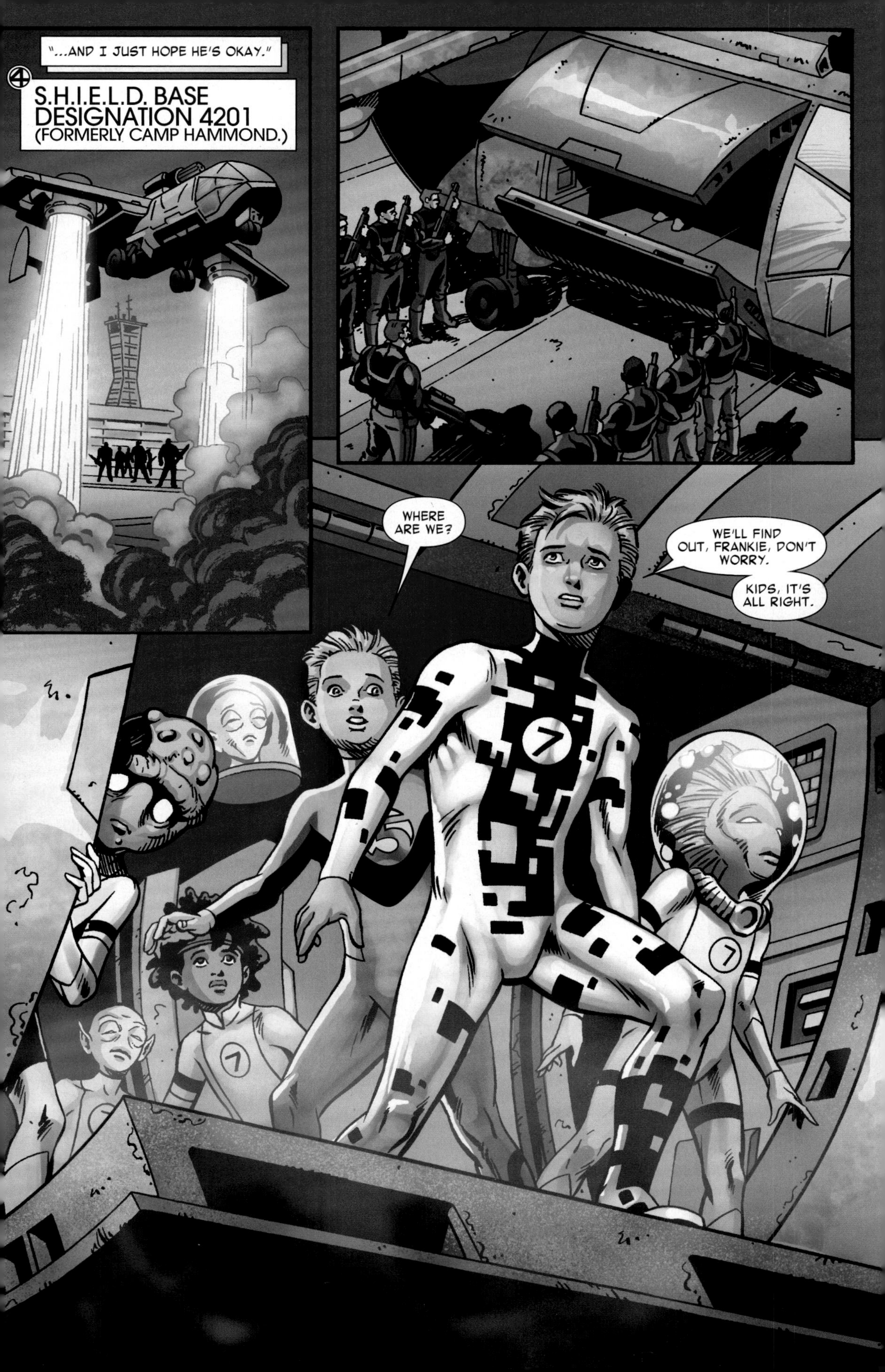
"...AND I JUST HOPE HE'S OKAY."
S.H.I.E.L.D. BASE DESIGNATION 4201 (FORMERLY CAMP HAMMOND.)
WHERE ARE WE?
WE'LL FIND OUT, FRANKIE, DON'T WORRY.
KIDS, IT'S ALL RIGHT.

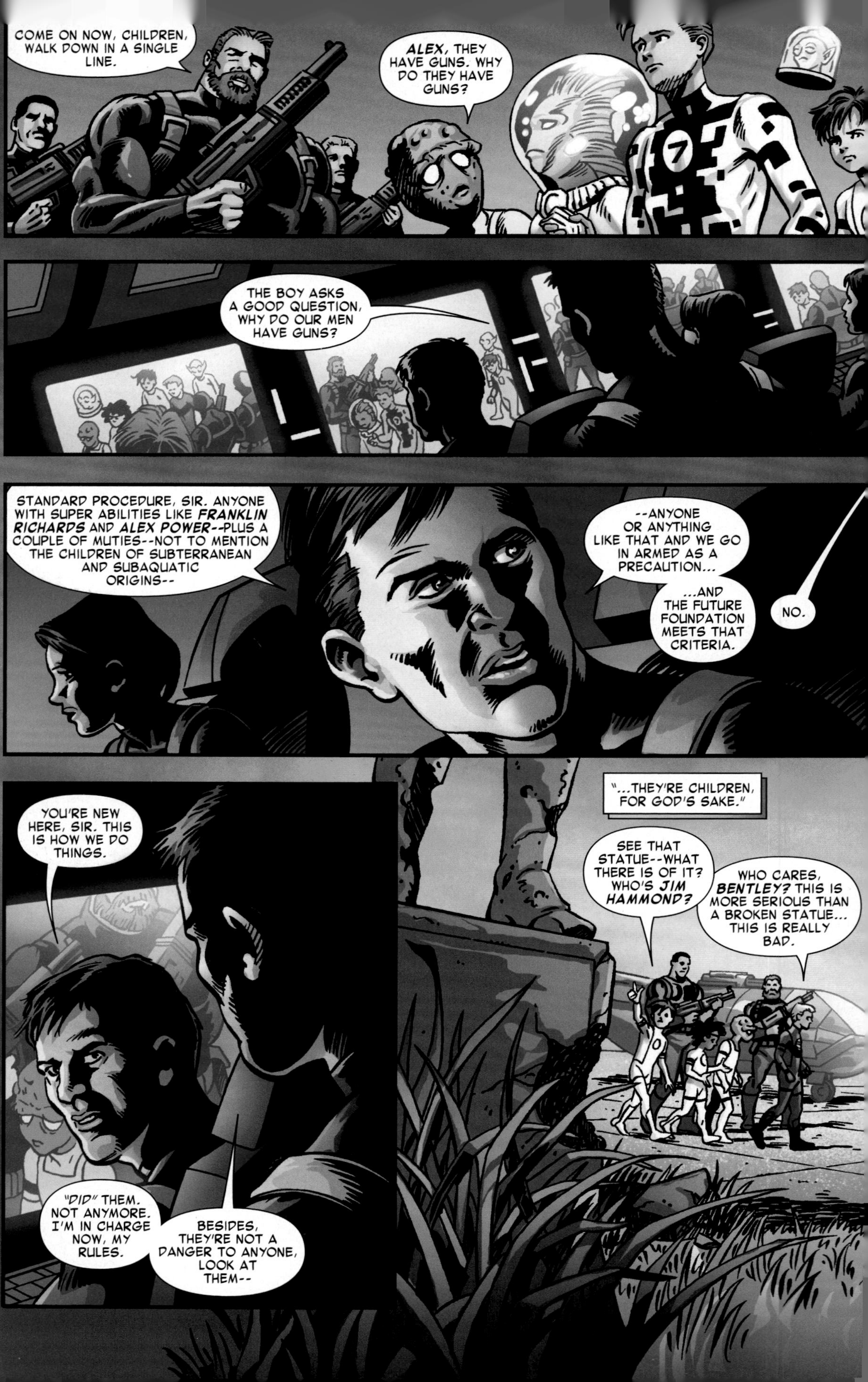
COME ON NOW, CHILDREN, WALK DOWN IN A SINGLE LINE.
ALEX, THEY HAVE GUNS. WHY DO THEY HAVE GUNS?
THE BOY ASKS A GOOD QUESTION, WHY DO OUR MEN HAVE GUNS?
STANDARD PROCEDURE, SIR. ANYONE WITH SUPER ABILITIES LIKE FRANKLIN RICHARDS AND ALEX POWER--PLUS A COUPLE OF MUTIES--NOT TO MENTION THE CHILDREN OF SUBTERRANEAN AND SUBAQUATIC ORIGINS--
--ANYONE OR ANYTHING LIKE THAT AND WE GO IN ARMED AS A PRECAUTION...
...AND THE FUTURE FOUNDATION MEETS THAT CRITERIA.
NO.
YOU'RE NEW HERE, SIR. THIS IS HOW WE DO THINGS.
"DID" THEM. NOT ANYMORE. I'M IN CHARGE NOW, MY RULES.
BESIDES, THEY'RE NOT A DANGER TO ANYONE, LOOK AT THEM--
"...THEY'RE CHILDREN, FOR GOD'S SAKE."
SEE THAT STATUE--WHAT THERE IS OF IT? WHO'S JIM HAMMOND?
WHO CARES, BENTLEY? THIS IS MORE SERIOUS THAN A BROKEN STATUE... THIS IS REALLY BAD.

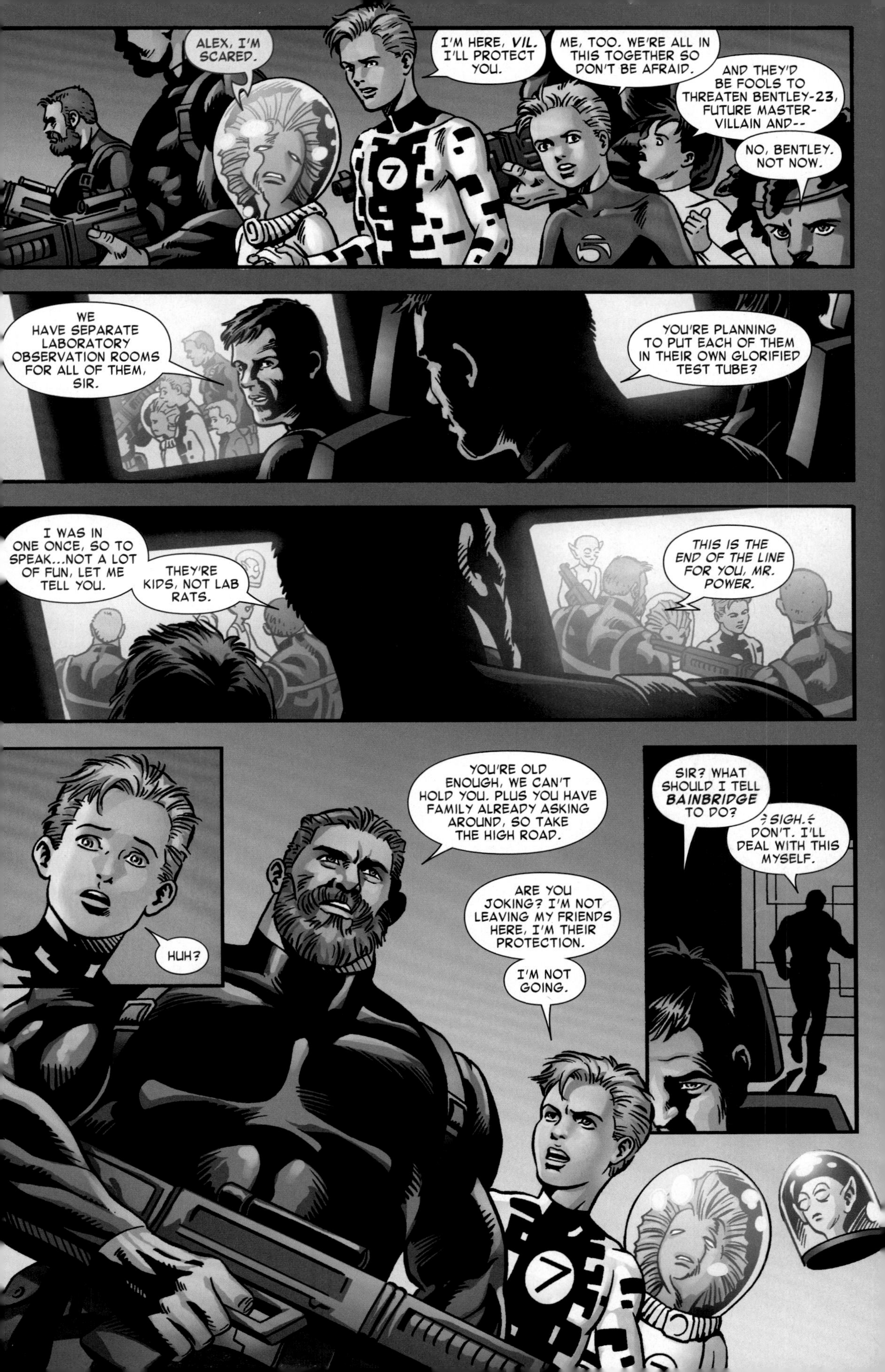
ALEX, I'M SCARED.
I'M HERE, *VIL.* I'LL PROTECT YOU.
ME, TOO. WE'RE ALL IN THIS TOGETHER SO DON'T BE AFRAID.
AND THEY'D BE FOOLS TO THREATEN BENTLEY-23, FUTURE MASTER-VILLAIN AND--
NO, BENTLEY. NOT NOW.
WE HAVE SEPARATE LABORATORY OBSERVATION ROOMS FOR ALL OF THEM, SIR.
YOU'RE PLANNING TO PUT EACH OF THEM IN THEIR OWN GLORIFIED TEST TUBE?
I WAS IN ONE ONCE, SO TO SPEAK...NOT A LOT OF FUN, LET ME TELL YOU.
THEY'RE KIDS, NOT LAB RATS.
THIS IS THE END OF THE LINE FOR YOU, MR. POWER.
HUH?
YOU'RE OLD ENOUGH, WE CAN'T HOLD YOU. PLUS YOU HAVE FAMILY ALREADY ASKING AROUND, SO TAKE THE HIGH ROAD.
ARE YOU JOKING? I'M NOT LEAVING MY FRIENDS HERE, I'M THEIR PROTECTION.
I'M NOT GOING.
SIR? WHAT SHOULD I TELL *BAINBRIDGE* TO DO?
SIGH. DON'T. I'LL DEAL WITH THIS MYSELF.

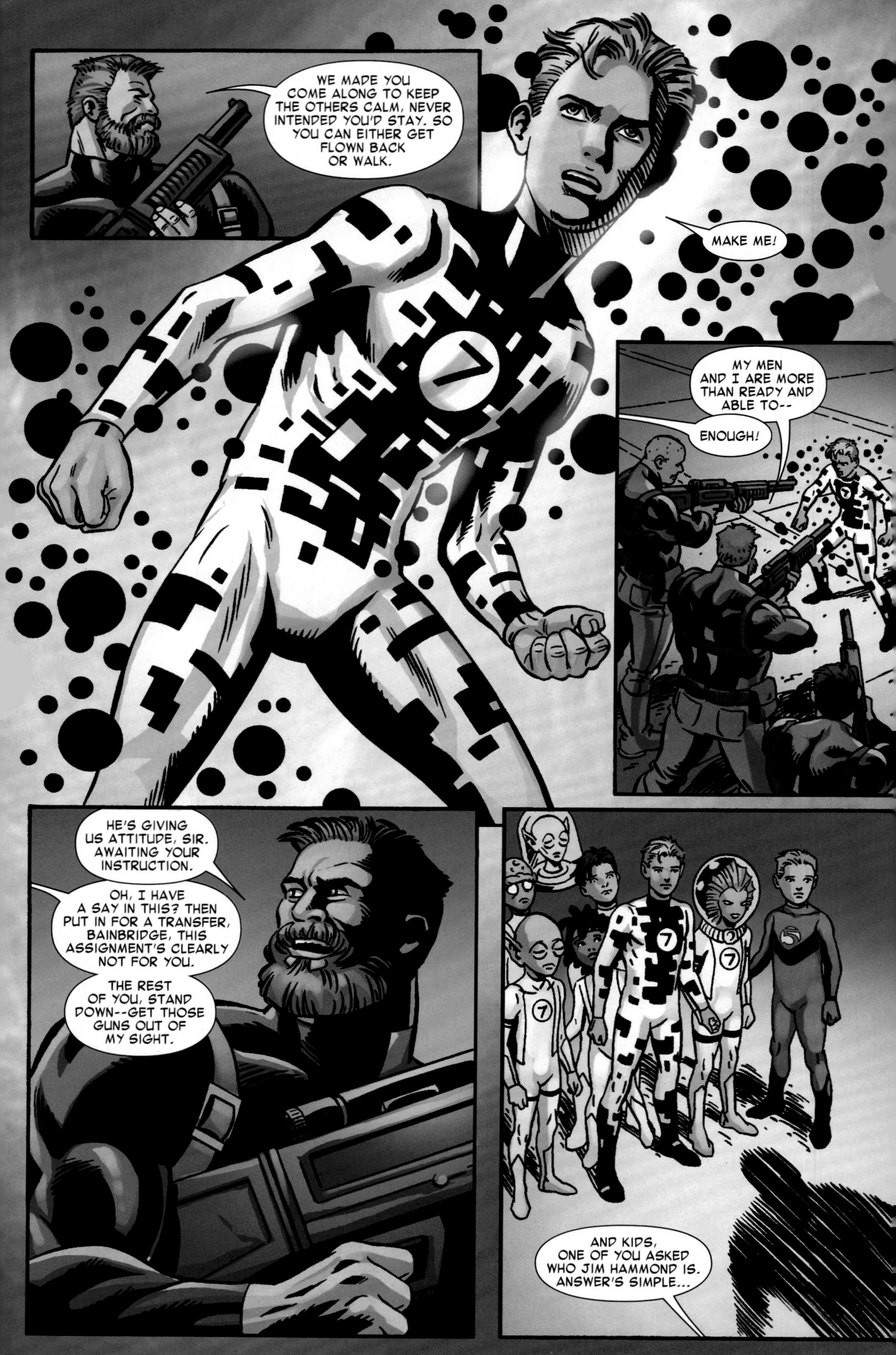
WE MADE YOU COME ALONG TO KEEP THE OTHERS CALM, NEVER INTENDED YOU'D STAY. SO YOU CAN EITHER GET FLOWN BACK OR WALK.
MAKE ME!
MY MEN AND I ARE MORE THAN READY AND ABLE TO--
ENOUGH!
HE'S GIVING US ATTITUDE, SIR. AWAITING YOUR INSTRUCTION.
OH, I HAVE A SAY IN THIS? THEN PUT IN FOR A TRANSFER, BAINBRIDGE, THIS ASSIGNMENT'S CLEARLY NOT FOR YOU.
THE REST OF YOU, STAND DOWN--GET THOSE GUNS OUT OF MY SIGHT.
AND KIDS, ONE OF YOU ASKED WHO JIM HAMMOND IS. ANSWER'S SIMPLE...

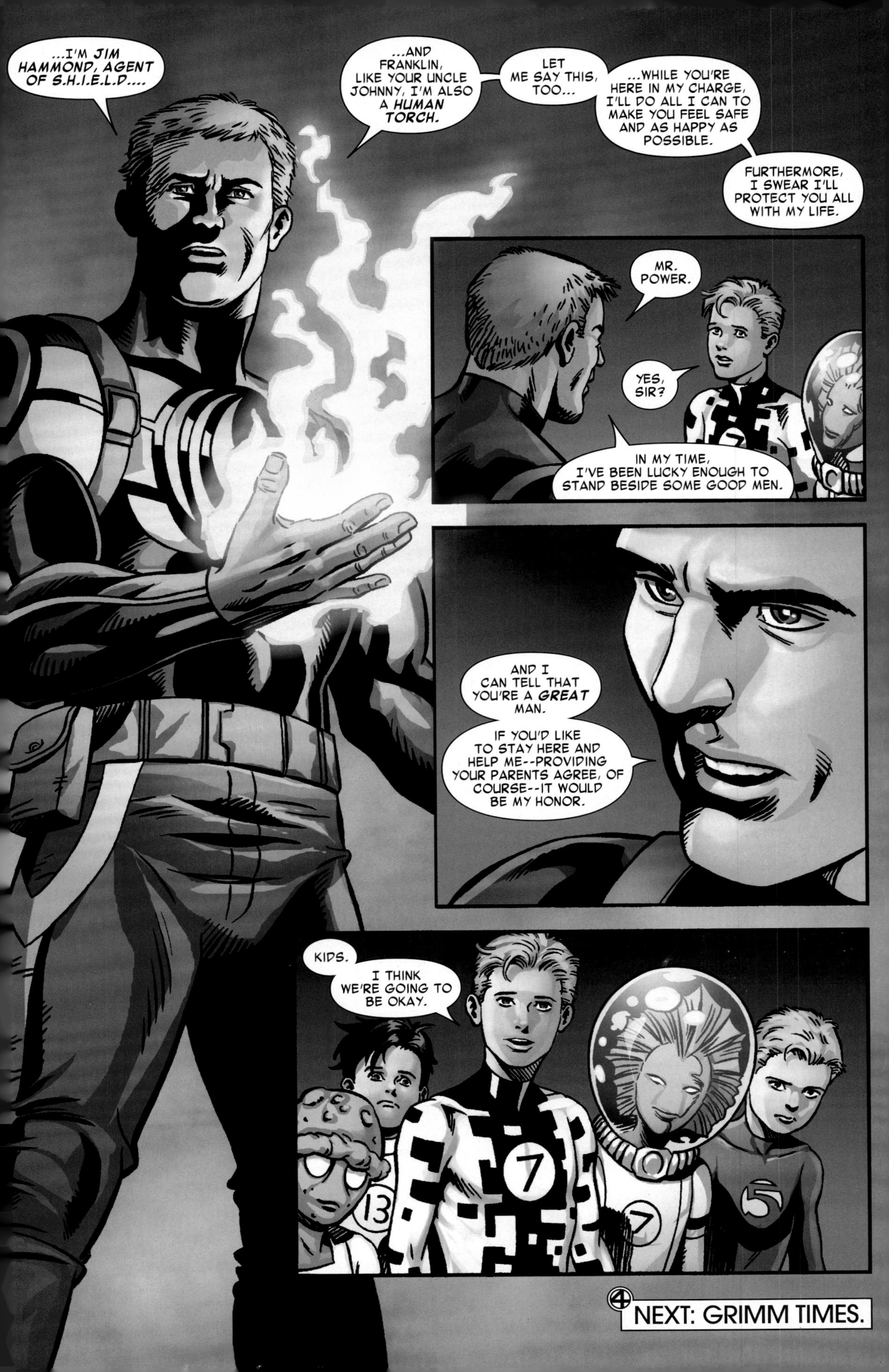

...I'M JIM HAMMOND, AGENT OF S.H.I.E.L.D....
...AND FRANKLIN, LIKE YOUR UNCLE JOHNNY, I'M ALSO A HUMAN TORCH.
LET ME SAY THIS, TOO...
...WHILE YOU'RE HERE IN MY CHARGE, I'LL DO ALL I CAN TO MAKE YOU FEEL SAFE AND AS HAPPY AS POSSIBLE.
FURTHERMORE, I SWEAR I'LL PROTECT YOU ALL WITH MY LIFE.
MR. POWER.
YES, SIR?
IN MY TIME, I'VE BEEN LUCKY ENOUGH TO STAND BESIDE SOME GOOD MEN.
AND I CAN TELL THAT YOU'RE A GREAT MAN.
IF YOU'D LIKE TO STAY HERE AND HELP ME--PROVIDING YOUR PARENTS AGREE, OF COURSE--IT WOULD BE MY HONOR.
KIDS.
I THINK WE'RE GOING TO BE OKAY.
NEXT: GRIMM TIMES.

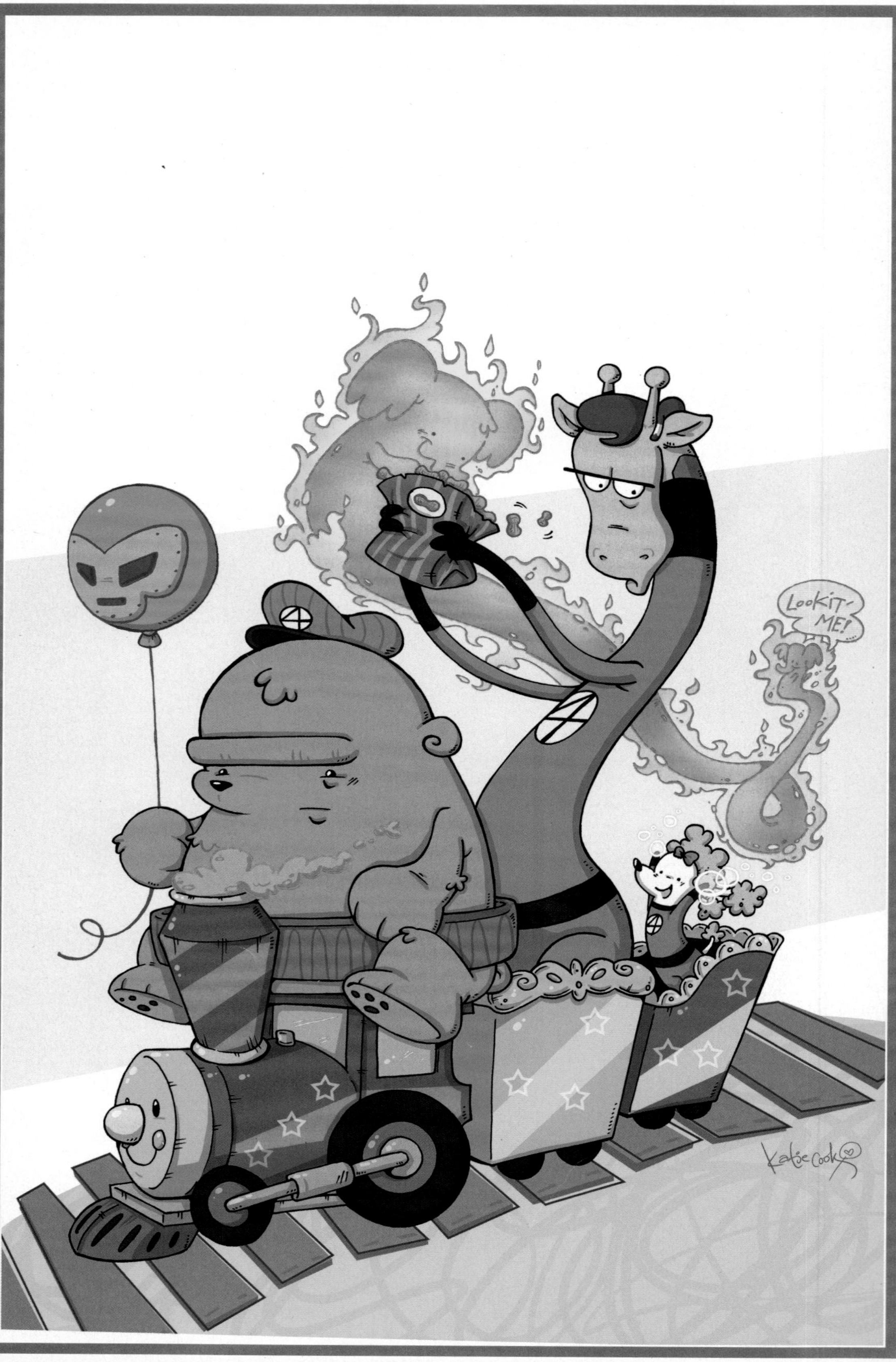
LOOKIT' ME!
Katie Cook

ONE • animal variant by Katie Cook

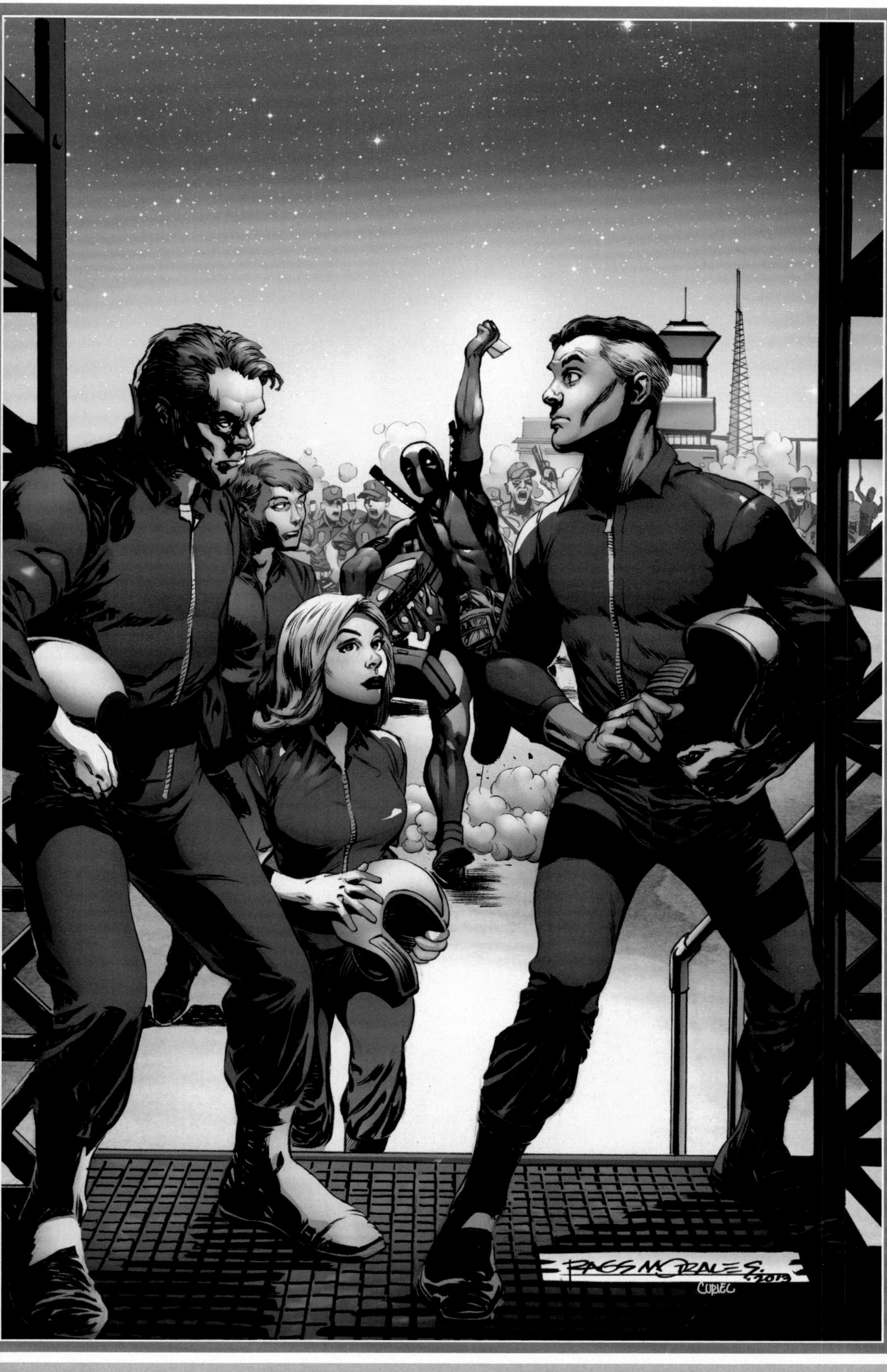
RAGS MORALES
2013
CURIEL

ONE • hastings variant by Rags Morales with David Curiel

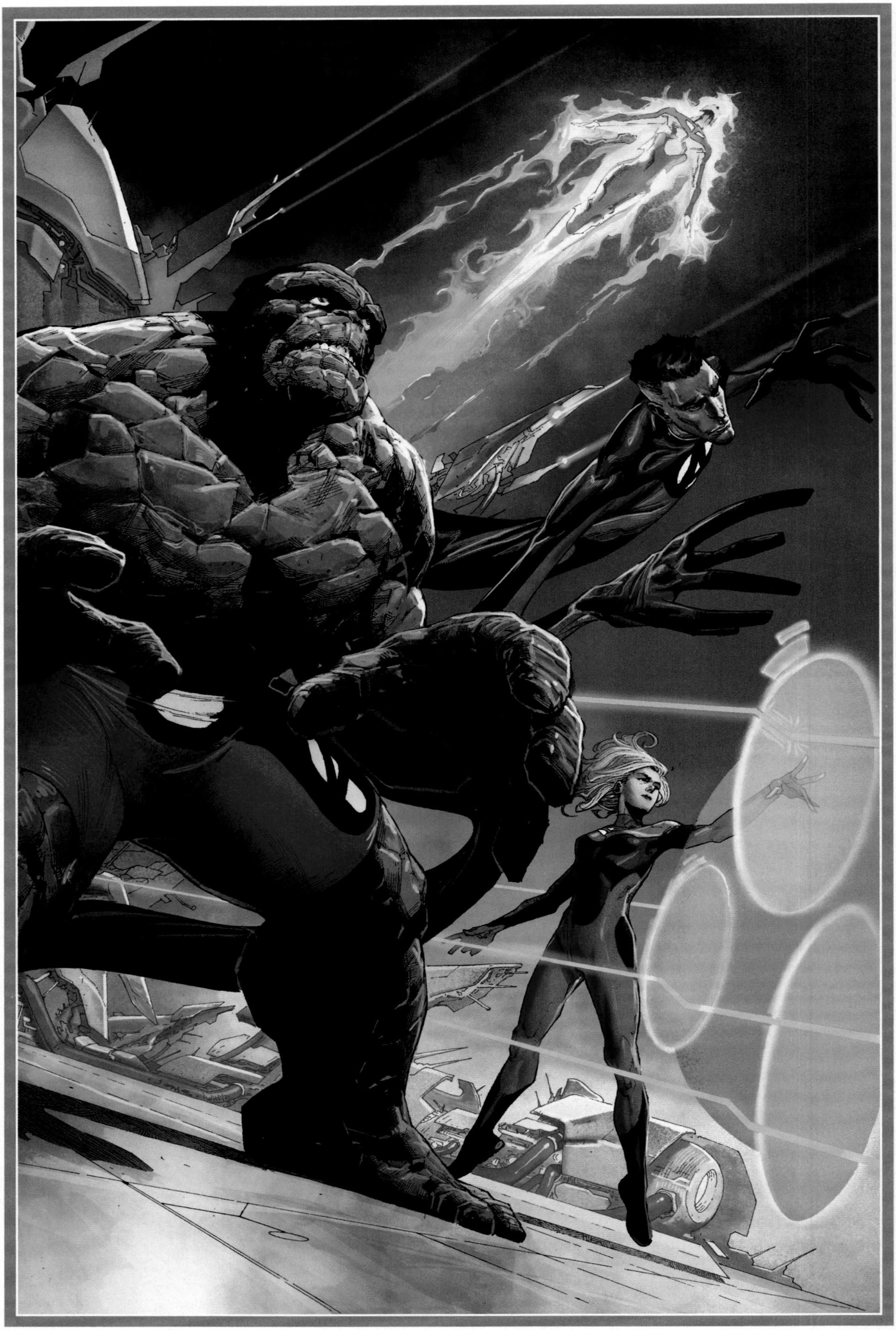

ONE • variant by Jerome Opeña with Dean White

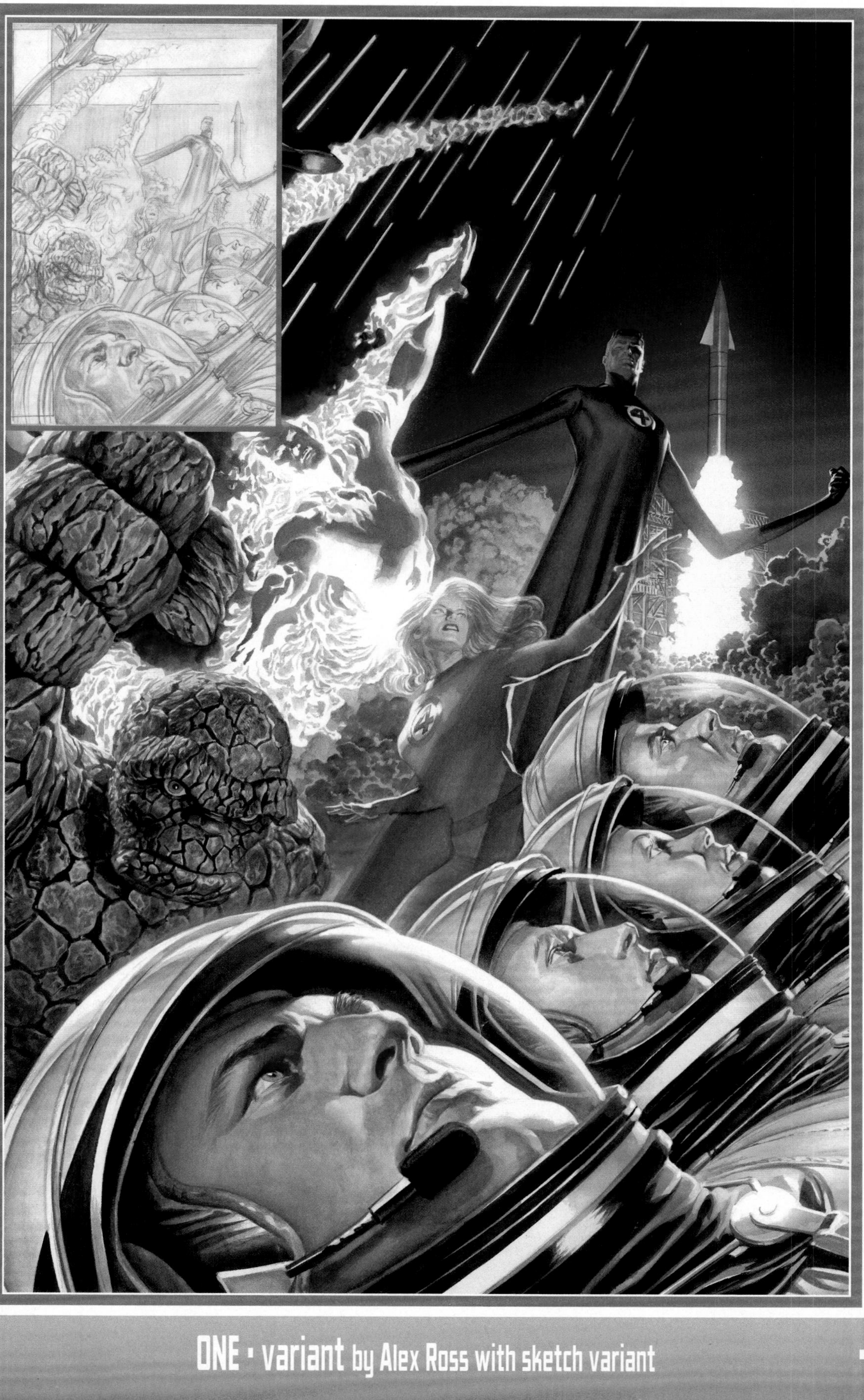

ONE • variant by Alex Ross with sketch variant

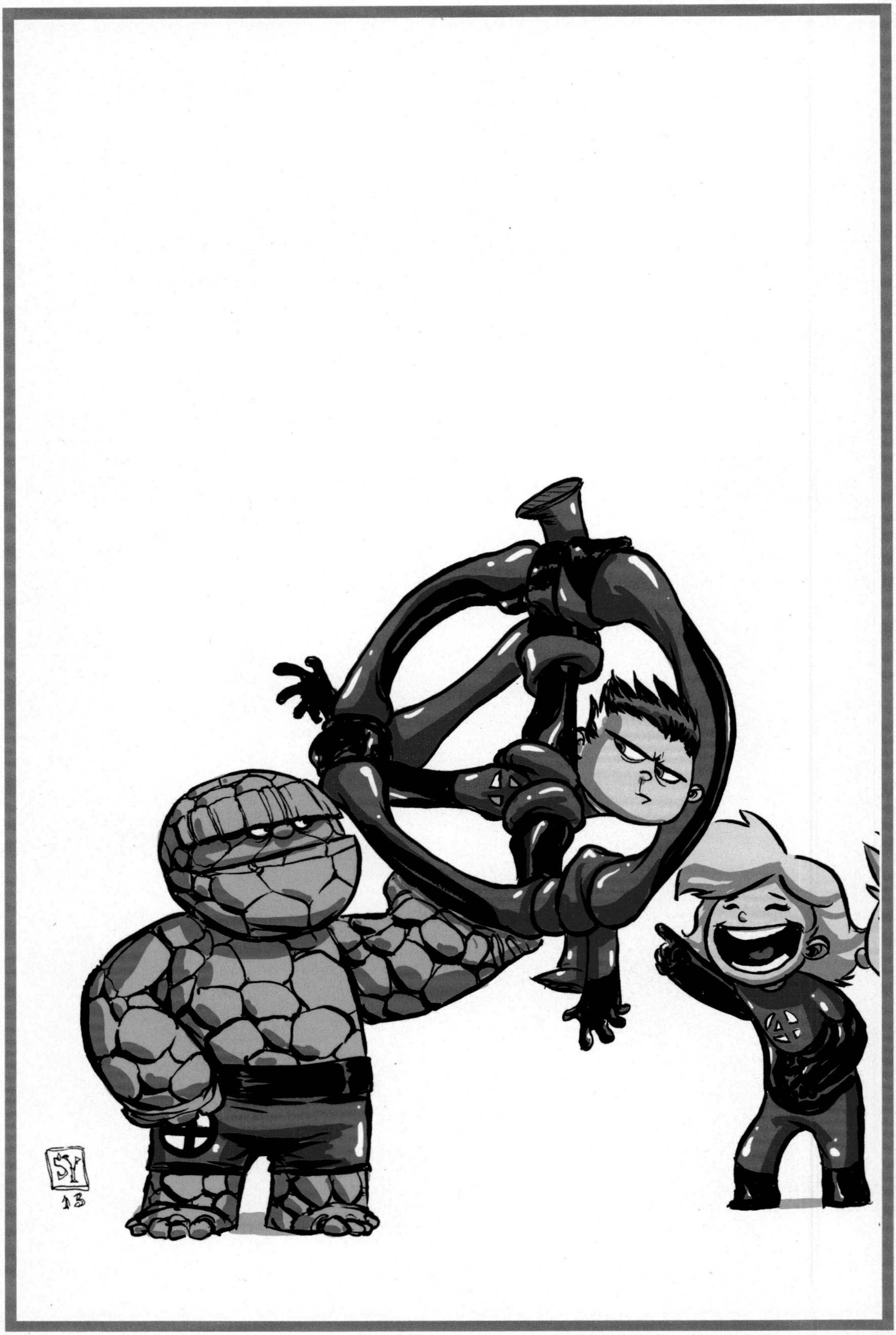

ONE • variant by Scottie Young

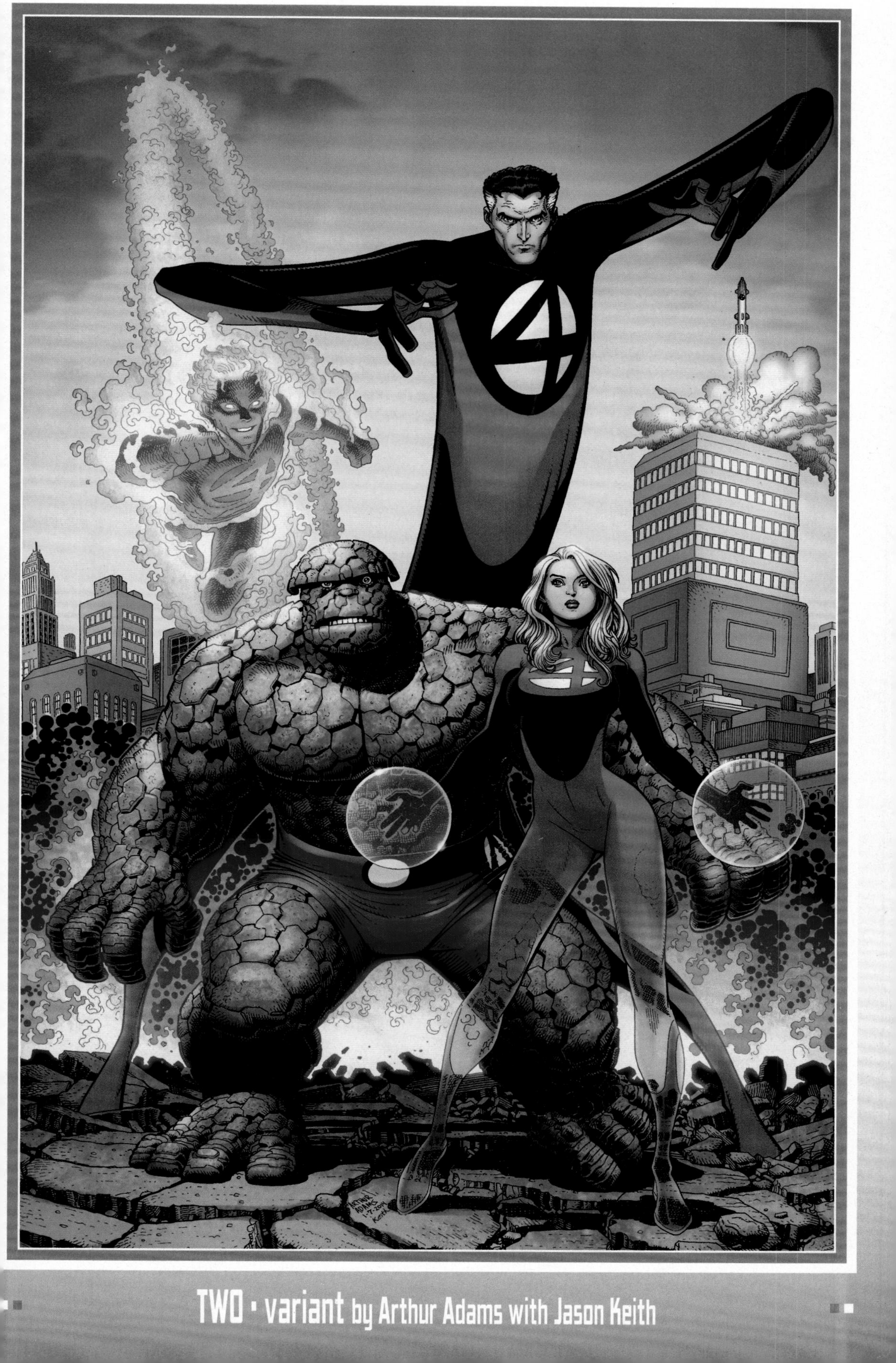

TWO • variant by Arthur Adams with Jason Keith

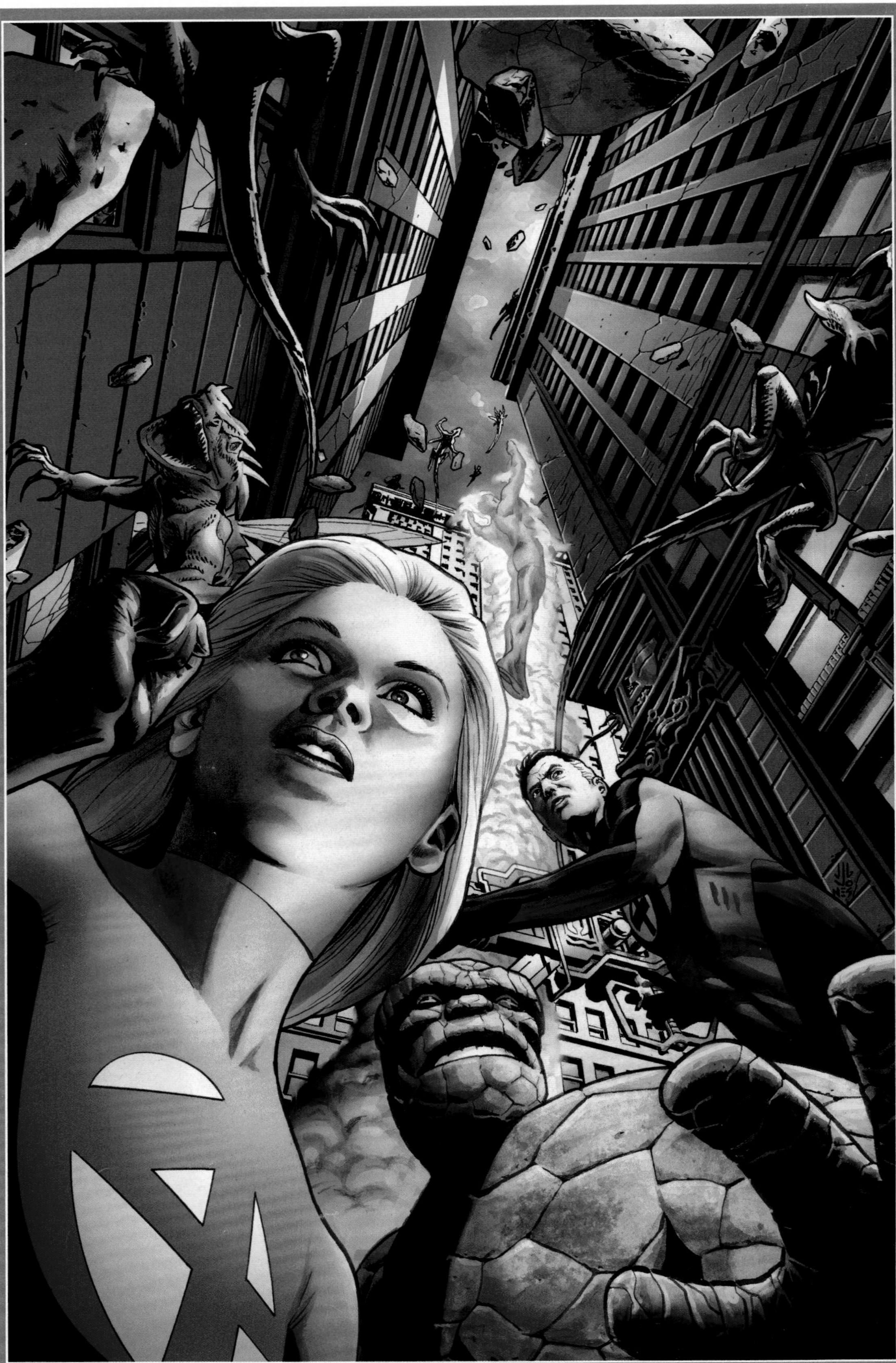

THREE • variant by J.G. Jones with Paul Mounts

FANTASTIC!

SPACE EXPLORERS GET SUPER POWERS One of the things I loved most about the FANTASTIC FOUR was the fact that they were astronauts. Kind of. I mean, it wasn't their full-time job but they got into a rocket and went into space. For a kid growing up at the tail end of the Apollo missions and watching reruns of STAR TREK religiously, anything that had to do with rockets and space was gold to me. Add in the fact that they all get super-powers and now you've got my complete, undivided, focused attention. Just ask my fourth grade teacher.

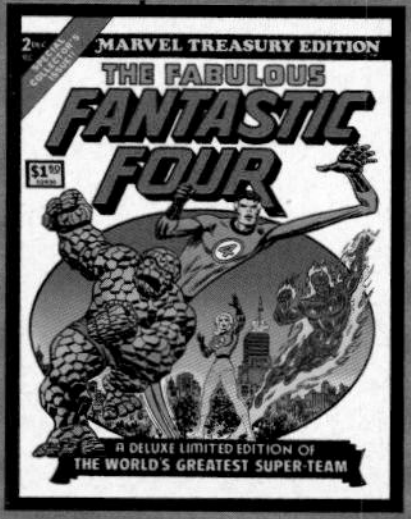
MARVEL TREASURY EDITION
THE FABULOUS
FANTASTIC FOUR
A DELUXE LIMITED EDITION OF
THE WORLD'S GREATEST SUPER-TEAM

COMIC BOOK TREASURE My first exposure to the first family of comics was THE FABULOUS FANTASTIC FOUR TREASURY EDITION. For those of you who don't know what a treasury edition is, you don't know what you missed. They were these huge, oversized 10" x 14" tabloid specials. Mainly reprints but in glorious giganto-vision. I read the heck out of the FF issue. Which meant dings, bends, rips. Eventually the comic book collector Mark Paniccia would look back and curse his slightly younger self for not taking proper care of it. Which would have meant touching it less. Which would have meant not reading it as much. Which would have meant not enjoying it as many times. Ah, the eternal conundrum of a comics fan!

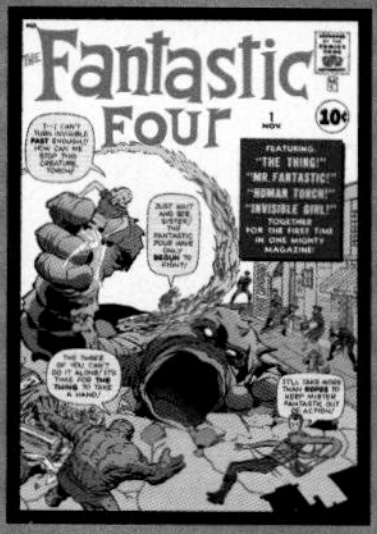
Fantastic
Four
10¢

COMIC BOOK TREASURE PART II One day in fourth grade a friend of mine brought something special to school. He pointed at his backpack and said, "Wait till you see what I got." He pulled out a stack of FANTASTIC FOURs, including the very first issue. It was one of those classic "found these in the trash" stories. He had some AVENGERS, too but all I cared about was the FFs. As class started and the teacher began writing math problems on the chalkboard, all I could think about was getting my hands on those books. I was willing to give my friend all of my hard-earned lawn mowing dollars but he didn't want to permanently part with them. He did lend them to me. And they were awesome.

HOME, JAMES Flash forward forty years (sigh, yes forty) and I am working for Marvel and Tom Brevoort has finally decided to pass the editorial torch. To me (Thank you, Tom). I call up James Robinson. He's writing ALL-NEW INVADERS for me. I tell him that the current creative team is cycling off, that I've just inherited the FANTASTIC FOUR and ask him if he'd like to pitch. He initially says no but as we start talking about the stories that we read as kids, I hear excitement in voice. He says, "Let me sleep on it." He sleeps on it. He calls me back with a pitch so dang good I almost cried. When he turned in the first script it was like he'd been writing these characters all his life. James made me feel like I was back home (or school) with the magic of those early issues. Powerful. Emotional. Fantastic.

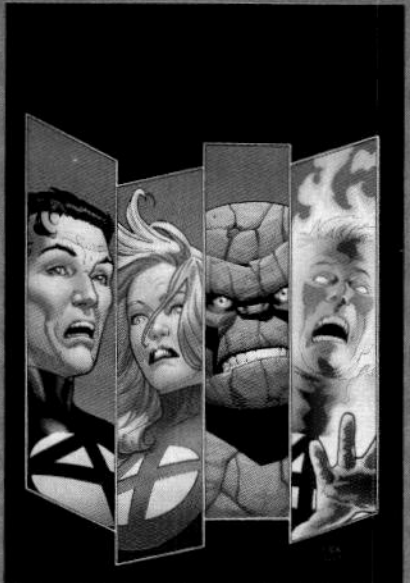

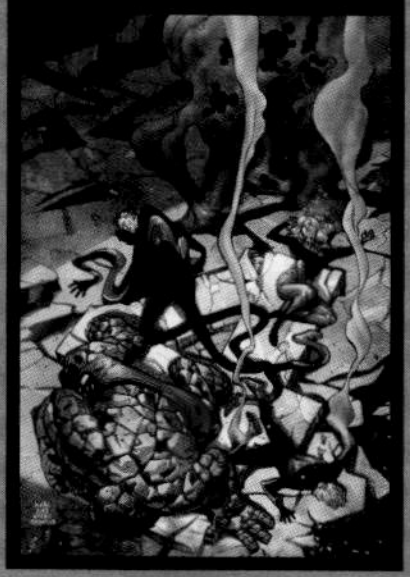

HOW I MET YOUR LEONARD
Leonard Kirk worked with me on the STAR TREK: DEEP SPACE NINE comic book I edited back at Malibu Comics. The guy was amazing. He could draw anything you asked. Anybody. Any place. He knew perspective like the back of his hand (whatever that's supposed to mean). We continued to work together on various projects. He did HUNGER for me and drew one of the best Galactuses I ever saw. That planted a seed. When I was going over a list of potential artists with James, just before I got to Leonard, he asks, "What about Leonard Kirk?"

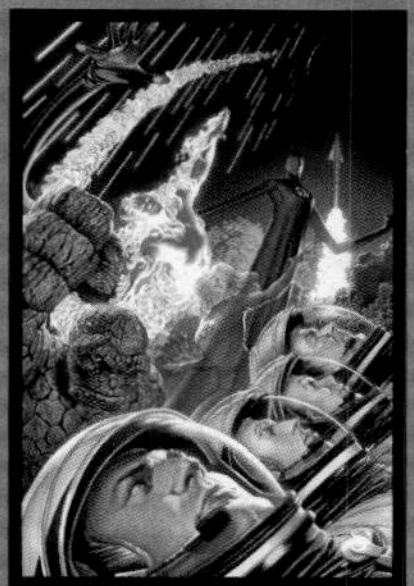

NEW VOYAGE So here we are. A new creative and editorial team. Along with James, Leonard and myself we have Karl Kesel (no stranger to FF fans), Jesus Aburtov, Clayton Cowles and Emily Shaw. I don't think there's anyone here that hasn't experienced the thrill of the series at some point in their comic book reading life and we hope to thrill you during our run, to do what all those before us did. And while those are some big space helmets to fill, I think we got the right stuff. Visors down. Seatbelts on. 3, 2, **1...TAKE OFF!**

Mark Paniccia
Marvel Comics

Sketchbook of the Fantastic

Hey Fantastic Fans! We thought it might be fun to take a peek at some early stages of development for the series. Here are some of artist Leonard Kirk's initial sketches.

YOU KNOW, THERE'S REALLY NO NEED FOR ME TO BE CRAMPED IN HERE LIKE THIS!
FANTASTIC FOUR UNIFORMS 2.
KIRK 2013

UPDATING THOSE UNSTABLE MOLECULES

The first thing we talked about was the costumes. James, Leonard and I discussed going back to blue, but since this was a bold new direction, we thought now was the perfect opportunity to do something completely unexpected. When all was said and done, Leonard did about nine versions. Since this arc is about the fall of the Fantastic Four, we decided red would help message that our characters were in danger. Here's one of the early designs.

JET SETTING

Leonard came up with this design for a new Fantasticar, not only wanting it to look cool and different, but practical for a certain blue-eyed member of the team: Not as 'uniform" as earlier models. I want Ben's segment to really stand out both because he is the biggest AND the fact that he used to be a fighter pilot and test pilot. I'd love to see that part of his history played up a bit. Also, as we'll see with more detail later, the controls in Ben's section are BIG to accommodate his massive hands and feet.

FANTASTIC FOUR
FANTASTICAR
BACK
FRONT
LITTLE WINGS POP OUT
TOP
SIDE
KIRK 2013

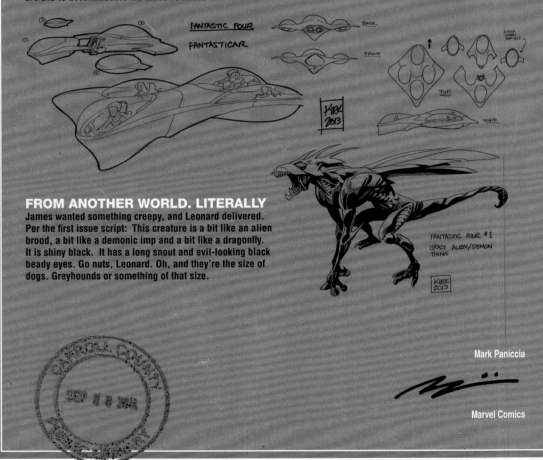

FROM ANOTHER WORLD. LITERALLY

James wanted something creepy, and Leonard delivered. Per the first issue script: This creature is a bit like an alien brood, a bit like a demonic imp and a bit like a dragonfly. It is shiny black. It has a long snout and evil-looking black beady eyes. Go nuts, Leonard. Oh, and they're the size of dogs. Greyhounds or something of that size.

FANTASTIC FOUR #1
CRAZY ALIEN/DEMON THING
KIRK 2013

Mark Paniccia

Marvel Comics